Computer Supported Cooperative Work

For further volumes:
http://www.springer.com/2861

Dave Oliver · Celia Romm Livermore ·
Fay Sudweeks
Editors

Self-Service in the Internet Age

Expectations and Experiences

 Springer

Editors

Dave Oliver
Queensland 4703, Australia

Celia Romm Livermore
School of Business Administration
Wayne State University
Detroit, MI 48202, USA

Fay Sudweeks
School of Information Technology
Murdoch University
Murdoch, WA 6150, Australia

Computer Supported Cooperative Work ISSN 1431-1496
ISBN: 978-1-84800-206-7   e-ISBN: 978-1-84800-207-4
DOI 10.1007/978-1-84800-207-4

British Library Cataloguing in Publication Data
A catalogue record for this book is available from the British Library

Library of Congress Control Number: 2008937479

Printed on acid-free paper

Springer Science+Business Media
springer.com

Contents

Contributors

Madhumita Banerjee Essex Business School, University of Essex, Southend-on-Sea SS1 1LW UK, mbaner@essex.ac.uk

Stuart Barnes University of East Anglia, Norwich NR4 7TJ United Kingdom, stuart.barnes@uea.ac.uk

Chris Barry Department of Accountancy and Finance, National University of Ireland, Galway, Ireland, chris.barry@nuigalway.ie

Phillip W.J. Brook School of Management, College of Business, University of Western Sydney, Australia, p.brook@uws.edu.au

Alex Broom School of Humanities and Social Science, University of Newcastle, Callaghan NSW 2308 Australia, alexander.broom@newcastle.edu.au

Vanessa A. Cooper RMIT University, Melbourne VIC 3001 Australia, vanessa.cooper@rmit.edu.au

Joerg Evermann Victoria University of Wellington, PO Box 600, Wellington 6140, New Zealand

Mary Tate Victoria University of Wellington, PO Box 600, Wellington 6140, New Zealand, mary.tate@vuw.ac.nz

Neveen Awad Farag School of Business Administration, Wayne State University, 5229 Cass Avenue, Detroit MI 48202 USA, nawad@wayne.edu

Mark Freeman School of Information Systems and Technology, University of Wollongong, ollongong NSW 2522, Australia, mfreeman@uow.edu.au

Beverley Hope United Arab Emirates University, PO Box 15551, Al-Ain, United Arab Emirates, bhope@uaue.ac.ae

Les Killion School of Arts and Creative Enterprise, Faculty of Arts, Humanities and Education, Central Queensland University, Rockhampton QLD 4702 Australia, l.killion@cqu.edu.au

Sharman Lichtenstein Deakin University, Burwood VIC 3125 Australia, sharman.lichtenstein@deakin.edu.au

Celia Romm Livermore School of Business Administration, Wayne State University, 5229 Cass Avenue, Detroit MI 48202 USA, celia_romm@hotmail.com

Rachel McLean The Business School, Manchester Metropolitan University, Manchester M15 6BH UK, r.mclean@mmu.ac.uk

Dave Oliver 45 Mirrawena Avenue, Farnborough QLD 4703 Australia, dodave@gmail.com

Line Lervik Olsen BI Norwegian School of Management, Oslo, Norway, sangeeta.singh@bi.no

Helen Richardson Salford Business School, Manchester M5 4WT UK, h.richardson@salford.ac.uk

Celia T. Romm School of Business Administration, Wayne State University, 5229 Cass Avenue, Detroit, MI 48202 USA, celia_romm@hotmail.com

Sangeeta Singh BI Norwegian School of Management, Oslo, Norway, sangeeta.singh@bi.no

Ross Smith RMIT University, Melbourne VIC 3001 Australia, ross.smith@rmit.edu.au

Fay Sudweeks School of Information Technology, Murdoch University, Murdoch WA 6150 Australia, sudweeks@murdoch.edu.au

Ann M. Torres Department of Marketing, National University of Ireland, Galway, Ireland, ann.torres@nuigalway.ie

Marilyn A. Wells School of Management and Information Systems, Faculty of Business and Informatics, Central Queensland University, Australia, m.wells@cqu.edu.au

Introduction

Dave Oliver, Celia Romm and Fay Sudweeks

This book follows previous texts: Celia Romm and Fay Sudweeks (eds) (1998), *Doing Business Electronically: A Global Perspective of Electronic Commerce*, and Fay Sudweeks and Celia Romm (eds) (1999) *Doing Business on the Internet: Opportunities and Pitfalls*. Not only is this current book about doing something, but it also aims to present insights into how electronic commerce impacts upon the lives of everyday people; in other words, how electronic commerce is received, as well as how it is 'done'. Accessing the Internet on a regular basis has become an established activity for many people. This activity gives academics and researchers the opportunity to observe and study the nature and effects of this engagement in society. The influence of the Internet in our social fabric also provides the incentive for organizations to implement a web presence.

As expressed in the title *Self-Service on the Internet: Expectations and Experiences*, we aim to present the expectations or reasons for the availability of various services on the Internet, and social responses to these developments, i.e. the experiences. These are the two main dimensions to the chapters presented in this book.

The major component in the title is *self-service on the Internet*. The term electronic commerce is too restrictive for our purpose as it tends towards commercial overtones, which do not especially concern us. We are specifically focusing on self-service from an array of information from fields as diverse as dating and IT problem solving. In other words, self-service in this book refers to access to a range of services from the highly specialized to the routine. Much Internet activity is of a self-service nature. Google is used by people who want to find out something for themselves and typifies the essential nature of self-service on the Internet. We have a website Google, which is accessed by somebody who is seeking information on some topic via the Internet. In such an encounter that person is serving himself or herself with information. However, Googling is not the only way of serving ourselves on the Internet as these chapters demonstrate.

D.Oliver(✉)
45 Mirrawena Ave, Farnborough QLD 4703 Australia
e-mail: dodave@gmail.com

There are a great many websites that present information in a way that is designed to enable people to serve themselves by accessing the information they require.

The chapters in this book are necessarily limited to a relatively small range of topics: small that is compared to the range of topics that could be found on the Internet. Most of the chapters relate to websites that serve commercial organizations and therefore meet business objectives. Many organizations have turned to the Internet in order to enable self-service activities by customers, and the impacts of these on consumers are examined in a number of chapters. However the topics that are presented and discussed in this book are potentially important to many people. The contributors to this work present insights along the dimensions of expectations and experiences of self-service on the Internet from a wide range of contexts. The book begins with chapters that address self-service on the Internet that concern personal issues including dating, health and education. We then move on to chapters concerning self-service on the Internet that cover the lifestyle oriented services of travel and tourism and the more routine areas of shopping and banking. The final set of chapters includes a chapter on an organizational application of self-service on the Internet on IT support and a chapter which has a global coverage. Many of the chapters include assessments and impressions of Internet users in these areas.

For many people the Internet is somewhere to turn when seeking self-help in the areas of personal relationships and health.

Celia Romm and Dave Oliver, in their chapter on Social Networking and e-Dating, explore how individuals use the Internet to extend their personal relationships. Then we have a chapter from Alex Broom which identifies intriguing aspects of how different individuals respond with a variety of possible types of engagement with the Internet in coping with their illness. Both our personal relationships and our health are integral to our well being and it is instructive to explore how people may choose to serve, or not to serve, themselves from the Internet in these intimate areas of life.

Next we have two chapters on self-service and the Internet in higher education. Marilyn Wells and Phil Brook explain a self-service approach to a university course they have taught over a number of years. Their self-service educational philosophy is played out in this course and the practical implementation of the course involves a number of Internet-enabled self-service features. Mary Tate explores the online service quality of a university website using an established service quality instrument. This study is not concerned with self-service within a specific university course but rather self-service to a range of university services. An outcome of her study is a proposal for a variation in the instrument used to measure self-service quality.

Areas of life more oriented towards leisure and pleasure are the focus of the next two chapters. Les Killion writes on tourism and travel and he identifies the emerging role of self-service on the Internet in both of these areas. He discusses both web-based services and those obtainable from travel agents and he looks at how each type of service provision is likely to develop in the future. His chapter reports some experiences, attitudes and behaviours of tourists and travellers who have both served themselves on the Internet and made use of travel agents. Chris Barry and Ann Torres make a critical evaluation of Irish low-cost airline websites and they critically assess the interactional capacities of a number of design interfaces presented. They examine the human–computer interface qualities of these websites, taking a professional ethics perspective, and identify many screens which have seemingly opaque information presentation.

The next three chapters are concerned with shopping, and in particular shopping for groceries. Mark Freeman examines the usability of online grocery store websites and the uptake of this mode of shopping. He explains why grocery shopping on the Internet is more complicated than, for example, shopping for leisure items. Dave Oliver and Celia Romm also consider online grocery shopping but from the specific perspective of the division of work between supplier and customer. Self-service is usually assumed to require more tasks being taken on by the customer and this issue is explored in their chapter on grocery shopping. Rachel Mclean and Helen Richardson present a critical analysis of e-shopping discourses, also with some emphasis on grocery shopping. This chapter motivates the reader to think critically about self-service aspects of e-shopping and related issues of how individuals are positioned in the e-order of things.

The following two chapters examine self-service Internet banking. Madhumita Banerjee studies Internet banking as one of a number of possible channels whereby customers may conduct dealing with a bank. She studies the attracters and detractors of Internet banking and finds that many potential users of Internet banking aspire to receive more person-to-person support from their bank, to either establish or enhance their confidence in using this mode of self-service. This discussion has similarities with the chapter by Les Killion on travel and tourism, where it is reported that some people preferred to self-serve certain services using the Internet but for others sought personal contact. Sangeeta Singh and Line Olsen examine how attitudes towards the service supplier, in this case banks, are affected when a self-service technology is used. They study how the established relationships between satisfaction, affective and calculative commitments, and loyalty are affected when the service is provided through a technology interface as opposed to service personnel.

The next chapter by Vanessa Cooper, Sharman Lichtenstein and Ross Smith is set in the context of inter-firm self-service or B2B as opposed to the business to consumer B2C setting explored in the other chapters. In their analysis they explore issues relating to the provision of IT support to business customers through web-based self-service. The issue of the willingness on the part of business customers to take up the work of serving themselves appears also in this study, although this appears as a relatively minor point among a very wide range of complex issues that emerge in the discussion of this way of doing business.

The final chapter integrates many of the issues raised in the previous chapters. Dave Oliver, Celia Romm and Neveen Awad Farag report on a broad ranging macro level study of a very large number of websites across a range of industries, countries and cultures. Their chapter presents a model that includes a number of explanatory variables for self-service on the Internet.

We expect this book will appeal to all who have an interest in the Internet or social change, as well as those students and academics who have a focus on social impacts.

Acknowledgements We wish to acknowledge those who have played a part in producing this work. The contributions of the Authors are prominent, self-evident and indispensable. Without the many hours each has spent researching their field to the depth of scholarship required for a work of this standard, we would have nothing to present to you, the reader. As well as writing their chapters, all of the Authors have participated in the reviewing of other chapters using a double-blind review process. Others we would like to acknowledge for assisting with reviewing chapters are Tony Dobele, Naimatullah Khan, Ken Howah Rob McDougall and Mohammed Huque of Central Queensland University. Dave Oliver wishes to express his gratitude to his wife Lyn for her support in promoting the written quality of the chapters.

Chapter 1
Social Networking and eDating: Charting the Boundaries of an Emerging Self-Service Arena

Celia T. Romm and Dave Oliver

Abstract This chapter focuses on social networking and eDating as emerging areas of self-service. Following an overview of the theoretical aspects of self-service, two models or typologies for categorizing business models in the two areas are presented, namely, one typology for social networking services and another for eDating services. The chapter concludes with a discussion of the psychological, social, legal, and other implications from the models, as well as suggestions for future research that emanate from the issues presented in the chapter.

1.1 Introduction

We define social networking websites as online services that focus on the building and verifying of social networks for whatever purpose. Indeed, social networking websites offer a range of services. Some are merely blog-hosting services, some offer the option of joining groups temporarily (through chat rooms) or for a longer period of time (through electronic bulletin boards, newsgroups, or online groups). Some social networking services encourage their members' creativity through music and video sharing services or enable members to meet and possibly marry (eDating services).

The objective of this chapter is to discuss social networking and eDating services as emerging areas of self-service. To accomplish this goal, we will start by explaining in some detail what self-service is about. We will then proceed to discuss the reasons that social networking and eDating can be seen as examples of self-service. Next we will consider the business models on which the social networking and eDating industry is based, categorizing them according to a number of categories and subcategories. We will conclude this chapter with a

C.T. Romm (✉)
School of Business Administration, Wayne State University, 5229 Cass Avenue,
Detroit, MI 48202, USA
e-mail: celia_romm@hotmail.com

D. Oliver et al. (eds.), *Self-Service in the Internet Age*,
DOI 10.1007/978-1-84800-207-4_1, © Springer-Verlag London Limited 2009

discussion of the research and other implications from the discussion in this chapter.

1.2 What Is Self-Service?

Following Romm et al. (2005) and Oliver et al. (2005), we define self-service as "a process in which aspects of the customer service experience that used to be provided by the company's employees are now provided through the interaction of customers with the company's website." Examples of self-service where customers perform functions that used to be performed by employees can be found in many new and long established industries. For example, in the past, grocery shopping involved shop employees retrieving items that customers wished to purchase. These days, when self-service is practiced, it is the customers who select their purchases, place them in a cart, and carry them to the cashier. It is expected that in the future, the process will be extended to include automatic scanning of purchases and automatic debiting of the customers' bank account as they walk out of the store, without any direct involvement of store employees. Other industries where self-service is common are fast food, where waiters have been replaced by customers' selecting and carrying their food to the table themselves; health, where new mothers are expected by hospitals to care for their new born babies as part of the "rooming-in" practice instead of having nurses care for them, as used to be the case several decades ago; and banking, where customers now conduct banking services through ATM machines.

A relatively recent development in the self-service area is for customers to be served online. Indeed, many companies establish an e-commerce presence (a company website) precisely because they consider a website a natural platform for self-service by their customers. This phenomenon is evident in many industries, for example, banking (where customers are encouraged to conduct transactions online) and travel (where customers can book flights and hotels online).

As indicated by a number of researchers, self-service websites can be categorized into two main types:

1. *Informational websites.* This type of website provides information about companies, services, or products. Many companies that offer informational websites (online newspapers, search engines, weather forecasting, etc) do not charge customers for their services. Instead, they generate profits through selling advertising services on their sites.
2. *Transactional websites.* This type of website involves an Internet-mediated transaction such as placing an order, making a bank transfer, or booking a flight. By conducting automated transactions through their websites, companies can greatly reduce the cost of transactions that were previously conducted by employees. For example, airlines can offer customers greatly

reduced fares when they order tickets online, relative to the price of the same ticket ordered from a travel agent, through the telephone, or face-to-face.

As indicated in the previous sections, the proliferation of online self-service and the heavy investments that companies are willing to make to create the infrastructure that enables such services are motivated by expectations of profit. In other words, companies expect their short-term investment to eventually lead to long-term cost cutting.

However, the benefits from online self-service are also clear to customers. As indicated by Meuter et al. (2000), Bitner (2001), and others, consumers elect to avail themselves of self-service technologies for a number of reasons which are specific to them and not to the company that provides the service. These include:

1. ease of use
2. avoidance of service personnel
3. saving time
4. availability of the service when and where the consumer requires it
5. saving money

A recent investigation into the manner in which companies use their websites to support self-service by customers (Oliver et al. 2007) revealed that three variables affect this process: "industry ", "culture ", and "level of technology development". This work was based on the instrument reported in Romm et al. (2005) and Oliver et al. (2005) for measuring website content. The scale was applied to a sample of over 140 websites from more than 20 countries, measuring the extent to which the websites contained self-service features.

The results of the study indicated the following:

First, that industry made a difference to the extent to which self-service features were present in companies' websites. Thus, while websites of companies in the construction and building industry contained few self-service features, websites in the gas and electricity industry (irrespective of culture) made extensive use of these features.

Second, the study indicated that culture made a difference. Thus, while English speaking countries, like the US, Canada, the UK, and Australia had a relatively large number of self-service features in their companies websites (irrespective of industry), developing countries were less likely to do so, again, irrespective of industry.

Finally, the study demonstrated that within the group of English-speaking countries (US, Canada, UK, and Australia), technology development has an impact on the prevalence of self-service features in a company's website, with the US, being the highest on the technology scale, also displaying more self-service features in its companies' websites than the other countries.

It should be noted that social networking and eDating websites were *not* included in the above study. Still, as we will demonstrate in the following sections, at least some of the implications from the above research might be relevant and applicable to self-service in the social networking and eDating arena.

1.3 Are Social Networking and eDating Self-Service Industries?

In the context of this chapter, we consider social networking and its subcategory, eDating, examples of self-service because they involve the interaction of customers with websites that provide them with services that could have been delivered to them through face-to-face interactions with company employees. When we consider the various subcategories of the social networking industry, it is easy to demonstrate that each subcategory represents a "migration" of the service from a face-to-face to an online environment, and hence is an example of a self-service industry. Let's consider some of the major subcategories of the industry as examples of this phenomenon.

The most obvious example of a social networking service that replaces an interaction with company employees are the virtual communities that are established by companies to sell the company products to each other (Amazon.com uses this feature extensively), those which enable customers to support each other on the use of company's products (Dell uses this feature in its virtual support communities) or those which elicit ideas for new products from customers. However, one can also consider services like FaceBook or MySpace as examples of services that used to be provided face-to-face (such as in clubs, churches, or other social gatherings) and are now made available online. Finally, eDating (including all its subcategories) can be seen as an example of an industry that used to be conducted by professionals (matchmakers) and is now undertaken on a self-service basis by customers who interact with other customers via eDating websites.

1.4 Business Models in the Social Networking Industry

As for the reasons for establishing social networking websites, some of the earliest services have been created by companies as virtual communities of customers. They were intended to serve as platforms for conducting market research, venues for customer support, and means for promoting customer loyalty. Some companies (e.g., Amazon.com) used their social networking services for selling their products by enabling customers to read other customers' comments about the products and services that the company sells. Some companies, e.g., eBay, took the concept of community one step further, inviting their users to buy and sell from each other through the biggest auction house in the world.

Recently, corporations have been establishing social networking websites as a means for connecting employees within and beyond the company boundaries. The websites are intended to enhance employees' social connectivity with the hope that better connected employees are more effective managers of the company's environment. Business associations are creating similar networks to connect business professionals by industry, functions, geographic areas, and areas of interest.

The best indication that social-networking websites are becoming big business is the recent acquisition of YouTube by Google for 1.6 billion dollars (Delaney et al. 2006). The social networking video website, developed by its 29-year-old CEO, Chad Hurley, and its 28-year-old chief technology officer, Steve Chen, in their garage in 2005, has managed to increase its hit rate from 0 to over 100 million visitors per month in one single year.

Most commentators agree that the reason for this phenomenal growth is that social networking websites are the Internet's Holy Grail because they provide an entry point onto the Web for consumers (Delaney et al. 2006). This role of gate keepers that social networking websites play enables them to be the key to a revolution not just in how we conduct business through e-commerce but also in how we live our social lives.

Despite the proliferation of social networking websites and the enormous attention that they have been getting in both the popular and the business media, we are not aware of any research published in the leading journals in information systems that focuses on the social network industry. To respond to this, the major objective of this chapter is to start a process of charting the terrain of social networking. As the first step in this process, we propose a categorization model for social networking websites, identifying the place of eDating websites in the social networking landscape. Next, we present a categorization of eDating services. Finally, we describe an on-going research project that explains the business models that underlie each of the different categories in our model. We conclude this chapter with suggestions for future research that emanate from the eDating categorization model.

1.5 Categorizing Social Networking Business Models

The social networking landscape to date can be divided into a number of different types of services. While all of them share the same purpose, namely, to provide an electronic platform that supports social networking between users, the different "players" in the social networking "playground" offer different means for achieving this goal (Delaney et al. 2006; Jesdanun 2006; Markman 2006; Marshall 2006; Jordan 2006).

A useful theoretical concept that can help us chart the social networking terrain is that of the "business model ". One of the most widely quoted definitions for this concept has been proposed by Osterwalder (2004, p. 14). According to his definition, a business model "synthesizes the different conceptualizations into a single reference model based on the similarities of a large range of models".

Osterwalder describes a business model as consisting of nine related building blocks, including:

- Value propositions. The company's offers that bundle products and services into *value* for the customer. A value proposition creates *utility* for the customer.
- Target customer segments. The customer segments a company wants to offer value to. This describes the groups of people with common characteristics for which the company creates value. The process of defining customer segments is referred to as *market segmentation*.
- Distribution channels. The various means of the company to get in touch with its customers. This describes how a company goes to market. It refers to the company's *marketing* and *distribution* strategy.
- Customer relationships. The links a company establishes between itself and its different customer segments. The process of managing customer relationships is referred to as *customer relationship management*.
- Value configurations. The configuration of activities and resources.
- Core capabilities. The capabilities and competencies necessary to execute the company's business model.
- Partner network. The network of cooperative agreements with other companies necessary to efficiently offer and commercialize value. This describes the company's range of *business alliances*.
- Cost structure. The monetary consequences of the means employed in the business model.
- Revenue model. The way a company makes money through a variety of revenue flows.

Another, simpler way to define the concept of a business model is to consider it as a combination of *who* the company chooses to do business with, *what* it chooses to sell, and *how* it chooses to go about it.

Considered from this perspective, the different types of social networking services that have been described in the previous sections share the same *what*, in that they all provide electronic platforms for social networking among their customers, but they differ on the *how* and *who* in that they negotiate the relationships between customers differently and attract different kinds of customers. Figure 1.1 shows a two by two model that categorizes the social networking area in terms of the business models that it involves.

As indicated in Fig. 1.1, the social networking arena can be divided into four major subcategories. These subcategories can be seen as a continuum, where each subcategory represents a higher level of involvement on the part of company that supports the service in the interactions between customers.

Fig. 1.1 Social networking
websites categorization
model

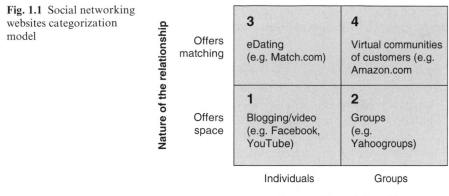

Thus, while cell no. 1 (subcategory 1) in the model represents a relatively low level of involvement of the company in the interactions that occur between its customers, cell no. 4 (subcategory 4) represents a relatively high level of involvement by the company in the interactions between customers that take place on its website.

The subcategories in the model (or the cells) are the product of an interaction between two dimensions or continuums. These two dimensions are:

1. *The nature of the relationship between the company and its customers.* This dimension consists of two "values": (i) provision of space for networking; and (ii) provision of matching services. We distinguish between the simple provision of a space for social interactions (such as the space that is provided by MySpace, FaceBook, YouTube, or SecondLife) and the active matching of individuals with other individuals or groups (such as through YahooGroups, Amazon.com, or Match.com). Companies that specialize in simply providing space for social networking focus on advertising as their main source of income, while companies that provide active "matching" of customers tend to charge users for the matching process and/or for other transactions that are associated with the "matching". These transactions could be between the company and its customers or between customers.
2. *The scope of the relationship between the company and its customers.* This dimension consists of two "values": (i) individuals; and (ii) groups. We distinguish between the provision of networking services primarily to groups (such as the creation of groups on YahooGroups or on Amazon.com) and the provision of networking services primarily to individuals (such as the provision of "space" to individuals through MySpace, FaceBook, YouTube, or SecondLife).

Based on these two dimensions, the model distinguishes between the following four types of social networking business models:

1. *Focus on creation of space for individual bloggers* (the least involvement from the company that provides the service). Examples of this type of service would be MySpace, or FaceBook . These services provide a space for bloggers to set up a presence on the website. Even though bloggers can join groups and can contact individuals that are members of the service, the company does not get involved in these interactions in any active way. YouTube is another example of this type of service. Even though the company does provide an added service, the ability to display one's home videos and to see videos of other members, the company does not actively "match" users with other users. A similar concept is demonstrated by SecondLife , a virtual reality website that offers customers the opportunity to create a "home" and interact (through avatars) with other users. Here again, even though the company offers users "space" and enables them to interact with each other, it does not actively match them.

2. *Focus on creation of space for groups* (the next level of involvement by the company that provides the service). An example of this type of service would be YahooGroups and the chat-room services that accompany it. Even though the company invites users to select the groups that they wish to join and/or establish, and even though users can be contacted by other users through the service (if they choose to make their website public), the company's involvement in the activities that take place within the groups is minimal and the benefits that it reaps from helping individuals match themselves with appropriate groups are minimal too.

3. *Focus on matching individuals with other individuals* (the highest level of involvement by the company that provides the service). All eDating services would fit this category because they represent instances where individuals are matched with other individuals based on criteria that the users specify and/or on criteria that the company gleans from information that is provided by users.

4. *Focus on matching individuals with groups* (the next level of involvement by the company that owns the service). An example of this type of service would be the virtual communities established by companies for their customers. The virtual communities serve different purposes ranging from customer support (Del.com), to active selling of the company's products (Amazon.com). The principle in all cases is that new prospective buyers are invited to interact directly (Del.com) or indirectly (Amazon.com) with a group of people who share their interest in the company's products and services. We consider this an example of relatively high level of involvement by the company because the company developed unique "matching" algorithms to create the group(s) and to match individuals with groups. The major contribution of the company here is in the matching process. And,

yes, the matching process is not intended just for social networking but for selling the company's products and services.

We consider the fourth subcategory of the model an example of the highest level of involvement by the company because the company does not just set up the platform that enables the social interaction between users but actually provides value-adding matching services. In this model, even though users are expected to establish a webpage (or a profile, as it is usually referred to) and even though some services do provide discussion forums and even chat-rooms, the major service that the company provides is the matching of individual users to each other. And, yes, just like the previous type of social networking service, here too, the company is making a profit by charging both parties a fee for its matchmaking service.

It should be noted that even though the above model suggests that the categories are distinct, SecondLife, a new player in the social network arena, demonstrates that several of the above types can be combined into one service. The uniqueness of SecondLife is that while offering users "space" to build their home (which appears to represent the first subcategory in the model), it also encourages users to engage in buying and selling among themselves, charging them for each of these transactions. This unique business model makes SecondLife a combination of subcategory 1 and subcategory 4 in our model.

1.6 eDating as a Subcategory of Social Networking

Considering eDating a subcategory of the social networking arena indicates that even though it shares the same purpose, i.e., it focuses on social networking, targets different customers (those who are specifically interested in connecting with romantic or sexual partners), and conducts the business transaction differently by providing a much more interventionist involvement of the company in the networking interactions of the customers. When it comes to eDating, the company that owns the service is in the business of actually matching customers with other customers, a service that the other social networking services do not provide. Furthermore, the company charges users for this service, which the other social networking services do not do.

It is important to note that because eDating services charge customers for being matched with other customers, they are essentially similar to auction sites. In both cases, the value-adding contribution from the company that owns the service is the matching of users to other users. In both cases, it is difficult to distinguish between buyers and sellers, as users may alternate between the two roles throughout their involvement with the service. Finally, in both cases, the business model does not rely on advertising but on direct charging of users for the matching service that the company provides.

Given how similar the eDating business model is to auction models, can we consider it part of the social networking arena? We believe that we can do this because unlike other auction services, eDating services do not involve buying and selling of goods or services (a financial transaction between users). Instead, users in the eDating model are engaged in social interactions where, if anything, they might be considered as buying and selling each other. As such, even though eDating is an extreme case of company involvement in the transactions that occur on the website, this business model does fit within the social networking category.

1.7 Categorizing eDating Business Models

Even though eDating services share a similar business model in that they all target individual customers and offer a matchmaking value-adding service, not all eDating services are the same. The following sections offer a categorization of eDating services that follows the same principle as the above categorization, namely, we will consider again *who* the customers are, *what* the service that is being offered is, and *how* the service is provided. Figure 1.2 presents a pictorial depiction of the eDating categorization model.

As indicated in Fig. 1.2, the eDating categorization model is based on two dimensions: (i) attributes; and (ii) behaviors.

1.7.1 Attributes (Physical Versus Personality)

This dimension refers to the amount of information about the dater's attributes offered in the website. A low ranking on this dimension will mean that the website provides a minimum amount of information about the dater's attributes. This will most likely include information about the dater including

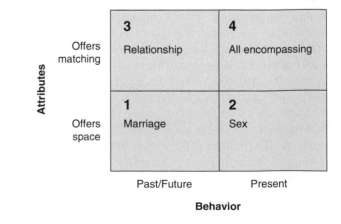

Fig. 1.2 eDating categorization typology

picture, voice message, and physical attributes. A high ranking on this dimension means that the website provides in-depth information about the dater's personality traits, including questionnaire-based data that enable the website to assess the personality of individual daters objectively as a basis for matching them with other daters (e.g., eHarmony , Chemistry.com , etc).

1.7.2 Behavior (Past and Future Versus Present)

This dimension refers to the amount of information about the dater's past, present, and future behavior offered by the website. A low ranking on this dimension means that the website provides a minimum amount of information about the dater's behavior. In most cases, this will include essay-type information written by the dater (or based on questions provided by the website) on the dater's preferred activities, hobbies, places visited, etc. A high ranking on this dimension will include information about the dater's actual behavior in the present, such as, profiles visited by the dater in real-time, or actual behavior vis-à-vis these profiles (perusal, chatting) also in real-time. A strong emphasis on real-time behavior in general, such as the option of communicating with other daters via instant messaging, also suggests a high ranking on the Behavior dimension. A new category of eDating websites offers rating of daters by other daters. This too can be seen as an example of a high ranking on the "Behavior" dimension because it represents reporting on real-time behavior of individual daters. The recent introduction of classified advertisements on Face-Book represents the same integration or conversion of business models.

1.7.3 Combining the Two Attributes to Produce Four Types of eDating Websites

1. *Marriage-oriented websites.* Low on attributes/low on behavior. Examples of this type of website are JDate (for Jewish daters), or Asian matrimonial websites that are strongly oriented toward marriage. This subcategory of eDating website serves a niche market of daters with special needs (religion, sexual affiliation, ethnicity, handicaps) who wish to date specifically for the purpose of marriage. Daters trust the service to select for them daters with desirable attributes and are satisfied with a minimal amount of information about other daters other than the fact that they are members of the desired group. The information that is provided in this type of websites includes pictures of the daters and basic demographic information. The more developed versions of this type (JDate) offer open-ended questions for daters to write about themselves. The less-developed versions (Asian websites) have no such features.

2. *Sex-oriented websites.* Low on attributes/high on behavior. Examples of this type of websites include AdultFriendFinder, or Passion.com , which cater to sexually oriented daters. Here the emphasis is on the visual, with the service providing primarily pictures of potential daters and some information about their demographic attributes and sexual preferences. Many of these websites offer features like real-time chat that allows interested daters to contact other daters in real-time, including via voice mail. Even though personality tests are not available, the real-time communication features provide information about behavior that is not available in the previous type of websites, hence, differentiating this subcategory of eDating websites from the previous one.

3. *Relationship-oriented websites.* High on attributes/low on behavior. An example of this type of website would be eHarmony. The website's original business model emphasized the in-depth questionnaires developed by the psychologist originator. Daters were administered these questionnaires prior to being offered a small number of hand-picked dates considered by the service to be "perfect" for them. In addition to information about the personality of the prospect, daters initially received minimal information about the prospect's demographics, behavior, etc. Indeed, the service did not initially provide even a picture of the prospect. Contact with prospects was also severely restricted by the service. Daters were not allowed free communication with each other and at least in the early stages of the online communication had to communicate with each other via prescribed questions provided by the service. A minimum of e-mail exchanges were required before free e-mail communication was allowed and no instant chat, voice mail, etc. were possible. Thus, the original design of the eHarmony website was intended to minimize information about real-time behavior and maximize information (or at least assurance) about the other dater's personality attributes.

4. *All encompassing websites.* High on attributes/high on behavior. Examples of this type of websites are Match.com , YahooPersonals, or LavaLife . These leading websites provide a richness of information about prospects' attributes that include, in addition to pictures and open-ended information, questionnaire-based data on the dater's personality traits. In addition, the website provides features that allow daters to assess the level and type of activity of other daters in real-time. They can see who viewed their profile, how active other daters have been in the recent past, and even (in extreme cases) what other daters are doing in real-time. The all-encompassing websites offer real-time communication via instant messaging and a high level of exposure via video or audio recordings that daters can attach to their websites. These provide high level of exposure because they eliminate the anonymity that is possible when daters communicate with each other on e-mail only. The high level of exposure to other daters can be perceived by some daters as invasive of their privacy, creating a sense of "surveillance" by other daters.

1.8 Discussion and Conclusions

As indicated in the previous sections of this chapter, our goal was to chart the boundaries of social networking and eDating as an emerging self-service industry. Our goal in this section is to consider the implications from this discussion.

We believe that the categorization models presented in the previous sections and the discussion of the business models that are the basis of the social networking and eDating industry have a number of implications. The first set of implications are related to research into the phenomenon that has been described in this chapter, namely, the proliferation of social networking and eDating services and the many different manifestations that they can take. The most immediate research direction from this chapter would be the construction of a scale that would allow researchers to measure the degree to which different eDating services contain features that correspond to the dimensions of the model. The scale would include items that describe "behaviors" and items that describe "attributes", with each category divided also into past/future versus present (for behaviors) and physical versus personality (for attributes).

Once the above scale is completed, it would be possible to test empirically whether the eDating industry can, indeed, be categorized into the four types of business models that were described in the previous sections of this chapter. It would also be possible to find out whether the four business models do, indeed, focus on the combination of behaviors and attributes that the model predict, e.g., whether the marriage websites are, indeed, low on both behaviors and attributes.

Another direction for the above research would include extending the sample of websites analyzed to different cultures. This extension will provide more robust support for the model and insights into the effect of culture on the manifestations of the model. Thus, it might be possible to demonstrate that even when a particular subcategory of the model is utilized (e.g., marriage websites), the actual combination of behaviors and attributes for a given type of website differs across cultures.

Another direction for future research that is based on the discussion in this chapter is to consider the business models in each subcategory of the eDating model as an environment . The eDating model implies that some combinations of behaviors and attributes represent a greater degree of exposure than others. Thus, a high level of "present" behaviors, combined with, a strong emphasis on "physical" attributes (a combination that is common in sex-oriented websites), exposes users more than a combination of "past and future" behaviors and an emphasis on "personality". Future research might explore empirically whether eDaters actually perceive websites that expose them more to other eDaters as more "invasive" of their privacy than other websites and whether such perception makes eDaters less inclined to use services that are seen as "too invasive".

Future research might also explore the impact that individual differences have on perceptions of eDating. For example, it would be interesting to find out if being a male or a female makes a difference to which attributes the individual would consider desirable in an eDating website. It would also be interesting to study the impact of culture on which attributes are welcomed in eDating websites, as well as the impact of other demographic variables like age, geographical location, ethnicity, and religion.

Finally, since this study focused on business models that are used by the eDating industry, it would be interesting to study the impact of choosing one or more of the business models that have been discussed here on the company's "bottom line". In particular, future research might explore whether the use of eDating models that are particularly invasive of daters' privacy in North America is behind the current saturation of the market in North America compared to Europe. It might also be interesting to find out whether as the industry matures, the more "inclusive" business models (such as the one exemplified by Match.com), which combine all business models under the same "roof" are the most successful ones. Obviously, if this is the case, our research would have immediate prescriptive implications to the eDating industry. However, given that this chapter does not focus only on the eDating industry, but also on the broader social networking industry, there is another set of more general implications that emanate from the discussion in this chapter.

The first set of issues that this chapter raises has to do with the self-service aspects of the social networking and eDating industry. If indeed, this emerging industry is a case where a service that used to be provided to customers by company employees is now provided on a self-service basis, does this transition represent an improvement of the service? Do customers perceive the services that are provided by social networking and eDating websites as enhancing their social life and their likelihood (in the case of eDating) of finding appropriate friends or marriage partners?

On the face of it, the answer to this question seems a resounding "yes". After all, as indicated in the earlier sections of this chapter, the social networking and eDating sector is thriving. However, the degree to which different types of user benefit from this industry is still an empirical question that requires further research. For example, one can argue that since the majority of customers on most eDating websites are males (Hitsch et al. 2005), the services are bound to favor females in terms of degree of choice and, consequently, level of satisfaction with the service. Does this mean that males and females are experiencing their "career" as eDaters differently? Does it mean that in order to be successful at eDating, males and females need to use different eDating strategies ? Does this mean that to enhance the level of satisfaction experienced by male eDaters, eDating services can (should) modify their business model to favor them?

Another related issue has to do with education. Given that social networking and eDating is becoming ubiquitous, should the educational system dedicate resources to training young people to be efficient eDaters? Should males and females get different instruction on how to conduct themselves on a social networking or an eDating website given that the environment in which they operate is not the same? Should the educational system consider eDating skills just as important for young adults as driving, cooking, and other "survival skills" have been in the past?

Another set of questions that the discussion in the previous section raises is related to the risks that eDating may entail. Recent popular publications discuss the fact that the risks to eDaters might involve, particularly in the case of female eDaters, the potential for violence (Loviglio 2007; Moraski 2007). Consequently, the popular literature is replete with prescriptions on how to conduct "safe" eDating.

Some eDating services (e.g., True.com) have based their business model on providing their customers with background checks on other eDaters' criminal record and matrimonial status, and on lobbying for such searches to be enforced by law on all services or for services that do not conduct such searchers to acknowledge it on their websites (Heydary 2006). Following this line of reasoning, an interesting direction for future research would be to explore the extent to which different eDating business models are perceived by eDaters as more or less safe, and what the service providers can do to enhance the sense of security of their customers.

Privacy concerns and the possible invasion of privacy that some eDating websites (the ones that involve a higher level of exposure) represent is another important direction for future research. As indicated in the previous sections, a business model that combines "present behavior" and "physical attributes" has the potential to be experienced by users as highly invasive of their privacy. Indeed, users might experience, particularly the emphasis on present behavior, as actual surveillance. Again, it would be interesting to empirically explore how different eDaters feel about the invasion of privacy that different eDating business models entail. Are males more comfortable with it than females? Are younger eDaters more comfortable than older ones? Does level of education or socio-economic status impact the degree to which eDaters are willing to tolerate different levels of self-exposure or invasion of their privacy?

The discussion in the previous sections also has some wider societal implications. One such implication is the possible potential for abuse of information that eDaters make public. The potential for criminal abuse has been discussed in the previous sections. However, there is also a potential for more "benign" abuse. For example, there are numerous reports in the popular literature of the use of information in social networking and eDating services by employers (Lavallee 2007; White 2007). These reports suggest that many employers use information that individuals have posted on social networking and eDating services (possibly a long time before the individual joined the labor force) as a basis for selection of candidates for jobs, promotion of employees, and even for harassment of employees on the job.

The potential for abuse of social networking and eDating services raises a set of other issues that involve the political and legal system. If, indeed, the social networking and eDating sector poses potential dangers, including dangers to children, should society regulate the industry to make sure that customers are more protected than they currently are? Should social networking services that cater primarily to children and teenagers (such as FaceBook) be expected to conduct their business differently to other services, including requesting customers to identify themselves and to prove how old they are? Should some practices (such as buying and selling) not be allowed on social networking services that cater to minors? Should eDating services be required to check their customers' criminal record or marital status? Should they be required to acknowledge on their website, in a manner similar to pharmaceutical companies, if they do not conduct such searches? Should eDating services that involve "ranking" of eDaters by other eDaters in a manner similar to eBay's rating of buyers and sellers be outlawed because this practice involves the potential for defamation of customers? Only the future will tell how many of these issues will be addressed by researchers and/or by society as a whole, and how this will lead to an evolution of the social networking and eDating industry as we know it today.

References

Bitner MJ (2001) Self-service technologies: What do customers expect? Marketing Management 10:1–10

Delaney K, Buckman R, Guth R (2006) Facebook riding a web trend: Flirts with a big-money deal. Wall Street Journal March 16:A8

Heydary J (2006) Regulation of on-line dating services sparks controversy. Wall Street Journal, September 26:B7

Hitsch GJ, Hortacsu A, Arieli A (2005) What makes you click? Paper presented at the QME Conference, University of Chicago, Chicago

Jesdanun A (2006). Facebook changes after privacy protests. Wall Street Journal January 17:B6

Jordan M (2006) Official sues students over MySpace page. Wall Street Journal June 15:B6

Lavallee A (2007) Firms tidy up clients' bad on-line reputations. Wall Street Journal June 13:B7

Loviglio J (2007) Two sex convictions in on-line dating case. Wall Street Journal June 16:A8

Markman JD (2006) Why YouTube is ready for prime time. Wall Street Journal January 5:A4

Marshall C (2006) Facebook opens its pages. Wall Street Journal April 23:B3

Meuter ML, Ostrom AL, Roundtree AI et al. (2000) Self-service technologies: understanding customer satisfaction with technology-based service encounters. Journal of Marketing 64:50–64

Moraski M (2007) Beware of digital Don Juans. Wall Street Journal June 16:B5

Oliver D, Romm C, Farag-Awad N (2007) Self-service on the Internet: an explanatory model. Paper presented at 20th Bled eConference eMergence: Merging and Emerging Technologies, Processes, and Institutions, Bled, Slovenia, June 3–6 http://domino.fov.uni-mb.si/Proceedings

Oliver D, Romm C, Farag NA (2005) Are you being Served - exploring the role of customers as employees in the digital world. Paper presented at CollECTeR Europe, Furtwangen, Germany

Osterwalder A (2004) The business model ontology: a proposition in a design science approach. In Theses presente a l'ecole des hautes etudes commercialles de l'université de Lausanne, Lausanne

Romm C, Farag NA, Oliver D (2005) Turning customers into employees - research in progress. Presented at *6th Annual Global Information Technology Management Conference*, Alaska, USA

White E (2007) Employers reach out to recruit with Facebook. Wall Street Journal January, 11:A3

Chapter 2
The Role and Implications of the Internet in Healthcare Delivery

Alex Broom

Abstract Drawing on a study of the Internet usage of Australian men with prostate cancer , this chapter investigates how access to information and online support affects men's experiences of disease and, in particular, the possible implications of Internet-informed patients for the doctor/patient relationship. The data reveal that accessing information and/or support online can have a profound effect on men's experiences of prostate cancer, providing a method of taking some control over their disease and limiting inhibitions experienced in face-to-face encounters. However, it is also clear that some medical specialists view Internet-informed patients as a challenge to their power within medical encounters and, as a result, employ disciplinary strategies that reinforce traditional patient roles and alienate patients who use the Internet.

2.1 Introduction

In the context of health and well-being, the Internet is playing an increasingly crucial role in shaping patient's experiences of disease, lay-expert relations and broader societal conceptions of disease. In particular, the presence of health-related information, social support and therapeutic products online has opened up the possibility of a 'virtual' liberalisation of health-related knowledge and clinical expertise (see Broom 2005a, 2006b). Recent research published in the medical and social science literature suggests that information seeking on the Internet is regularly health-related (Ahmann 2000; Cline & Haynes 2001; Diaz et al. 2002; Hardey 1999; Fox & Rainie 2002) and that patients (and health consumers) are *increasingly* relying on the Internet to make critical health decisions, often bringing Internet material into medical consultations as an aid to decision making (see Anderson et al. 2003; Berland et al. 2001; Cotten 2001; Friedewald 2000; Pemberton & Goldblatt 1998). Moreover, online forums related

A. Broom (✉)
School of Humanities and Social Science, University of Newcastle, Callaghan NSW
2308 Australia
e-mail: alexander.broom@newcastle.edu.au

D. Oliver et al. (eds.), *Self-Service in the Internet Age*,
DOI 10.1007/978-1-84800-207-4_2, © Springer-Verlag London Limited 2009

to health and well-being are increasingly popular with patients, allowing them to 'chat' to others about their health condition/s, treatment programmes and encounters with medical professionals (see Broom 2005b; Burrows et al. 2000; Dudley et al. 1996; Lamberg 1997; Loader et al. 2002; Rainie & Fox 2001; Sharf 1997; Zrebiec & Jacobson 2001). Furthermore, whereas previously a 'second opinion' was generally only available through local and informally linked health professionals, the Internet provides international and cross-cultural comparisons of therapeutic advice from the 'safety' of one's own home.

As such, an Internet-mediated form of health self-service has emerged within contemporary therapeutic culture that, whilst limited in scope (i.e. many patients still require face-to-face clinical care), is allowing individuals to access expert advice, social support services and some therapeutic interventions *independently* from their medical professional/s. In order to understand the implications of such developments, social sciences have, in recent years, examined the range of impacts the Internet is having in healthcare delivery, resulting in a considerable body of work addressing the potential implications for a range of differently positioned stakeholders (e.g. Anderson et al. 2003; Broom 2005a,b; Burrows et al. 2000; Hardey 1999, 2002; Nettleton 2004; Seale 2005; Seale et al. 2006; Sharf 1997; Ziebland 2004; Ziebland et al. 2004). This work has produced numerous ideas and hypotheses regarding the impacts of the Internet for patients, professionals, therapeutic modalities (i.e. biomedicine versus alternative practices) and state-enforced regulatory processes (i.e. pharmaceutical benefits schemes and government-led quality control initiatives). The Internet, some have argued, by educating the public and empowering consumers, is contributing to the democratisation of medical knowledge and the emergence of 'patient-as-expert' (for more discussion see Broom, 2005c). It is thus breaking down elements of the expert/lay divide and fundamentally changing patient's expectations of care.

Internet-based self-service in health delivery raises several key concerns regarding the role of the patient, the nature (and legitimacy) of knowledge and the position (and influence) of the clinician in treatment and decision-making processes (Broom 2005b,c). Moreover, the Internet has also been linked—albeit tentatively—to an increasingly pluralistic therapeutic landscape (see Broom & Tovey 2008 forthcoming). The increased democratisation of healthcare knowledge online is viewed, at least by some social commentators, to increase the profile of (and be supportive for) alternative therapeutic models of care, thereby *further* challenging mainstream healthcare professionals and organisations. Within the medical literature, such concerns have been expressed in the form of debate about the 'risks' associated with increased access to information, support and health products online (e.g. Kiley 2002; McKinley et al. 1999; Schmidt & Ernst 2004; Whiting 2000), including the potential for harm and adverse effects as patients explore different therapeutic options (i.e. alternative medicines). Such arguments remain largely unsubstantiated and have been viewed by some as a means of circumventing the rather dramatic increase in public support for alternative therapeutics and waning deference to biomedical expertise (see Broom & Tovey 2008 forthcoming).

This chapter engages with such issues through an examination of the impact of the Internet from the perspectives of 33 Australian men suffering from prostate cancer . As such, it examines the interplay of patient roles, new information technologies, gender inequality and expert-lay relations. More specifically, it examines the complex and at times contradictory effects of the Internet on these men's relationships with their doctors and broader experiences of disease. Whilst the limitations of the Internet are evident in their accounts, the results of this study *also* illustrate the powerful role of the Internet in improving aspects of these men's experiences of disease and treatment processes. Specifically, the results indicate the powerful role self-service in healthcare may have within contemporary therapeutic landscapes. However, the mixed responses of healthcare professionals suggest potential barriers to patient empowerment and the actualisation of new patient roles as engendered in much social science literature hitherto. Ultimately, at least from the results of the study reported on here, the reactions of some medical specialists to Internet-informed patients will have considerable implications for the impact of new information technologies and forms of self-service in healthcare delivery.

2.2 Prostate Cancer, Masculinities and Men's Health

Prostate cancer is the second most common cause of cancer-related death in Australian men (Frydenberg 1998; Frydenberg & Wijesinha 2007). It is largely a disease of men over 60 years of age but also can occur in those under 40 years. Despite common perception, it accounts for more deaths in men than breast cancer does in women (see Frydenberg & Wijesinha 2007). In 2004, in Australia there were 10,512 new cases of prostate cancer and 2852 deaths (AIHW 2004). Despite these high rates of morbidity and mortality of prostate cancer in Australia, public awareness and support services lag behind those for comparable diseases such as breast cancer. As such, the Internet is an increasingly important source of information and support for men with prostate cancer (see Broom 2005a,b). Research to both assess its effects for those men currently using it, and its potential for those who are not, is essential to reap the full benefits of this new technology.

Cultural constructions of masculinity within Australian society, and indeed internationally, have been shown to be influential in men's health outcomes (see Broom 2004). Media portrayals of the 'bullet-proof', 'hard' man (Saunders 2000), contribute to a socio-cultural environment in which some men are less able than women to recognise physical and emotional distress and to seek help (Reddin & Sonn 2003). Statistics back up the importance of gendered social relations in mediating health behaviour and outcomes. For example, for most illnesses men are less likely than women to consult their general practitioners, yet their hospital admission rates for diseases such as coronary heart disease and stroke are higher (Broom 2004; Bradlow et al. 1992; Cameron & Bernardes 1998). Australian men have higher death rates than women for all major causes of death. Furthermore, their use of health services is 40 percent lower than Australian women (Broom 2004). Men are said to be less aware of potential risks to their health and this seems to be true in the case of the male and his prostate.

The reluctance of men to consult medical professionals and seek social support is amplified for prostate cancer sufferers who at various stages in the course of the illness and its treatment may experience problems with sexual performance and continence (Broom 2004; Hines 1999), resulting in a fear of humiliation. This is compounded by the fact that the majority of men with prostate cancer are over 60 years of age—an age group not as accustomed as other groups to taking an active role in their health or treatment decisions (Beisecker & Beisecker 1990). Furthermore, physicians often do not deal well with 'the male mentality' and tend to be uninformed and uncomfortable with male problems (Walsh 2000). As a result men are often unaware of where to turn to for health information and support (Broom 2004, 2006).

2.3 On Method and Methodology

After reviewing the literature and obtaining ethics approval, meetings were arranged with local support group organisers to explain the study, and with their support, the author sent information letters to group members, asking them to participate in the study. Eventually, 25 men were recruited from 3 face-to-face support groups operating in Victoria, Australia. Overall, 37 percent (25/68) of those approached through the support groups agreed to take part after follow-up and reminder letters. The remaining eight responded to an article written about the current study in a personal computer magazine, which requested that readers with prostate cancer interested in participating in the study contact the author. The description of the study in the information letter, outlining the focus on men's Internet usage, meant that the majority of the men who responded (28/33) were current Internet users. To provide some comparison with the Internet users, five men were interviewed who had never used the Internet. The sample was not designed to be representative of all men prostate cancer, rather, the purpose was to get a sample that would allow an investigation into the effects of Internet usage on disease experiences. In total, 33 men were recruited. Interviews continued until the sample included men with a range of prognoses, who had been through a range of treatments.

2.3.1 The Interviews

All the respondents were subsequently interviewed in their own homes for between 1 and 2 hours. In two cases, the men's wives were present in the interview. The interviews were relatively unstructured, exploring the impact of the Internet on their coping and decision-making ability, and the implications of becoming 'Internet informed' for interactions with medical specialists. Empowerment, enhanced sense of control, and 'risk' emerged as important themes, with many men talking spontaneously about the benefits of the Internet in terms of empowerment and heightened sense of control, and others about their fears around the accuracy of information and the authenticity of relationships on the Internet. It is these three themes, 'empowerment', 'control' and 'risk', which are examined in this article.

The method for this project draws on the interpretive traditions within qualitative research, in which the researcher seeks an in-depth understanding of the experiences of the respondents and, in particular, how they made sense of the role of the Internet within their experiences of disease. An in-depth exploratory approach to data collection was taken aimed at documenting the subjective and complex experiences of the respondents rather than merely reflecting on such things as frequency of Internet usage, sources of information and the type of information retrieved. A focus was maintained on unpacking the complex ways in which the Internet has affected the lives of the respondents, building theory from their narratives rather than imposing it on them (see Charmaz 1990).

2.4 Results: The Internet, Self-Help and Maintaining Control

It is important to emphasise at this point that there is no one archetypal effect of the Internet on disease experience. Experiences and attitudes differed for each patient and were influenced by many different factors such as disease stage, age, literacy, socio-economic status and social support networks. However, whilst embracing the complexity of effects and perspectives within such a heterogeneous group of men, one is able to identify certain themes within their accounts which provide an idea of the effects the Internet can have on patients' experiences of disease. The role of the Internet in enhancing these respondents' power and control over their disease and decision-making processes were prominent themes within the interviews. One respondent talked about this in relation to an online community:

> In terms of the actual outcome it [the Internet] probably doesn't make any difference. In terms of people's need to feel that they are in control of the situation. . .if people have confidence in their treatment they're more likely to have a positive outcome. I wasn't stressed out by the information I gained, I just thought I was in greater control. . . that's what I thought (1 year post-treatment, organ-confined disease, Internet user).

Another respondent comments:

> I found [the online community] extremely useful. I'm one of these people who has a high need for information and knowledge. Knowledge is power. I like to be in control of my situation and the way I want to do that is by knowing what is going to happen. . .That need for knowledge or need for control means I really need that

information to feel ok. There are some people who are really quite happy just to not
have that information. I'm not one of those (6 months post treatment, organ-confined
disease, Internet user).

Several of the men who had used the Internet stated that online information
sources (and in some cases, online communities) provided an invaluable method
of seeking knowledge and thus control over their treatment process. As the
above respondent notes, the information provided by online forums provided
clarity in terms of treatments options, and as a result, diminished his reliance on
his specialists, allowing him to "take control of my treatment instead of having
to rely on my specialist". Although several of the respondents reported that
their Internet usage did not necessarily influence the actual decisions made, and
certainly not the physiological outcome of treatment, it was seen as greatly
improving the decision-making process by reducing the uncertainties involved
in making a treatment decision.

It has been suggested by some members of the medical community that the
Internet is problematic, or even harmful, due to its tendency to either sway
patients away from conventional cancer treatments or mislead them in relation
to their 'efficacy' (see for example Kiley 2002; McKinley et al. 1999; Schmidt &
Ernst 2004; Whiting 2000). Moreover, fear of increased consumer access to
alternative knowledge has contributed to the labelling of Internet usage as an
activity that represents dissatisfaction with conventional medicine. One respondent discusses his approach to alternative treatments and the Internet:

[The Internet] is quite good for people who might be trying alternative treatments who
say, no, I don't want the knife. I didn't go down that path. I was happy that my
urologist had advised me correctly and that I had made the right decision to so I wasn't
really seeking alternative information. I had made up my mind that I wanted to have
surgery and then it was a matter of concentrating on achieving fitness to be able to have
it happen. So I wasn't really looking around on the Internet for information other than
stuff on surgery (1.5 years post treatment, organ-confined disease, Internet user).

Contrary to the fears of the medical community, for the majority of the men
interviewed here, accessing support and information online did not increase
their negativity or scepticism towards biomedical cancer treatments. Rather,
the result was clarification of the subtleties involved in particular biomedical
treatments, enabling a significant proportion of the respondents to experience a
heightened sense of control and therefore enter into a comprehensive negotiation with their specialist and make what they perceived to be an informed
choice.

The reaction of medical specialists to Internet-informed patients was of
particular interest in this study. One respondent's response to the question of
what effect information seeking had on his encounters with medical professionals was:

A lot of the medical community basically see it as loss of control. The standard advice is
if you want information about your condition ask your doctor. They don't like it when
you seek information from other sources...it [is] the standard, well, you're not

medically trained, you're not competent to understand this, we will interpret it for you. This is back to, we have exclusive control over this area of knowledge type mind set. I felt that particularly in contact with the urologist I saw. (6 months post-treatment, organ-confined disease, Internet user)

Like this respondent, the majority of the men who had used the Internet felt that their information-seeking was effective and that they were competent to decipher the 'good' from the 'bad'. Despite this they were acutely aware that their specialists may view this as outside the 'patient's role', or, as the above respondent suggests, as a challenge to his/her authority (see also Broom 2005b,c, 2006). This same respondent states later in the interview, "I don't feel completely comfortable sharing the information that I have found with my specialist", reflecting a pattern in the men interviewed here of being 'disapproved of' in terms of his Internet usage and information seeking. Another respondent explained his specialist's reaction when he disclosed his use of the Internet in the consultation:

I asked him questions and he answered them and I said, "well listen, I was on the Internet last night and I've got all these questions for you". And he goes, "oh, look you've got to be careful when you go on the Internet", and he's telling me, "keep away, steer away, because information overload is just no good for you". And I thought to myself, hmm, that's thick, for me, and I like the Internet, I like reading, I'm right into it and this bloke is telling me to keep away from it. "That means I leave it up to you and I rely totally on you for information" – he goes, "yes". And I said, "well, how do I know what to ask you." He said, "oh you just do." I said, "hmmm...". And he didn't like that. (Pre-treatment, organ-confined disease, Internet user)

This perception of feeling 'Disapproved of' is a significant barrier to patient–clinician communication that inevitably results in higher levels of anxiety, confusion and frustration. The behaviours of specialists, as illustrated in the above excerpt, may discourage patients from asking questions and entering into an open dialogue with them about their treatment preferences and concerns. The reaction of some specialists to the apparent threat of a disruption to the lay/expert divide within the consultation is to create a dynamic relationship whereby the patient feels 'bad' for attempting to understand or question the information being provided by the specialist. This produces a complex process of contesting, redefining, and in some cases, reinforcing the dominance of the passive patient role in the treatment process.

As was the case for several of the respondents, there is clearly a discrepancy between what the above respondent viewed as his role in the treatment process and his specialist's expectations of the patient's role. Thus, increased access to information and support online does not necessarily result in better doctor–patient communication. Being 'well informed', and attempting to engage in a comprehensive dialogue in treatment decisions, may in fact result in hostility, irritation and a less satisfactory level of care. This has the effect of reducing patient control and power in decision making, thus complicating claims of the liberating nature and positive effect of the Internet on disease experience. The narratives of several of the respondents reveal that patients may feel their level of knowledge seeking creates a barrier to receiving effective care from their specialist. Control or power, then, cannot be seen as confined to any one particular facet of a patient's experience, since feelings of power and control are in part determined by the reception of patients' Internet usage by medical specialists.

2.4.1 Patient Empowerment Online

In the current study, the respondents were asked how their Internet usage affected their decision-making ability. One respondent talked about him and his wife's use of the Internet:

> The information available on the Internet was a revelation. It was a real revelation to us. We were reading reports and information about different treatments right up to the minute – material that just wasn't available anywhere else. We picked the bones out of each particular subject. We could log on to brachytherapy and a new world opened up to us. We were able to then sort out statistical information about cure rates, and define centres of excellence. We finally felt as if we had some control over things. (Mid-treatment, extracapsular disease, Internet user)

For this respondent, the Internet allowed him to 'do something' rather than just being "told what to do by our specialist". It provided him with a sense of purpose and control, having a profound effect on his ability to deal with his cancer. Being a very active person, this respondent strove to be able to "throw my energy into getting better", and the Internet, he suggested, provided a vehicle for him to feel like there was something he could do. Furthermore, it provided him with the resources to help other men with prostate cancer by explaining to them what was happening to them based on the information he retrieved from the Internet. The Internet gave him the knowledge and skills to counsel his friends and take a leadership role in the face-to-face support group he attends, dramatically improving the quality of his life. As he put it, "it made me feel like I had some power over this disease, I could understand it, so I could fight it".

Despite the powerful and liberating effect of the Internet for several of the respondents, findings from the current study indicate that for others, it was a case of too much information too late. Although several of the men found important information on the Internet, by the time they began searching and became computer savvy enough to find useful information, they had either already begun a particular treatment regime or had already gone through surgery. As a result, for several of the respondents, searching the Internet became more a matter of discovering information they felt they should have known before making a treatment decision. Several expressed regret regarding how much more useful the Internet would have been if they had been exposed to it immediately after diagnosis, and in particular, before making a treatment decision:

> The Internet wasn't really very useful in helping to make the decision but it certainly made a tremendous difference in your background information for either accepting what was decided or regretting the decision. I think that that it was extremely useful in reassuring me that that had been the right decision. . .I suppose decisions have to be made in real life before you get all the information. (Mid-treatment, extracapsular disease, Internet user)

This excerpt captures one of the many practical limitations of the Internet for patients. Often the testing, diagnosis and treatment take place over a number of weeks or just a couple of months, leaving little time for research, let alone learning to use communication technologies such as the Internet. Moreover, for several of these respondents there was considerable self-imposed, and sometimes clinician encouraged, pressure to make a quick decision to 'get the cancer out' as soon as possible, even in the case of low grade, non-aggressive tumours that are relatively slow growing. As a result, searching the Internet was about making sense of the treatment process they had been through or exploring alternatives if treatment had been unsuccessful. In particular, they often sought information about side effects and how successful their surgery/radiation treatment was compared with others (whether their situation is typical or whether something 'went wrong').

2.4.2 The Internet and 'The Patient's Role'

The Internet is, to a certain degree, generating new dynamics between doctors and patients by providing patients with the information and support necessary to understand and at times question medical decisions (see Broom 2005a,b). In the following excerpt, a respondent talks about his specialists' attitudes towards patients seeking information from the Internet and other sources:

> I more than think, I know what their attitude is. We extensively searched the Internet [and] at one urologist's office I was asking about certain information and this went on for some time. I went back to his secretary and we are paying the bill. He was talking into a dictaphone and he was making the referral to somebody else and he said, "[patient's name] is somewhat difficult and over-informed". . .The first urologist that I went to said, "have an operation", he didn't even discuss other forms of treatment. No, they definitely don't really like well-informed people. (1 year post-treatment, organ-confined disease, Internet user)

As this respondent experienced first hand, the Internet tests the limits of the 'conventional' doctor–patient relationship, having a levelling effect (but not necessarily making them level) in a relationship historically marked by an imbalance of power. However, this can result in specialists adopting various strategies to discourage this 'levelling' such as giving patients the impression that they are disapproved of or treating men who ask questions as 'problem patients'. Another respondent responds to the question of why specialists are resistant to questioning and informed patients:

Well they are probably that busy or whatever that it's all dollars and cents to them. The thing that really disheartened me was that I went away rather shocked like anyone is when they are told they have got cancer and I made a list of things to ask him in the next consultation. I had two foolscap sheets of questions. . .I said to him could you please tell me what my Gleason score[1] is. He said "oh, you've got some questions have you", and I said yes and he said, "oh, show them to me", and I gave him the two pieces of paper and he just grabbed them like that [shows me] and went [ticking motion] yes, no, yes, no. . .not applicable, yes, no, and handed them back to me.

AB: Why do you think your urologist reacted like that?

Why. . .when you park you car, one parking officer won't even speak and will write out the ticket, but the other bloke will give you a bit of a warning. It's attitudes. . .that happens in all professions I guess. (4 years post-treatment, organ-confined disease, Internet user)

The reaction of this specialist is an example of a strategy to avoid dialogue and reclaim the consultation model whereby it becomes merely a process of, at best, one-way information provision (see also Broom 2005b). His response of "yes, no, no" and ticking the questions listed by the respondent disempowers the respondent by not allowing him to initiate a dialogue to work through his concerns. This specialist ignores the respondent's request for his Gleason score, reacting, according to the respondent, as if it was inappropriate and "suspicious for me to want this type of information". This is one example of the various strategies employed by some of the respondents' specialists to limit the success-fulness of their attempts to understand and question medical decisions and initiate a dialogue within the consultation.

It is tempting to romanticise the effects of the Internet and the empowering nature of information. However, as a number of the respondents suggested, the empowering nature of the information they retrieved from the Internet and other sources was dependent on how receptive providers and specialists were to their desire to take part in decision-making processes. Financial constraints combined with a desire to "deal quickly" with their disease meant that several respondents felt that they could not afford to spend a lot of time "shopping around" for sympathetic specialists. One respondent explains the limits to the potential of the Internet:

You can be empowered to be happier with decisions that are made for you and you also can participate more to a degree in the decision but it's still dependent on finding a consultant or even the hospital which is reactive to this situation or sympathetic. That seems to me to be the difficulty in that, in my case, or in the individual case, you can't go to 4 or 5 specialists. Sooner or later you have to make a choice. (Mid-treatment, suspected extracapsular disease, Internet user)

---

[1] The Gleason system evaluates how effectively the cells of any particular cancer are able to structure themselves into glands resembling those of the normal prostate. The ability of a tumour to mimic normal gland architecture is called its *differentiation*, and a tumour whose structure is nearly normal (well differentiated) will probably have a *biological behaviour* that is not very aggressively malignant.

The benefits of information are constrained by a number of factors, including an individual's skill in accessing and comprehending it, and the amount of time (both perceived by them and prescribed by the specialist) that they have to actually make a treatment decision, and their access to receptive medical professionals. Several of the men interviewed could not afford to get a second opinion or to choose their own specialist. Even though they had access to a substantial amount of information, they either could not afford to see other specialists or opt for limited, costly treatments such as HDR Brachytherapy[2]. Furthermore, their resistance to getting a second opinion was amplified by the fact that they thought it would "slow down" their progress and mean their cancer would be worse when they were eventually treated. The view seemed to be that it would "irritate" their specialists to seek a second opinion or to be presented with information that questioned their advice and possibly result in them receiving less effective care. Thus, information was only one variable in determining whether the respondents were empowered to make an informed decision, with other structural constraints severely limiting their ability to negotiate satisfactory treatment processes.

2.4.3 Trust and Uncertainty

A number of the respondents, particularly the non-users, were suspicious of the Internet, and talked consistently about their reliance on the expertise and advice of their medical specialists. In the following excerpts, two respondents talk about whether or not patients should seek information and be 'active' in making treatment decisions:

> Even now I ask myself: these people, they sit in front of their computers and they search the Internet and they read this but for what reason? Maybe they are chasing something that's not there...I figure if you go to a specialist and you don't follow his advice it's bordering on stupidity – he's the expert and I trust his judgement. (6 years post-diagnosis, hormone treatment for secondary disease, non-Internet user)

> I don't think that's my job. I sort of believe you've got to judge your surgeon. I know he goes overseas to conferences. I think you've sort of got to assume that they're up with the latest, um, you've got to hope that they have got a steady hand [laughs] and just go from there. I would be weary of designing me own treatment. (3 years post-treatment, organ-confined disease, non-Internet user)

The latter respondent articulates a common feeling of a lack of ability to judge information and a heavy reliance on the expertise of the specialist. This same respondent was then asked why he did not seek information or support

---

[2] Brachytherapy is an advanced cancer treatment. Radioactive seeds or sources are placed in or near the tumour itself, giving a high radiation dose to the tumour while reducing the radiation exposure in the surrounding healthy tissues. The term "brachy" is Greek for short distance, and brachytherapy is radiation therapy given at a short distance: localized, precise, and high-tech.

from the Internet. He responds, not in relation to the Internet explicitly, but rather, the futility, in his view, of trying to take control of his treatment process:

> Even though I had been diagnosed with cancer, which is a word everybody fears, I guess I'm fairly accepting of the situation. If I've got little or no control over it... When I went into hospital for this they said, you know, do you want to be a public or a private patient. If you're a private patient you have a doctor of your own choice. Well, I mean, who am I going to pick, I've never had that operation before, obviously, or I wouldn't have a prostate. Am I going to say, well, gee, bring us in the yellow pages and I'll pick one out. So, at the end of the day you sort of go with something but you've got the stress. . .I mean you've got the stress of your own situation and your family is under stress, you're exploring this information and you have got to make good judgments and you can't actually necessarily judge the source. (3 years post-treatment, organ-confined disease, non-Internet user)

This respondent vividly articulates the sense of loss of control that a significant proportion of the respondents (not just the non-users) experienced attempting to make treatment decisions. The provision of options, such as public/private, gives a perception of choice, whereas clearly this choice almost constricts the previous respondent in the sense that information is not provided for him to actually make the choice. There are no performance criteria for particular doctors provided. The choice, from the perspective of this respondent, is meaningless because he has no knowledge, and in his mind has no way of gaining the knowledge, to make a decision that would produce the better outcome.

For three of the non-Internet users, reliance on their specialist was not considered a negative thing, rather, the intelligent option. As suggested in one of the earlier excerpts, they considered it "stupid to try and learn what they [specialists] already know". Reliance was viewed as the 'safe' option, and using the Internet, as one respondent put it, "is a stupid thing to do. I think they [other men] are probably grasping at straws anyway. Why bother? My specialist knows his stuff". These narratives illustrate the complex needs of men with prostate cancer and the importance of not assuming that all men want to self-educate or develop a sophisticated understanding of the treatment options available.

2.4.4 Masculinity and Managing Risk in Cyberspaces

A theme that emerged from the interviews was the potential of online communities to allow men to 'open up' and reduce the 'risk' they might feel in sharing their experiences in face-to-face situations. One respondent spoke about his experience of using an online community, reflecting on the benefits of this new medium in terms of an effective forum for him and other men, to talk about the more sensitive aspects of their disease experience:

> One of the things you find is an amazing openness and frankness about these sort of matters that I'm sure men if they were meeting face to face would not talk about. I mean it's amazing stuff when you actually look at it that if they were sitting around a table in

a room. I'm fairly positive they would not be talking about such intimate details because it's a community out there...we're doing it through this medium and we can be a lot more frank. We could discuss things that if we knew each other face-to-face, we wouldn't have been quite as frank and open. There's the anonymity, there's the disembodiment which is slightly different than anonymity. Anonymous is, your not known and you have all these people who...you're able to project in a way that isn't having any comeback on you...in terms of your not having to deal with the face-to-face reactions or anything like that. It is disembodying from you, from what you're putting there. It's away from me. It's out there. (6 months post-treatment, organ-confined disease, Internet user)

This respondent's comment suggests that the Internet can provide a haven for some patients (in this case men) to talk about the more sensitive aspects of their disease experiences; discussions that, according to this respondent (and several others interviewed), would not occur in a face-to-face situation. The Internet presented a number of these men with a method for managing the 'risk' of sharing sensitive information with other men. The 'risk' of attempting such a dialogue in face-to-face situations is precisely that of not being able to share their experiences at all.

Several of the respondents suggested that the Internet distanced them from their disease and their symptomology. They found it much easier to share their experiences, if only at first, if they perceived them to be dislocated from their body. Seen in the previous excerpt, there is a differentiation between being anonymous, which this respondent sees as negative, and being disembodied, which he views as a positive state with regard to feeling able to share his experiences. The separation of 'embodied self' from the 'disembodied-but-diseased self' allows some of these men to open up to other men and seek information and support—an opening up that may not have occurred in a face-to-face situation. This perceived disembodiment allows a controlled transition towards intimacy and mutual support.

For several of the men interviewed, the protection felt online helped them extend themselves, allowing different types of interactions and personal growth. This perception of anonymity or disembodiment in online forums may in fact lead people to reveal more about themselves than they do face-to-face (Joinson 2001). As suggested by the following respondent, the 'risk' of expression may be amplified in the case of prostate cancer as societal perceptions of manliness and the nature of the disease and treatment (incontinence, sexual dysfunction, etc...) make open face-to-face discussion problematic for men:

Some men don't want to be face-to-face. Maybe they're frightened of it, maybe they don't want to travel the distances. Maybe they're scared of being ridiculed or something...all sorts of reasons like that. Maybe they're bit anxious about having the problem and not wanting to share it with other people. I think that's men for you. Some will find it easier to talk online. (3 years post-treatment, organ-confined disease, Internet user)

The ability to 'lurk' and, not necessarily, post messages was also viewed as a significant advantage of online communities. In particular, men could

participate without feeling the pressure to actually share their specific experience as may be felt in face-to-face situations. One respondent discussed different
levels of participation in his online support group , and the benefits of 'lurking'
for patients attempting to find information and support:

> In terms of people being active there's a hard core, whose names you will see just about
> everyday, of about 10 or 12. There's a much wider group of about 50 who constan-
> tly...every couple of months they will bounce up. So they are obviously sitting there
> monitoring it, they will respond to something that interests them. And then there is a lot
> more who are lurking, who occasionally...someone will come on and say, "well, I've been
> lurking on this site for three or four months, now I have a specific question to ask". But
> there are also people that are obviously just monitoring it and not actually contributing
> anything...maybe they'll make the occasional contribution. It suits some people to post
> messages but not others. (2 years post-treatment, metastatic disease, Internet user)

For this respondent, 'lurking' is an invaluable characteristic of this community, allowing participants who do not feel able to ask questions, to benefit from
the interactions of the more active participants. The respondents who used
online communities reported going through stages of needing more or less
information and support, with periods where they would post more than once
a day and times when they would not post at all for months. The point of
making a decision about treatment and the period immediately following
treatment were, according to several of the respondents, the times that they
posted the most messages. There was a collective understanding of the dynamic
nature of the need for information and support during disease and treatment
processes. The acceptability of both varying and low levels of involvement
within such groups was appealing for a number of the respondents.

There was a clear division amongst the respondents as to the context in which
they were willing to share their experiences and their perceptions of what
constituted 'risk'. The respondents who used online support networks emphasised the importance of being able to get information and support from a 'safe'
distance and the value of a forum that was separate from their 'everyday life'.
However, several of the respondents who attended face-to-face support groups,
particularly those who had never used the Internet, were adamant of their
suspicion of communication that wasn't face-to-face and the importance of
being able to "see who I am talking to". These reflect two different ways of
managing 'risk' within this particular group of men. The 'risk' for those using
the online support group s was having to share their experiences in a public
situation—to be exposed to the 'public' gaze and reveal themselves to other men
face-to-face. Online support group s presented as a way of negotiating this
'risk', and a 'safe' way of sharing, receiving and providing emotional support
and information. However, for others, online support groups presented a
serious 'risk' in terms of authenticity of relationships (who am I talking to)
and information (they could tell me anything). As is shown in the following
discussion, for these respondents, not searching the Internet or being involved
in online support groups was considered a method of reducing 'risk'. One
respondent talks about the 'risk' of online communities:

> I would be very wary of [online communities]. For the same reason as the Americans are finding out when they are interrogating these [terrorists]. They are getting fed wrong information, sometimes deliberately, and they're going out and bombing innocent people on the basis of information extracted out of these people.

AB: How does that relate to prostate cancer?

> Well, if I talk to you I can gauge that you are a fine young man and so on and so forth. If it's an anonymous person on the Internet and I was talking about sexual things, I wouldn't know if it was a female who's getting some sort of kicks out of it. Also, it's a pretty asocial sort of activity isn't it. If I sit in there on my computer and my wife's in there watching the TV. If I, this was not a cause of friction, but, it's not very...she's a sort of widow sitting in their on her own. If I get the Internet and I'm on there every night doing things she could be wondering, oh, is he talking to some girl in America – that's what the next-door neighbour did. She was talking to some bloke in America. As a consequence her marriage has gone. (3 years post-treatment, organ-confined disease, non Internet user)

For this respondent, the concept of communicating via a computer is bizarre and devious. He could not think of sharing any personal details unless he could see the person face-to-face. Furthermore, his social group had demonised the Internet as a corrupting force in light of what happened to the next-door neighbour's marriage. Justification for not using the Internet and/or online support group s generally ranged from concerns regarding the stigma of being "on the Internet" (i.e. being viewed as "promiscuous" or "unfaithful"), to the perceived risk of being "fed the wrong information". These concerns represent the 'flip side' of the benefits described by the men who had used online support groups who viewed anonymity and secrecy as conditions allowing them greater personal disclosure, and considered the multiplicity of views offered in chat rooms not as potential sources of misinformation or deception, but rather, as opportunities to hear descriptions and perspectives other than those provided by their medical specialists.

2.5 Discussion

This study showed considerable support for the potential of the Internet to provide patients with a sense of empowerment and greater control of their disease. The results indicate that accessing information and/or support online can have a profound effect on men's experiences of prostate cancer. For a number of the respondents, the Internet was an essential coping strategy, and in particular, a method of taking some control over their disease. The immense value of the Internet lies in its role as source of information that empowers patients in decision making, providing some balance to traditional imbalances in knowledge and power in doctor–patient encounters, thereby improving communication and satisfaction with treatment processes. Regardless of whether their Internet usage changed the actual decisions made, the majority of the men viewed it as greatly improving their ability to reduce the uncertainties involved in making a treatment decision.

However, this study *also* highlights the limitations of the Internet for patients, particularly in terms of the responses of their medical specialists. The accounts of these men illustrate the impact of specialists' responses to Internet usage in terms of patients feeling respected, competent, and able to engage in decision-making processes. The evidence presented suggests that increased access to information and support online does not necessarily result in better doctor–patient communication. Being 'well-informed' and attempting to actively engage in decision-making processes may in fact result in hostility and irritation within the medical consultation. Specialists may react by employing strategies which implicitly or explicitly discredit the ability of patients to become informed via the Internet, presenting serious barriers to shared decision making and to the acceptance of the importance of information seeking for their disease experiences.

It is clear that, whilst many doctors embrace Internet-informed patients (see Broom 2005c), for some medical specialists, Internet-informed patients challenge their power within the medical encounter, resulting in the employment of strategies to reinforce paternalistic dynamics and alienate patients who use the Internet. This has the effect of reducing patient control and power in decision making, thus complicating the potentially positive influence of the Internet on disease experience. This 'backlash' against Internet-informed patients presents a considerable barrier to reaping the benefits of the Internet as a source of information and support, with serious implications for doctor–patient communication and thus quality of care. Medical specialists must provide encouragement, guidance and support to patients in relation to their Internet usage in order to achieve the maximum benefits from this potentially empowering and liberating source of information and support.

This study also illustrates the potential of online support group s to provide men with a unique and potentially liberating source of support and information, limiting inhibitions felt in face-to-face encounters, thereby fostering increased expression of emotion and intimacy. The potential benefit of online support groups lies in their ability to allow some men to transcend cultural expectations of masculinity (non-emotive, strong, well, tough, inexpressive etc.), and share personal experiences that they would not in a face-to-face situation. For several respondents, the 'risk' of expression was reduced with the anonymity of the Internet and the perceived safety of 'doing it at home'. However, for the men who chose not to use online forums, 'risk' consisted of the potential for deception and misinformation.

Whilst online health (or eHealth) is a relatively new social phenomenon, it represents an important shift in self-help culture in the contexts of health and wellbeing. Moreover, it is having, as has been shown in the study examined here, important impacts on the interplay between the public/consumer and professional organisations/expertise. As such, further research is needed to explore the various and contextually specific effects of this complex and constantly evolving socio-cultural forum, on contemporary information exchange, knowledge production and social interaction.

Acknowledgments Thanks to SAGE Publications for permission to reprint the parts of this Chapter previously seen as an article published in *Qualitative Health Research* Vol. 15 No. 3.

References

Ahmann E (2000) Supporting families' savvy use of the Internet for health research. Pediatric Nursing 26:419–423

AIHW (2004) Australia's Health. Australian Institute of Health and Welfare, Canberra

Anderson J, Rainey M, Eysenbach G (2003) The impact of cyberhealthcare on the physician/patient relationship. Journal of Medical Systems 27:67–84

Beisecker A, Beisecker T (1990) Patient information-seeking behaviours when communicating with doctors. Medical Care 28:19–28

Berland G, Elliot M, Morales L, Algazy J, Kravitz R, Broder M, Kanouse D, Muñoz J, Puyol J, Lara M, Watkins K, Yang H, McGlynn E (2001) Health information of the internet: accessibility, quality and readability in English and Spanish Journal of the American Medical Association 285:2612–2621

Bradlow A, Coulter A, Brooks P (1992) Patterns of referral. Oxford, Health Services Research Unit

Broom A (2004) Prostate cancer and masculinity in Australian society: A case of stolen identity? International Journal of Men's Health 3:73–91

Broom A (2005a) Virtually he@lthy: A study into the impact of Internet use on disease experience and the doctor/patient relationship. Qualitative Health Research 15:325–345

Broom A (2005b) The eMale: Prostate cancer, masculinity and online support as a challenge to medical expertise. Journal of Sociology 41:87–104

Broom A (2005c) Medical specialists' accounts of the impact of the Internet on the doctor/patient relationship. Health 9:319–338

Broom A (2006) The impact of the Internet on patients' expectations. Nature Clinical Practice Urology 3:117

Broom A, Tovey, P (2008) The role of the Internet in cancer patients' engagement with complementary and alternative cancer treatments. Health: An Interdisciplinary Journal for the Social Study of Health, Illness and Medicine 12(2):139–156.

Burrows R, Nettleton S, Pleace N, Pleace N, Muncer S (2000) Virtual community care: social policy and the emergence of computer mediated social support. Information, Communication and Society 3:95–121

Cameron E, Bernardes J (1998) Gender and disadvantage in health: men's health for a change. Sociology of Health and Illness 20:673–693

Charmaz K (1990) 'Discovering' chronic illness: Using grounded theory. Social Science and Medicine 30:1161–1172

Cline R, Haynes K (2001) Consumer health information seeking on the Internet: the state of the art. Health Education Research 16:671–692

Cotten S (2001) Implications of Internet technology for medical sociology in the new millennium. Sociological Spectrum 21:319–340

Diaz J, Griffith R, Ng J, Reinert S, Friedmann P, Moulton A (2002) Patients' use of the Internet for Medical Information. Journal of General Internal Medicine17:180–185

Dudley T, Falvo D, Podell R, Renner J (1996) The informed patient poses a different challenge. Patient Care 30:128–138

Fox S, Rainie L (2002) Vital decisions: How Internet users decide what information to trust when they or their loved ones are sick. Pew Internet & American Life Project, Washington DC

Friedewald V (2000) The Internet's influence on the doctor-patient relationship. Health Management Technology 21:7980

Frydenberg M (1998) Management of localised prostate cancer: state of the art. Medical Journal of Australia 169:11–12

Frydenberg M, Wijesinha S (2007) Diagnosing prostate cancer - What GPs need to know. Australian Family Physician 36:345–347

Hardey M (1999) Doctor in the house: the Internet as a source of health knowledge and a challenge to expertise. Sociology of Health and Illness 21:820–835

Hardey M (2002) 'The story of my illness': Personal accounts of illness on the Internet. Health 6:31–46

Hines S (1999) Treating early prostate cancer: Difficult decisions abound. Patient Care 33:82–91

Joinson A (2001) Self-disclosure in computer-mediated communication: The role of self-awareness and visual anonymity. European Journal of Social Psychology 31:177–192

Kiley R (2002) Does the internet harm health? British Medical Journal 324:238

Lamberg L (1997) Online support group helps patients live with, learn more about the rare skin cancer CTCL-ML. Journal of the American Medical Association 277:1422–1424

Loader B, Muncer S, Burrows R, Pleace N, Nettleton S (2002) Medicine on the line? Computer-mediated social support and advice for people with diabetes. International Journal of Social Welfare 11:53–65

McKinley J, Cattermole H, Oliver C (1999) The quality of surgical information on the Internet. Journal of the Royal College of Surgeons of Edinburgh 44:265–268

Nettleton, S (2004) The emergence of e-scaped medicine? Sociology 38:661–679

Pemberton P, Goldblatt J (1998) The Internet and the changing roles of doctors, patients and families. Medical Journal of Australia 169:594–595

Rainie L, Fox S (2001) Online communities: Networks that nurture long-distance relationships and local ties. Pew Internet & American Life Project, Washington DC

Reddin J, Sonn C (2003) Masculinity, social support, and sense of community: the men's group experience in Western Australia. The Journal of Men's Studies 11: 207–224

Saunders C (2000) Where are all the men? Patient Care 34:10

Schmidt K, Ernst E (2004) Assessing websites on complementary and alternative medicine for cancer. Annals of Oncology 15:733–742

Seale C (2005) New directions for critical internet health studies: representing cancer experience on the web. Sociology of Health & Illness 27:515–540

Seale C, Ziebland S, Charteris-Black J (2006) Gender, cancer experience and internet use: a comparative keyword analysis of interviews and online cancer support groups. Social Science and Medicine 62:2577–2590

Sharf BF (1997) Communicating breast cancer on-line: support and empowerment on the Internet. Women and Health 26:65–84

Walsh N (2000) Men are out of touch with health care system. Family Practice News 30:42

Whiting R (2000) A healthy way to learn: The medical community assesses online healthcare. Information Week 60

Ziebland S (2004) The importance of being expert: the quest for cancer information on the Internet. Social Science & Medicine 59:1783–1793

Ziebland S, Chapple A, Dumelow C, Evans J, Prinjha S, Rozmovits L (2004) How the internet affects patients' experience of cancer: a qualitative study. British Medical Journal 328:564

Zrebiec J, Jacobson A (2001) What attracts patients with diabetes to an internet support group? A 21-month longitudinal website study. Diabetic Medicine 18:154–158

Chapter 3
Self-Service and E-Education: The Relationship to Self-Directed Learning

Marilyn A. Wells and Phillip W. J. Brook

Abstract Self-service via the Internet is becoming a common method of selling goods or services as customers have access to retailers' websites whenever the "need" takes them. Higher education institutions are increasingly offering e-education which means that traditional teaching methods need modifying. Traditional teaching often consists of presenting and expanding upon material found in a prescribed text and delivering this content in lecture, seminar or workshop mode. Studies have confirmed that students learn more effectively when they can discuss the material with others and treat learning as a collaborative process. This chapter reports a case study, where students were required to decide on their level of involvement, discuss and propose the criteria for assessment evaluation, share ideas, concepts and understanding amongst themselves: in effect, self-directed learning. The learning environment used computer-mediated tools, such as discussion forums and chat rooms, and the case study assesses both the expectations of the teaching staff and the experiences of the students, and relates the outcomes to self-directed learning in a self-service environment.

3.1 Introduction

This chapter discusses the expectations of the authors and the experiences of students during a third-year undergraduate subject in Knowledge Management. This is presented as an example of self-service e-education and, in particular, of the acquisition and sharing of knowledge. In the context of this chapter, self-service e-education is understood as the way in which a learner accesses educational resources through self-initiated learning activities mediated by electronic communication. The underlying principle used to inform the teaching and learning strategy was that of collaborative learning where the students had

M.A. Wells (✉)
School of Management and Information Systems, Faculty of Business and Informatics, Central Queensland University, Australia
e-mail: m.wells@cqu.edu.au

D. Oliver et al. (eds.), *Self-Service in the Internet Age*,
DOI 10.1007/978-1-84800-207-4_3, © Springer-Verlag London Limited 2009

some determination of the assessment strategy and criteria. Over a period of 6 years, the strategy was gradually refined and adapted to different circumstances of the learners, following the principles of action-based research tempered by a pragmatic adoption of theory-in-use ideas.

A model of collaborative learning underpinning our discussion shown in Fig. 3.1 emerged as the result of teaching a core third-year knowledge management class (a capstone subject) in an information systems degree at the University of Western Sydney (UWS). In essence, the subject involved having students research, populate and maintain a knowledge repository (KR) as the vehicle for acquiring both common knowledge and uncertain knowledge. The latest version of the subject also required students to attempt to teach classmates how to use the KR.

Following a discussion of the educational philosophies that informed our work, the chapter describes the way in which these philosophies were adapted to the study. This is followed by a detailed discussion of the changes that were made over the period of the study, and the insights that were obtained. These insights are then brought together in a discussion on their application to self-service education.

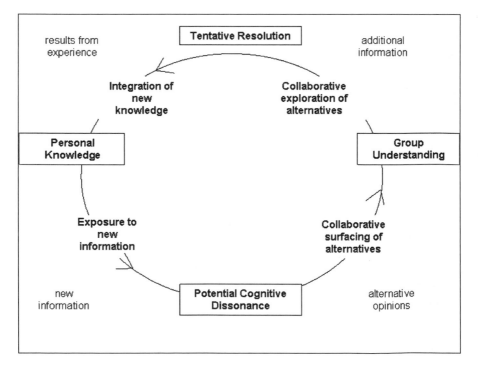

Fig. 3.1 A model of collaborative learning (Wells and Brook 2004)

3.2 Educational Philosophies

3.2.1 Transmission Models

Some academics favour the traditional methods of face-to-face lectures and tutorials, while others prefer to use technology to support their teaching. One group views traditional methods as enabling personal and more immediate contact between academics and students and sees technology as keeping the student at arm's length. They believe that technology distances students from the source of learning, namely themselves. Advocates of the traditional view emphasise the role of the lecturer as a source of leadership in the subject matter, and see the personal contact possible between academic staff and students, and the opportunities for feedback within the smaller groups, as the strengths of the traditional approach. An alternative view is that the use of technology enables the academic to adopt the role of facilitator who assists the students to progress through a subject while being available when needed (Wells and Brook 2003).

The traditional versus non-traditional extremes outlined above are rarely encountered; and the learning and teaching model used is usually a combination of both approaches. This chapter seeks to inform those involved in learning and teaching about the experience gained by adopting some of the principles of student self-directed learning in a technology-centred subject, and the use of student-centred conversations as a path to knowledge acquisition. For those students, who by choice or necessity, have to study independently and at some distance from others (that is, using self-service e-education), the use of an appropriate teaching and learning model by the educators is a key issue.

Teaching and learning as we understand them today have been part of human culture since the development of language; even before language people learnt through the transfer of tacit knowledge, by observing and practising what others did. What is particularly interesting is that these ancient educators taught in a way that reflected a belief that learning was an active process, not a passive process of receiving information. It was not until the Christian church started to recruit children for the priesthood that formal classrooms were established (Knowles 1990). These classes required children to learn religious texts and rituals by rote, and this model of a formal classroom with a teacher "up the front" became the basis for teaching that persists to this day. The term "pedagogy" has its roots in ancient Greek: the "leading of children" or, more conventionally, "the science of teaching children" (Knowles 1990).

Andragogy is "the science of teaching adults" (Knowles 1990), and it is the definition of "adult" that is important to our work. By adult, we mean a person who fulfils at least some of the social roles conventionally associated with adulthood in our society (such as employment, marriage and parenting) rather than a narrower age-related definition. By adopting this definition, we are recognising that our students are socially aware and have experiences that are (or should be) relevant to their learning. Perhaps a better term for our students is "adult learners".

In the " transmission model " of teaching, the educator is considered to be an expert in a particular body of knowledge, and her or his task is to impart this knowledge to her or his students. In the university context, this is often through the "lecture and tutorial" format, where the expert lectures on a topic, and the students (ideally) discuss the material in smaller groups during tutorials, where questions may be raised about the material. To test the extent of the students' learning, tests and examinations are held: if they reach a certain "mark" (usually 50%) – they "know" at least half of what has been presented to them, and they "pass".

3.2.2 The Collaborative Model

This chapter examines the theoretical basis and a supporting case study of an approach to learning and teaching that involves students creating their own class knowledge-base situated in the framework of the four-stage model of collaborative learning proposed by Wells and Brook (2004), shown in Fig. 3.1. Collis and Moonen (2006) suggest that the value of student contribution to a subject lies in the student-oriented activities of discovering and creating key features of self-service learning, and in further discussion and comparison as to why they, as a student group, made a specific selection or contribution to a topic. This together with a reflective activity on why and how the result was achieved reinforces the overall learning process. This links with creating a social network amongst the students enabling them to discuss and compare their activities with others in the subject.

By having students research, populate and maintain a KR, the aims were to focus firstly on the students' self-reliance in discovering both common and uncertain knowledge, and then to have them collaborate in order to understand the material and integrate it into their existing knowledge. These two aspects of learning are key elements of self-service e-education. By gaining an insight into how these tasks were performed we sought to reach a deeper understanding of a teaching methodology that could be applied consistently to self-service e-learning.

The model shown in Fig. 3.1 depicts exposure to new information, which may generate cognitive dissonance with existing knowledge. Through a collaborative process, involving surfacing of alternatives, an understanding is reached, and a tentative resolution formed. A result of testing the tentative resolution against experience is that the new knowledge is integrated with existing knowledge. When applied to a collaborative learning environment, the model provides a framework for designing collaborative learning situations, irrespective of whether that environment is face-to-face or Internet based.

In educational environments, it is possible that the interest is only in "certain knowledge" (also termed foundational knowledge) – that is the accumulated knowledge of a specific topic. Our work attempts to differentiate between "certain knowledge" and "uncertain knowledge": that which we know and that which relies on questioning or reasoning for discovery (Hamada and Scott 2000). Students regularly engage in discourse with their colleagues and academics (Bruffee 1995) and are ready to start extending their knowledge developed from "uncertain knowledge" (Rockwood 1995).

One approach for students to acquire "certain knowledge" is to incorporate a cooperative structure as the learning environment to transmit this foundational knowledge, with collaborative structures for transmitting "uncertain knowledge" (Bruffee 1995). Charmaz (2000), citing both Guba and Lincoln (1994) and Schwandt (1994), suggests using a constructivist approach to the creation of knowledge: knowledge will have different meanings for different people. Therefore, this framework enables students to undertake knowledge transfer, acquisition and its realisation through working in a group (Panitz 1997); collaborative learning on the other hand is more concerned with inquiry and discovery of knowledge.

A key element of collaborative learning is the social context (Kimber 1996), and this then leads to the *accountability* of participants in carrying out the learning tasks, especially the negotiation amongst the group that is required (Arnseth et al. 2001). This accountability is in part respect for peers' knowledge and perceptions that are brought to the learning environment (Panitz 1997). Kimber (1996) names three conditions as necessary for the integration of new information with prior knowledge: recollecting prior knowledge, a similar situation and context, and opportunity for elaboration. Stahl (2000) proposes as a model of knowledge building a cycle of personal understanding integrated with social knowledge building.

Dillenbourg (1999, pp. 5–6) proposed four ways of managing the collaborative learning environment to increase the likelihood of interaction:

- Set up the initial conditions;
- Use a collaboration contract;
- Specify the rules of interaction; and
- Monitor those interactions.

If the collaborative situations are carefully designed, including the initial situation, the composition of the groups and the means of interaction, they are more likely to be successful. It may be difficult to select initial conditions appropriate to a particular situation (Dillenbourg et al. 1996). Many studies have concluded that collaborative learning environment s lead to improved outcomes over traditional means (see, for example Lehtinen et al. 1999 for a review of this research). One way of conceptualising learning is via the metaphors of acquisition and participation (Sfard 1998). The acquisition metaphor considers learning to be the gaining of something within the individual, whereas the participation metaphor considers knowledge to be an aspect of practice and discourse. Collaborative learning is grounded in the participation metaphor, and as a consequence issues such as the social setting emerge as important factors. However, there remains a component that relates to what the individual gains from the collaborative learning setting (Lehtinen et al. 1999).

"Learning" has many aspects, one of the more important being the nature of the substantive material that is part of the learning environment, which may range from open-ended discussions (Craig et al. 2000) to focused tasks in decision making (Wild and Griggs 2002). It is not clear whether critical thinking activities should be seen as one of the ways in which the collaborative learning environment should be conducted, or whether the ability to think critically is one outcome of participating in a collaborative learning exercise (Wells and Brook 2003).

While a discussion regarding an appropriate curriculum for any specific university subject is beyond the scope and purpose of this chapter, one aspect is directly relevant to how a collaborative learning environment is conducted in practice. This is the issue of shared versus private knowledge, and the importance of this for subject results as perceived by the students. One of the philosophical viewpoints for any subject using a collaborative setting is the assertion that the more somebody shares knowledge, the more knowledge they are able to gain (Tissen et al. 1998). This sets up a tension between the stated goal of sharing knowledge as a criterion for collaborative learning (Dillenbourg 1999), and the goal of individual students to maximise their individual results by retaining knowledge discovered during the process of participating in the collaborative exercise.

3.2.3 e-Learning

The non-traditional adopters are of the view that using IT to teach IT concepts provides long-awaited technological support for open access for all: study-at-anytime, anywhere. In this approach, the person in charge (the teacher or learning facilitator) assumes the role of "guide", helping students to work through the subject material and being available to assist when needed. The role of guide requires both the students and lecturer to change. The student needs to change from expecting to receive "the word" to becoming active in searching, evaluating and transforming information into knowledge. The lecturer needs to understand that students will not always make the transformation in a consistent manner. If participants are not able to understand that a different perspective is needed for self-directed e-learning, both the students and teaching staff will find the experience frustrating and possibly revert to a more traditional format (Hamburg et al. 2003).

From the point of view of self-service and e-learning, there are two important consequences of the above discussion: the learning environment needs to recognise the individuality of the learner, and the information presented as part of the learning exercise is necessarily incomplete. One of the claimed benefits of self-service e-learning is the flexibility it offers the learner; however, if the learning experience is not presented in such as way as to recognise that learners are individuals with potentially differing needs, the usefulness of the learning experience may be confined to fact memorisation, rather than deep understanding. These points will be discussed further later in this chapter. With this in mind, we now turn to a discussion on one way the learning experience can be made effective in a self-service/e-learning environment: through the use of collaboration.

E-education or e-learning has the ability to improve the opportunities for students to exchange knowledge and skills. An online community as an e-learning environment is a convenient method of communication, particularly for students who are studying part-time or those who can not attend regular class lessons because of distance or some other reason (Gilbert et al. 2007).

The concept of learning being available to students on a 24/7 basis has limitations with issues such as social interaction, which is an aspect of face-to-face classes. We see learning as a shared process that emerges with participation over time. The social interaction of students serves to make their individual and joint experiences visible to others joining in the discourse, and therefore presents differing perspectives of that experience and viewpoint (Singh et al. 2007). Web-based learning management systems (LMS) contain chat rooms for synchronous collaborative discussions and asynchronous discussion forums that enable students to post comments on specific topics. Students have the ability to access subject materials at a time of their own choosing. E-learning requires students to adapt to potentially differing time zones for synchronous communication with colleagues. This lack of same-place/same-time contact with class colleagues makes the establishment of an effective virtual community an important feature when facilitating the transition from traditional to e-learning environments (Hamburg et al. 2003).

E-education requires a different model from that of a retail environment (for example), where customers can choose to shop at a convenient time for them, as students and teachers are possibly constrained by the lack of social interaction with their peers, whereas lack of social interaction is not necessarily a factor when purchasing online. This potential discontinuation of interaction shifts the responsibility to the student to decide on the time of study as well as the method of communication. Whilst some educators argue for initial face-to-face meetings to overcome the lack of socialisation of the class (Nicol et al. 2003), Salmon (2000) argues the reverse and claims that face-to-face meetings could inhibit online interaction by reducing online communication skills.

Many educational institutions use some form of online support for their students, whether it is a basic use of a LMS to post subject content, e-mail lists or a more sophisticated use of interactive media. Central Queensland University (CQU) makes extensive use of interactive video streaming to communicate with students situated on different campuses. The students have the ability to view the class interaction during specific class time or access a recording at a time of their own choosing. The traditional class lecture is recorded, using Interactive System Learning (ISL), and a link made available for students via the CQU subject website. An objective of setting up this mode of blended e-learning was for CQU to create an inclusive environment for students regardless of their location (Luck 2000).

3.2.4 The Self-Service Model

The term "self-service" is used to differentiate between interactions that involve the consumer and the provider (personal service) and interactions that involve the consumer and a non-human agent, possibly a computer-enabled device, (self-service) (Meuter et al. 2000). Everyday examples of self-service include ATMs, pay-at-the-pump petrol stations, self-check-in for airlines and self-registration at motels. From the providers' viewpoint, access to their products (banking, petrol, seating and accommodation) is made available without requiring a person to be present, thus (presumably) increasing sales and/or decreasing costs; meanwhile the consumer benefits from an increased availability of product and convenience (Walker and Johnson 2006). Alcock and Millard (2006) suggest that if self-service is done well, everyone should win. The actions described are limited in scope and may be satisfactorily achieved without interaction with service staff, whereas in educational environments interaction is an essential ingredient.

The majority of the research into self-service has been on commercial applications, in services such as self-service banking. In these commercial contexts, there is a clear distinction between the consumer and the provider, in that the provider of the self-service facility sees the opportunity to sell more, sell to a different group or to cut costs. In self-service education, this distinction between consumer and provider is not so clear-cut. In collaborative learning environment s, students learn from each other rather than from the provider, which constitutes a consumer to consumer service. If education is seen as a commodity, and subject to market forces, then this commercial view of self-service would seem to apply to an education product in a similar way to any other product. If however, education is seen to have unique attributes beyond a commodity, then these other aspects of self-service that are unique to education require (and deserve) discussion and research. As educators, we believe that there is something special about self-service education, and that we need to explore some of the issues that we see as pertinent for this educational experience.

However, despite apparent benefits to the consumer of self-service, some still prefer the human touch in their dealings with organisations. In particular, in situations that involve uncertainty, such as problems not catered for by the self-service facilities, people prefer face-to-face contact (Walker and Johnson 2006). Uncertainty in an educational environment is almost a given: it would be an impoverished learning experience where the learner was not challenged to think and ask questions, propose alternative viewpoints or seek further information.

In the education context, time constraints may mean that the learners cannot suspend their studies until contact with a tutor is made as the interruption may jeopardise the success of the learning experience. This time-based dimension for self-service education necessitates access to (ideally) a person, or, failing that as a 24/7 service, some form of repository that can be used to provide at least an interim answer to the learners' needs. Compared to commercial transactions, self-service in an educational environment is therefore more challenging for both the learner and the developer of online courses.

As part of the move away from traditional, classroom-based education, there is an increased focus on the use of "blended learning", that is, the use of more than one mode of instruction (for example, face-to-face and industry placements), although it is usually associated with e-learning. Of particular interest in this work is the use of Web-supported learning, the use of the Internet as one aspect of the learning environment, rather than Web-based learning, which implies a reliance on an electronic medium (Fresen 2007). With an opportunity to engage in both face-to-face and Web-mediated teaching and learning, we were able to gain practical experience of the issues concerned with blended learning, especially those issues that are pertinent to self-service e-learning. As discussed earlier, the need for self-service learners to have access to resources other than those provided by technology means that there is a need to understand what forms this support may take.

One of the issues surrounding the use of blended e-learning is whether it suits the learning styles of the learners, that is, the question of whether people prefer the more traditional (face-to-face) learning style or technology-mediated learning environments. The discussion of this issue can be conveniently considered in two parts: the preferences of the learners themselves and the quality criteria required of the learning environment, both the technology and the human element.

In a study of the preferences of tertiary students for traditional versus technology-mediated courses, Jones and Martinez (2001) observed that, where a choice is available, *conforming learners* (those preferring a highly-structured learning experience) preferred the traditional learning environment. On the other hand, *transforming learners* (those who are self-motivated and independent) are likely to perform well in online environments. In the context of this chapter and the work we have undertaken, the issue to be addressed is the extent to which our approach caters for both ends of the spectrum of learning orientations. More generally, should/can self-service/e-learning cater for all learning orientations? The study by Jones and Martinez (2001) concludes that "...the most successful web-based courses today are those designed for ... transforming learners" (p. 4).

The transition from a traditional classroom to a technology-mediated learning environment has been a gradual one, with early changes simply using computers to store files (often copies of lecture notes). As the software to support, a greater range of functionality (such as chat sessions, images and web pages) was developed along with an increase in general use of the Internet, the issue of the quality of the design of the learning environment became under investigation. A recent study by Fresen (2007) presents a taxonomy of factors related to the quality of web-supported learning environments. Fresen identifies six major classifications of factors related to the quality of web-supported learning (institutional, lecturer, instructional design, technology, student and pedagogical) in addition to important assumptions (such as a positive attitude by lecturers and the information literacy of the learners) and exogenous factors (such as class size and work commitments of the learners). It is evident that the quality of the web-supported learning environment (in terms of these factors) will have an important impact on whether the majority of learners across the orientation spectrum will be catered for, or whether it will be only those whose inherent orientation allows them to be effective regardless of the supporting learning environment.

3.3 The Approach Used in this Study

The collaborative and self-service e-education approach used by the authors contributes to the discussion amongst the academic community regarding the best method of teaching information systems and technology in a collaborative environment, whether the environment is entirely online or a mixture of online content supported by face-to-face teaching (blended learning). Computer-mediated communication is valuable to the distance learner who cannot attend regular class meetings as the tools on offer, such as chat, discussion forums and interactive classes create a social network of students (Woods and Ebersole 2003). Using interactive technology to support learning can have varying impacts depending on the pedagogical design used, and how students in differing situations interact with the technology (Godwin et al. 2007).

Developing from this approach is the issue of the students' responsibility in the process of converting information into knowledge. This approach has the students taking active responsibility for their own learning, with the lecturer acting as a guide or mentor in assisting the students to find their own information from diverse sources. Therefore, it embodies self-service, assisted learning and self-directed concepts.

Underlying the work reported in this chapter are beliefs about learners and learning. Rather than treating the students as inexperienced youngsters who needed to be exposed to information through a set curriculum, we took the approach that students would gain understanding through a process of discovery. Essentially, this is the antithesis of the transmission model of teaching. The alternative model adopted was to encourage students to learn by seeking out information for themselves and making sense of it in their own life context. There are two caveats on our use of this approach to teaching. Firstly, adult learners will be at different stages on their journey from youth to adulthood, and thus have varying degrees and variety of experiences: this difference needs to be recognised and catered for. Secondly, the constraints of the university setting previously described are real: we as educators have a responsibility to guide learners though a body of knowledge. However, we believe that by applying andragogical principles with undergraduates in either their final year at university or postgraduates, we are more effectively fulfilling our roles as educators.

In adopting this approach, the authors needed to be aware of their own context and the constraints this implied. Our work was the part of a structured university subject, and we needed to play our part in ensuring that the stated aims and objectives relevant to the course of study were satisfied. These constraints notwithstanding, we felt that our learning/teaching method was appropriate to the final (third) year of study: the students did have some foundational knowledge that we could build on, and in many cases, the students were employed in various capacities so that they did have experiences to draw upon. In order to effectively use the principles of adult learning in a university environment, we found it necessary to closely consider the ways in which knowledge is acquired by people, especially the impacts of the learning environment that exists in a tertiary setting. Several aspects of knowledge acquisition were found to be particularly relevant to our work, including

- the use of the principles of adult education;
- the characterisation of knowledge and knowledge acquisition used;
- the importance of collaboration to the acquisition of knowledge;
- the use of self-directed learning and technology and their impact on learning; and
- the cognitive dissonance that arose from the setting.

The use of case studies, research assignments, practical exercises, group work and industry placements are some of the methods used to teach the content of the curriculum. Nevertheless, the design of curricula, whether for an entire subject or a single module, continues to have as an assumption the need for an expert to transfer his or her knowledge. We do not claim that this is inappropriate, but rather that there is an alternative assumption available that may produce a better outcome.

As mentioned earlier, the foundational assumptions for our overall approach to learning and teaching are drawn from both andragogy (Knowles 1984, 1980) and more recent additions and extensions (Shapiro 2003). However, in order to provide a useful foundation for our work, we found it necessary to express the attributes of adult learners in terms of what would enable the development of concrete strategies for teaching and learning. In particular, we needed to understand better, how adults acquired and assimilated knowledge.

In order to cater for a diverse student population (that is, attempting to cover the entire spectrum of learning orientations), we designed our work to permit the students who were more comfortable working with others to have that support. In other words, we encouraged the students to form groups (although it was not mandatory) and to help each other in undertaking the tasks we requested. To facilitate this we provided a computer-based collaborative learning environment . By adopting this approach, we created a self-service/ e-learning situation. In this environment, members of the peer group interacted to test and explore ideas and their implications (Roschelle 1992), that is, to foster critical thinking skills.

The learning environment that we established could be classified as "blended", that is, it consisted of face-to-face interactions with the students, required the use of technology-mediated tools and encouraged students to collaborate in their work (both remotely and in person). Our work shows this environment can be successful (at least for this type of teaching and learning), and there are important implications for self-service/e-learning which are discussed later in the chapter.

3.4 Assessing Student Experiences of Self-Service Learning

The primary methodology is action research (Lee 2001; Baskerville 2001). Its iterative nature lends itself to the way educational environments are planned and taught. A provisional theory about the use of conversational online-facilitated learning first emerged after the presentation of the first class in 2001 and was informally tested in 2002. This formed the basis of subsequent presentations. Each delivery of the subject under discussion informed the next, and each delivery itself was modified as each cycle of the theory emerged. The central stages of diagnosis > planning > action > evaluation > learning (Susman and Evered 1978) are here as phases in the subject development, delivery and conclusion over a teaching period of 12 weeks.

However, we were concerned that our teaching be responsive to the needs of the students, so we also adopted a practical, theory-in-use approach (Brookfield 1987). In our work, this meant that we used the theories of teaching and learning discussed earlier as starting points for understanding, rather than as prescriptive ways of acting. The theory-in-use approach recognises that people continually adapt their ideas and formulations of the underlying structure in response to the circumstances. We believe that this was of considerable benefit to our work in that it enabled us to react to what was happening and to explore ideas as they arose.

The first formal phase of this research involved a study pertaining to knowledge gatekeepers in an educational environment, with the data gathered from surveys distributed to students in the Knowledge Management subject at UWS in 2003. The study extended to the classes in other years and includes data collected via the Student Evaluation of Educational Quality (SEEQ) surveys distributed to students at the conclusion of each semester at UWS in 2003, 2005 and 2006. All sets of survey responses were anonymous and the authors received the survey results after the release of the class results. The study is continuing into 2007.

Student feedback shows that the objective of developing students' critical thinking skills was achieved as the subject, and method of discussing the related topics encouraged them to think critically by increasing their ability to articulate their thoughts in a collaborative and supportive environment. A student notes that the "unit enables the students to think outside the square and gives us a learning experience that was fun and at the same time helped us to learn the unit topics." Student feedback from 2006 indicates that students appreciated being treated as adult learners and that the "teaching method gets you involved with the class discussion without imposing [on you]. ... treats us like adults and made the class fun/interesting as well as very informative."

3.5 The Context

One of the aims of the Knowledge Management (KM) subject is to give students an understanding of how knowledge is relevant to business. The KM subject extends the concepts that students encounter in prior semesters with other courses of the IS program. Whilst the other subjects take a more traditional perspective of the transfer of knowledge, the KM subject looks at the concepts of knowledge and knowledge management in the context of information systems and business, and the collaborative measures needed to transfer and acquire that knowledge. This KM subject did not have any set text, and the objective of the KR was to allow the students to discover their own knowledge and build their own textbook. The students were responsible for the identification of, and exercised quality control over, the documents offered for consideration for the repository. This enabled the students to explore the concepts presented both in the subject material and during online chat sessions (another strategy for exchanging ideas and information that reinforced other discussions).

The students initially found this a challenging concept as they had not previously had the opportunity to have such input into their own learning, nor had they been empowered to use the online LMS to such an extent. The intention was to create a community of learners who could use tools that they were comfortable with (chat and discussion forums) and communicate and exchange information with peers by building a social network (Woods and Ebersole 2003). In the processes described subsequently, the lecturers' played the part of facilitators not arbitrators.

3.6 Learning Situations in 2001–2003 and 2005–2006

In 2001, there was only one class. Contributions to the repository were anonymous and Blackboard® was used to create the repository. The lecturer was the only person who could determine which student had contributed which article

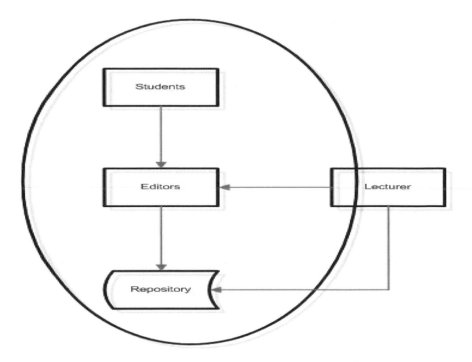

Fig. 3.2 Lecturer's interaction with 2001 class

summary. Refer to the framework in Fig. 3.2 for the interactive processes in year 2001.

In year 2002, the cohort used WebCT® as a platform for the repository and the lecturer gave students three sub-topics to research. In addition to the different structure (multiple classes), the subject was presented by a different lecturer.

The students decided, as a class group, the submission and evaluation criteria for the articles. It was a requirement that both classes use the same criteria when posting submissions; and therefore, one editor attended both classes and facilitated the discussions. By week 3, the students had agreed on the compliance criteria.

Unlike 2001, the students posted articles directly into WebCT discussion forums for the editors to assess for compliance before allocating to students for review. Contributions were not anonymous; user names were automatically logged and displayed against message postings. As in 2001, two students reviewed each paper; and as a control mechanism, if the reviews were widely different, the editor for that topic nominated another student to carry out a third review. In 2002, each class had its own repository, and in addition to building the repository, part of the assessment strategy was compulsory online chat sessions where the students discussed issues raised in the classes.

In 2002, the class structure was a basic business structure with offices in separate locations. Figure 3.3 shows the interaction between the lecturer,

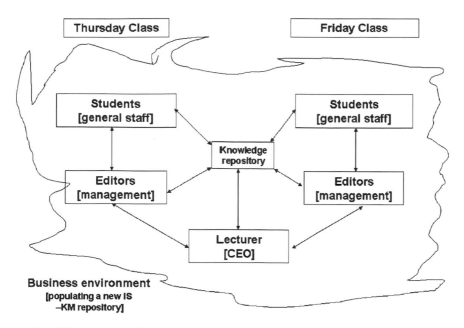

Fig. 3.3 2002 class interactions

editors and other students. In this instance, the editors undertook the roles of knowledge gatekeepers facilitating the sharing of knowledge via the repository.

In 2003, the classes shared one repository that included the initial submissions and reviewed articles, as well as the final selection of articles. Students found this an interesting way of learning and one comments that "article submission, reviews and repository process was excellent – definitely facilitated learning and understanding of concepts and topics." Another change implemented for 2003 was that the chat session groups were required to be made up of students from each campus and class with a maximum of six in each group. Students chose which group they joined. The SEEQ surveys indicate that students appreciated the interaction with students in other classes and commented that this interaction increased their knowledge of the topics discussed in the classroom. Among comments from students from the SEEQ survey are "weekly chat sessions definitely emphasised the lecture topics and enhanced understanding and learning" and "I really enjoyed the online chats, especially how we had to choose other people from other classes."

As a learning exercise, the students were again required to develop their own submission and evaluation criteria, though some students protested as they considered that the students in 2002 has already performed this task. The underlying purpose of developing class criteria was to focus student attention on the learning value of being responsible for their own outcome in the subject and once all students understood this, submission and evaluation criteria issues were resolved

Class environment

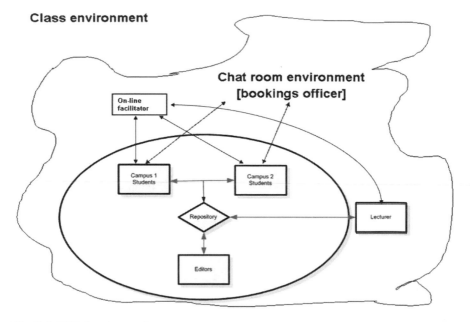

Fig. 3.4 2003 class interactions

quickly. The class structure for 2003 followed in principle the models for 2001 and 2002. Unlike 2001 and 2002, in 2003 the KM subject was presented at two separate campuses with the classes split into three: two at one campus (Monday morning and evening) and another campus on Wednesday evenings. Refer to Fig. 3.4 for the interaction between the classes, the online facilitator and the lecturer.

As in 2002, students were asked to volunteer for the positions of editor and bookings officer. In 2003, the students had 1 week to form groups with other classes and decide the day and the time for the chat session.

In 2005, there was only one class and campus involved with the KM subject. The lecturer was the same one as for 2002 and 2003. The class did not involve building a KR; neither did it include chat sessions. There was a class discussion forum, which the students accessed at all times and exchanged information about the topics discussed in class. Although there was the discussion forum, most class interaction took the form of ad hoc presentations with the lecturer selecting a topic and a group each week for the presentation. The group then presented the topic to the class in a form of their own choosing and the class commented on the presentations as a learning exercise in their essays. Comments from the 2005 SEEQ responses indicate that students found this offering as interactive and motivating as the previous classes where there was more online interaction, though one student did feel as though the class discussions always led back to the same point. Refer to Fig. 3.5 for 2005 interaction.

In 2006, and building on responses made in the 2005 SEEQ survey, where students indicated that they would like to build a repository, a different

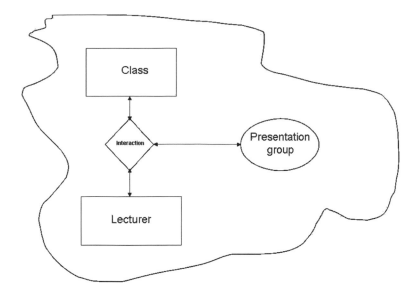

Fig. 3.5 Class 2005 interactions

approach was adopted. This year focused more on the underlying issues related to the creation of knowledge repositories and knowledge transfer. Students were required to create repository entries in the role of expert, that is, they were attempting to capture knowledge about topics where they were the subject matter experts. The students chose their own topic and worked in groups to accomplish their task. Once the entry was created, one or more of their peers used the entry to learn about the subject. Testing was performed to assess the degree to which the entry was successful in imparting knowledge. Refer to Fig. 3.6 for class interactions.

During the semester, the issues related to knowledge capture and transfer were discussed, and the practical experiences of the students were used as exemplars to aid understanding. The final outcome was a website structured as a KR. By developing a classification structure at the same time as creating their entries, the students were better able to appreciate their entry in a broader context. A survey response was "[This] unit enables the students to think outside the square and gives us a learning experience that was fun and at the same time helped us to learn the unit topics."

3.6.1 Case Study Summary

By the end of the 2001 semester, the students had produced a repository containing 117 articles, although the number submitted was a little greater than this due to duplicate material. With only a few exceptions (less than 5),

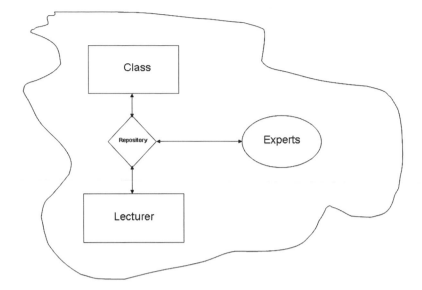

Fig. 3.6 2006 class interactions

all students achieved minimum submission levels, with some students contributing well in excess of minimum requirements.

In both 2002 and 2003, the students identified approximately 50 articles as worthwhile for inclusion in their "textbook" and most students achieved the minimum number of submitted articles. There were a few in 2002 who also contributed above the minimum requirements and did so out of interest in the learning process itself as there were no extra marks attached to their additional contributions. During both years, there were a few duplicate articles posted for evaluation and the editors rejected these articles. The number of rejections was minimal and the students involved accepted the decision of the editors as the students themselves had empowered the editors to make such decisions. In 2003, another factor was introduced: this was the online facilitator. The students were initially unsure as to the function of the facilitator as they considered themselves perfectly capable of entering into chat sessions without assistance. When it was explained that the facilitator was there to guide or prompt them rather than lead the conversations, they accepted the facilitator's presence during the chat sessions.

The year 2005 saw students taking an active involvement in the class with one group presenting their topic as a play and another group basing their presentation on an episode of the Simpsons television series, in which knowledge management was the target of the day. The lecturer did not have any input into how each group chose to present their topic; the choice was entirely each group's responsibility. The class of 2006 was encouraged to explore knowledge capture by using various media to capture their own expertise in a repository.

Along the way, the students came to understand the difficulties associated with transforming their expertise into a form usable by others.

3.7 Discussion

3.7.1 The Process

Early attempts at submissions varied enormously in terms of their substantive information content. Some students merely accessed the Web and copied information without analysis or comment, while other students took the trouble to undertake a more thorough research. In practice, the editors and reviewers proved to be fairly hard task-masters: they had no hesitation in rejecting submissions that did not meet the agreed criteria or contribute to the growing repository of information. Some students were content to achieve minimal submission levels, while others either provided well-researched and analysed submissions from the start, or actively used the feedback from the reviewers to improve their work. A student commented in 2003, "researching and reading is more effective way of learning [for me at least]. Challenging and motivating work."

At the beginning of each delivery for 2001–2003, students appeared to concentrate on the "mechanical" aspects of the tasks, such as establishing the repository. Much debate occurred about the format of submissions (headings, font to be used, spacing and so on), and how the posting would be carried out. Within 2–3 weeks, any issues of adhering to the standards that the students had set themselves disappeared, as editors rejected submissions if they did not comply with the agreed criteria. It was evident that the students were their own worst critics and the standard set by the class was overall quite high.

In conjunction with the submission criteria, the students were also expected to devise the review standards and agree on a ranking scale for each article. If the article reached a score of 3.5 out of 5 then it was placed in the KR. This exercise took place in the first few weeks of the semester and this topic was a major contributor to the online discussions during this time, as well as in the face-to-face class. This exercise was required of the students in both years 2002 and 2003, as the lecturer thought the activity of contributing to the subject structure would stimulate the students to take ownership of their own individual learning as well as that in the broader class environment (Collis and Moonen 2006). This proved to be the case, and the outcome was a cohesive cohort across different classes and days. The SEEQ survey for 2003 indicated that most students felt their personal contributions were listened to by the lecturer and the class (as a whole) and one student commented that there was a "great community of learning and good atmosphere."

In 2001–2003, the editors found their task very time consuming as the relatively tight time schedules meant that submissions had to be forwarded to student reviewers within 1 or 2 days of receipt, and the reviewers reminded that reviews were needed to be returned within a similar timeframe. Despite this demand on their time, the editors reported a very positive response to the task, saying that they learned much from the process. In recognition of their editorial work, they were not required to submit articles. Not everyone had a positive view of the editor–student relationship with one student commenting in 2003 that "communication between editors and students should be improved [for the next offering]."

In addition to recounting their personal experiences by relating them to what occurred during the semester, the students were also required to write about their understanding of the topics of knowledge, knowledge management and knowledge acquisition, using the repository creation and contents as examples. Through this requirement, they had to study the contents of the repository and form an opinion about its usefulness (or otherwise) for their writing. The students were explicitly told that they were to critique the repository (in terms of content and creation), not merely provide description. The reflective nature of the exercise further contributed to the students' ownership of their own knowledge (Collis and Moonen 2006). In 2005 and 2006, the reflective essay remained as a tool to reinforce students' learning, though the method of inter-action between the students changed. The student experience over the years under discussion appears to be similar in that they found the class processes and the self-service/self-directed concept of education to be beneficial to their learning of the subject topics.

3.7.2 Class Dynamics

In 2002 and 2003, the dynamics of each class were different and this caused the content of the class discussions to vary. In 2002, some students raised the issue of enforced collaboration during the online chat sessions with the comments relating to the desirability of sharing being voluntary (Wells and Brook 2004). In 2003, an online tutor facilitated the sessions and encouraged the students in sharing their knowledge. At first, students were very unsure as to what was expected of them and to what extent they were required to interact with the online facilitator. This finding is consistent with the study and conclusions regarding online tutors reached by Gilbert et al. (2007). Within a few sessions, the students appeared to understand very quickly how the online structure supported the subject's aims. Student feedback noted, "this subject used the WebCT tools differently from other courses and that the subject used the tools of their generation, i.e., chat rooms." In 2002, the students gave the subject a similar rating to that given by the 2001 students. In 2003, students were wary of sharing their knowledge with online classmates as it was difficult to gauge the extent of their participation in the discussion. This is similar to the findings of Nicol et al. (2003), where they reported that students in their study felt that familiar social cues were absent. In 2005 and 2006 where the emphasis was on collaboration and sharing rather than e-learning tools, students found that there were "excellent class interactions and involvement" and "that students were encouraged to participate in the class", which indicate that students may prefer a mixture of learning and teaching styles.

Two interesting comments emerged from 2001 to 2002, which were related to sharing knowledge and the "enforcement" component of the assessment regime. Again in the 2003 semester, there was an apparent reluctance to share relevant information with others – the rationale being that the individual student who discovered the information would not be able to use it to gain higher marks later in the semester if everyone had access to that information. It was made clear to all classes that their reflective writing was to be related to the repository and the processes undertaken to build it, and in fact if they were found not to be sharing information, they might lose marks. Many commented that this was quite contrary to other courses that the students had encountered in their university studies, and a specific comment was that "the method used in allowing students to collaborate opinions, ideas and experiences has allowed me to have a better understanding of various areas concerning management." In those courses, sharing was seen as something to be avoided: the students initially had a problem in understanding the difference between open collaboration, as this subject required it, and collusion as it is presented in other courses. The later years of this study did not have the same problems as the students were located on one campus and all attended the same class. The students in the later years were still required to interact with their peers via WebCT, though interaction was supported by face-to-face class work. A student noted in the SEEQ survey for 2006, "lectures were not very productive or challenging, possibly because students are mostly used to a lecture-based approach, rather than a discussion approach." This indicates that not all students are ready for a self-service style of education.

3.7.3 Overall

The lecturers had a level of expectation as to how the students would perform in later iterations of the subject, as students had already tested the model, shown in Fig. 3.1, to some extent in 2001. The 2002 class built on the experiences gained by the 2001 lecturer, and enabled the quasi business model, shown in Fig. 3.3, to drive the repository interaction processes. While the trigger for seeking new information was external, and although the general approach was prescribed, the rules relating to the repository were not. This enabled the lecturer's role to be one of mentoring rather than directing. The model of collaborative learning shown in Fig. 3.1, provides a convenient (post hoc) framework for understanding the processes involved in the exercise. Students noted that the time spent discussing the topics as a class allowed for identification of opinions and ideas that would have been missed out of a text book or in a lecture style class, and that everyone's opinion was valued. The SEEQ statistics for all years consistently report that the students' rating of the learning/academic value of the subject was above UWS average, as was the group interaction component.

As the lecturer was responsible for the subject, the articles were regularly reviewed for suitability. Despite the autonomy granted to the students, it would not have been acceptable to have inappropriate articles posted in the repository. In practice, there was no "wrong" information posted, and the students monitored the process themselves and clarification was sought in only a few cases. This reflected the lecturer's role as a source of advice, rather than a source of final arbitration. The students' preparation of a reflective essay on the processes they undertook to create the repository provided closure for the semester. In effect, this was a reflection on knowledge creation from their perspective.

A goal for this KM subject was to provide a consistent framework where the students could relate their learning experiences from KM to knowledge gained from other information systems subjects, and enable them to integrate that knowledge into their degree as a whole. The collaborative model shown in Fig. 3.1 enabled both lecturers to provide a reproducible learning framework for all 3 years, supporting the acquisition of non-foundational knowledge in an interactive environment.

During a conversational class, whether the conversations are held in a face-to-face environment or online sessions, students have many opportunities to interact with their peers and the lecturer. Students learn through engagement and participation (Waite et al. 2003), and the class environment centres on interaction. The lecturers introduce ideas to start the discussion cycles. Collaborative exploration of the topics and the issues surrounding them was the aim of this environment. In 2003, students indicated that some of the best aspects of the subject were "the collaborative nature of the lectures, the bulletin board, and building and using the KR".

Not all students became entirely autonomous learners even though most students achieved a good understanding of the learning process. All students made some progress towards understanding the issues related to creating, transferring, acquiring and managing knowledge. The students claimed ownership of in deciding as to what constituted a quality article, and this claim reflected collaborative engagement with their peers.

As reflected by the feedback at the end of the semesters, most students appeared to enjoy this method of learning and derived benefit from it. A student in 2006 makes the suggestion that "perhaps more interactive style with games, presentations, etc. which can assist the students to learn under a fun environment compared to the other units which have 3 hour lectures/tutorials." According to the SEEQ surveys from all years, the students reported finding the learning experience a positive one, both in terms of their final understanding of the issues related to knowledge and its management, and of the processes involved in creating that knowledge. Without exception, the students preferred this method of learning to the more traditional methods, and they were able to take new understanding and insight from the subject. Many suggested that this manner of teaching be used for other courses as this approach enabled them to take control of their own learning and they were appreciative of the collaborative nature of the subject design.

This appreciation of the essentially collaborative approach in the development of their autonomy as learners was a major outcome of the exercise. As reflected in their (anonymous) feedback, the semesters rated as a success with the students. From the perspective of the lecturer in charge, the semesters involved considerable work, but seeing students take responsibility for their learning was a rewarding experience.

3.8 Conclusion

Key points gained from the work include a clearer understanding of the role of technology in learning environments, the value and role of collaborative work between learners, and the value of educators as facilitators rather than more traditional transmitters of information.

While separately these insights essentially replicate the work of other researchers, we believe that the depth of the longitudinal study and the integration of the various components of the learning environment assist in understanding technology-supported, collaborative learning environments. Further, these outcomes are directly relevant to self-service/e-learning environments, in that the learners' requirements in these environments can be better understood, and therefore taken into account in the design and delivery of self-service e-education.

Students early in their tertiary careers may need more structured environments, such as cooperative learning. At a later stage, student-directed learning may be more appropriate as students move from encountering foundational knowledge to searching for non-foundational knowledge. The differentiation of foundational and non-foundational knowledge, and the related use of cooperative and collaborative learning environments, provides academics with a framework for selecting appropriate teaching strategies.

Enforced collaboration was also an issue with some students, with the comments related to the desirability of sharing being voluntary. Given the constraints of time and institutional assessment requirements, the need for some type of sanction for non-participation was necessary. It remains a problem for further investigation as to whether the task would have been as successful (or more successful) if submissions were voluntary.

Research in the area of student motivation and the link to self-directed e-education is a necessity as students' personality characteristics may lead them to success or failure in such a subject. Kim and Schniederjans (2004) propose that students should undertake a personality test to ascertain if they are suitable for e-education.

Moving from the traditional classroom to an e-learning environment is not simply a matter of making documents and such available electronically. It requires that the learning situations are carefully designed and tested. Our work with these classes over an extended time has provided us with substantial insight into the possibilities and constraints of e-learning. Starting with the earliest versions of the KR that the students created, through to the multi-media version produced in the last year of this study, our increased understanding of the benefits of technology has undoubtedly (by their own comments) been of benefit to the students. For those considering using e-learning environments, we would suggest that consideration be given to exploring the ways in which technology can support well thought-out teaching strategies.

From a self-service/e-learning perspective, the work discussed in this chapter has some important implications. Firstly, a learning orientation appropriate to the subject matter and its form will be an important factor in the learning outcomes: those who need face-to-face support will not react well to material that requires independent research. Secondly, and as a consequence of the first point, the e-learning environment needs to be designed in concert with the envisaged delivery mode. If truly remote delivery (no same-time support) is envisaged, then the level of detail and tasks set will be different to delivery modes that include some same-time support. Thirdly, regardless of whether the delivery is remote or includes support, the inclusion of opportunities for students to collaborate will provide an enriched experience for students. WebCT records the date and time of each posting and the posting log revealed that students were accessing the subject website at all hours. Some students seemed to favour mid afternoon and some late nights/early morning. This indicated the beneficial nature of this type of e-education with the site being available to students on a 24/7 basis.

One point that cannot be over-emphasised is that the success of any learning program is dependent upon the learning culture of the institution. This learning culture will affect how students react to e-education and in particular self-directed e-learning. Not all students are motivated or confident enough to pursue a course of study which requires them to have major input into their learning environment. Enabling students to access online study materials at times convenient to them creates a self-service environment where, compared to traditional settings, greater reliance is placed on a student's ability to service her or his own educational interests.

References

Alcock T, Millard N (2006) Self-Service – but is it good to talk? BT Technology Journal 24:70–78

Arnseth HC, Ludvigsen S, Wasson B et al. (2001) Collaboration and Problem Solving in Distributed Collaborative Learning. Computer Support for Collaborative Learning Conference (CSCL) Maastricht University Maastricht University, Holland

Baskerville R (2001) Conducting Action Research: High Risk and High Reward in Theory and Practice. In: Trauth E (ed) Qualitative Research in IS: Issues and Trends. Sage, Hershey USA

Brookfield SD (1987) Developing Critical Thinkers: Challenging Adults to Explore Alternative Ways of Thinking and Acting. Jossey-Bass, San Francisco

Bruffee K (1995) Sharing our toys – cooperative learning versus collaborative learning. Change Jan/Feb:12–18

Charmaz K (2000) Grounded Theory: Objectivist and Constructionist Methods. In: Denzin NK, Lincoln YS (eds) Handbook of Qualitative Research 2nd edn. Sage Publications Inc

Collis B, Moonen J (2006) The contributing student: Learners as co-developers of learning resources for reuse in web environments. In: Hung D, Khine MS (eds) Engaged Learning with Emerging Technologies. doi 10.1007/1-4020-3669-8_3

Craig D, ul-Haq S, Khan S et al. (2000) Using an Unstructured Tool to Support Peer Interaction in Large College Classes. Fourth International Conference of the Learning Sciences. Erlbaum, Mahwah

Dillenbourg P (1999) What do you mean by collaborative learning? In: Dillenbourg P (ed) Collaborative Learning: Cognitive and Computational Approaches. Elsevier, Oxford

Dillenbourg P, Baker M, Blaye A et al. (1996) The evolution of research on collaborative learning. In: Spada E, Reiman P (eds) Learning in Humans and Machine: Towards an interdisciplinary learning science. Elsevier, Oxford

Fresen J (2007) A Taxonomy of Factors to Promote Quality Web-Supported learning. International Journal of E-Learning 6:351–362

Gilbert J, Morton S, Rowley J (2007) e-Learning: The student experience. British Journal of Educational Technology. doi:10.1111/j.1467-8535.2007.00723.x

Godwin SJ, Thorpe MS, Richardson JTE (2007) The impact of computer-mediated interaction on distance learning. British Journal of Educational Technology. doi:10.1111/j.1467-8535.2007.00727.x

Guba EG, Lincoln YS (1994) Competing paradigms in qualitative research. In: Denzin NK, Lincoln YS (eds) Handbook of Qualitative Research (pp 105–117). Sage, Thousand Oaks, CA

Hamada T, Scott KA (2000) Anthropology and International Education via the Internet: A Collaborative Learning Model. The Journal of Electronic Publishing. http://hdl.handle.net/2027/spo.3336451.0006.105. Accessed 17 June 2007

Hamburg I, Lindecke C, ten Thij H (2003) Social aspects of e-learning and blending training methods. In: 4th European Conference E-Comm-Line. Bucharest, Hungary

Jones ER, Martinez M (2001) Learning Orientations in University Web-based Courses In: WebNet 2001: World Conference on the WWW and Internet. Orlando FL

Kim EB, Schniederjans MJ (2004) The role of personality in web-based distance education courses. Communications of the ACM 47:95–98

Kimber D (1996) Collaborative learning in management education: Issues benefits problems and solutions: A literature review. Royal Melbourne Institute of Technology University, Australia

Knowles M (1980) The Modern Practice of Adult Education: From Pedagogy to Andragogy Follett. Cambridge Books, NY

Knowles M (1984) Andragogy in Action. Jossey-Bass, San Francisco

Knowles M (1990) The Adult Learner: A Neglected Species, 4th edn/Gulf Publishing Company, Houston

Lee AS (2001) Challenges to Qualitative Researchers in Information Systems. In: Trauth E (ed) Qualitative Research in IS: Issues and Trends. Sage, Hershey USA

Lehtinen E, Hakkarinen K, Lipponen L et al. (1999) Computer supported collaborative learning: A review of research and development In: Giebers JHGI (ed) Reports on Education 10 Department of Educational Science. University of Mijmegan, Netherlands

Luck J (2000) Building a learning community using interactive videoconferencing. In: Research Report for the ISL Project. http://lifelonglearning.cqu.edu.au/2000/papers/luck.htm. Accessed 17 June 2007

Meuter ML, Ostrom AL, Roundtree RI et al. (2000) Self-service technologies: understanding customer satisfaction with technology-based service encounters. Journal of Marketing. 64:50–64

Nicol DJ, Minty I, Sinclair C (2003) The social dimensions of online learning innovations. Education and Teaching International 40:270–280

Panitz T (1997) Collaborative versus Cooperative Learning: A Comparison Of The Two Concepts Which Will Help Us Understand The Underlying Nature Of Interactive Learning. http://www.capecod.net/~TPanitz/Tedspage. Accessed 17 June 2007

Rockwood R (1995) National Teaching and Learning Forum 4:part 1

Roschelle J (1992) Learning by collaborating: Convergent conceptual change. The Journal of the Learning Sciences 2:235–276

Salmon G (2000) E-moderating: The key of teaching and learning online. RoutledgeFalmer, London

Schwandt TA (1994) Constructivist, interpretivist approaches to human inquiry. In: Denzin NK, Lincoln YS (eds) Handbook of Qualitative Research (pp 118–137). Sage, Thousand Oaks, CA

Sfard A (1998) On two metaphors for learning and the dangers of choosing just one. Educational Researcher 27:4–13

Shapiro SA (2003) From andragogy to collaborative critical pedagogy. Journal of Transformative Education 1:150–166

Singh G, Hawkins L, Whymark G (2007) An Integrated Model of Collaborative Knowledge Building. Interdisciplinary Journal of Knowledge and Learning Objects. 3

Stahl G (2000) A model of collaborative knowledge-building. In Fourth International Conference of the Learning Sciences (ICLS 2000). Ann Arbor MI

Susman GL, Evered RD (1978) An Assessment of the scientific merits of action research. Administrative Science Quarterly. 23:582–603

Tissen RJ, Andriessen D, Deprez FL (1998) Value-based knowledge management: creating the 21st century company: knowledge intensive people rich. Addison Wesley Longman, Amsterdam Nederland

Waite WM, Jackson MH, Diwan A (2003) The Conversational Classroom. In: Proceedings of 34th SIGCSE Technical Symposium on computer Science Education. Reno, Nevada

Walker RH, Johnson LW (2006) Why consumers use and do not use technology-enabled services. Journal of Services Marketing 20:125–135

Wells MA, Brook PWJ (2004) Conversational KM - Student Driven Learning. In: Lister R, Young A (eds) Proceedings of Sixth Australasian Computing Education Conference (ACE2004) Australian Computer Society Inc Dunedin NZ 30:335–341

Wells MA, Brook PWJ (2003) Learning about Knowledge Management through Enforced Collaboration using Web-Based Repositories. In: Ang J, Knight S (eds) Proceedings of 4th International We-b Conference (We-b 2003). Edith Cowan University, Perth Australia

Wild R, Griggs KA (2002) Collaborative telelearning: An experiment in remote project management. e-Service Journal 1:25–38

Woods R, Ebersole S (2003) Social networking in the online classroom: Foundations of effective online learning. EJournal 12–13(1). http://www.ucalgary.ca/ejournal/archive/v12-13/v1213n1woods-browse.html. Accessed 4 July 2007

Chapter 4
Stakeholder Expectations of Service Quality in a University Web Portal

Mary Tate, Joerg Evermann, Beverley Hope, and Stuart Barnes

Abstract Online service quality is a much-studied concept. There is considerable evidence that user expectations and perceptions of self-service and online service quality differ in different business domains. In addition, the nature of online services is continually changing and universities have been at the forefront of this change, with university websites increasingly acting as a portal for a wide range of online transactions for a wide range of stakeholders . In this qualitative study, we conduct focus groups with a range of stakeholders in a university web portal . Our study offers a number of insights into the changing nature of the relationship between organisations and customers. New technologies are influencing customer expectations. Customers increasingly expect organisations to have integrated information systems, and to utilise new technologies such as SMS and web portals. Organisations can be slow to adopt a customer-centric viewpoint, and persist in providing interfaces that are inconsistent or require inside knowledge of organisational structures and processes. This has a negative effect on customer perceptions

4.1 Introduction

Over the last 10 years, the emphasis of many websites has changed from providing information to transaction process ing (Hind 2005; McKay et al. 2000; Zeithaml et al. 1990; Zumpe & Madberger 2007). Universities have been at the forefront of online service provision. Online access to transactions such as enrolment, course delivery, course support and library lending is rapidly becoming a standard within the sector. Many universities now offer web portals, which provide an integrated front end to information and applications for various stakeholder groups. Ensuring that these services meet quality requirements is essential to ensuring business operations and stakeholder satisfaction.

M. Tate (✉)
Victoria University of Wellington, PO Box 600, Wellington 6140, New Zealand
e-mail: mary.tate@vuw.ac.nz

D. Oliver et al. (eds.), *Self-Service in the Internet Age*,
DOI 10.1007/978-1-84800-207-4_4, © Springer-Verlag London Limited 2009

However, measurements of the service quality concept have been characterised by a lack of consensus. Previous research has suggested that customer expectations are different in different business domains (Barnes 2001; Barnes & Vidgen 2002). We go a step further and argue that in a portal environment with multiple stakeholder groups, the expectations of different stakeholder groups within the same organisation may also vary. A qualitative, focus group approach has been successful in providing rich context and identifying domain-specific modifications to existing measures (Barnes 2001; Barnes & Vidgen 2002).

This chapter is structured as follows: firstly, we present a literature review covering stakeholder theory, e-service quality, web portals , and approaches to measuring service quality. Then we describe the methodology used, the findings, and finish with a discussion and some conclusions.

4.2 Previous Studies

We briefly review previous studies in stakeholder theory, online service quality and web portals. We then consider approaches to measuring service quality.

4.2.1 Stakeholders

A stakeholder has been defined as "any individual or group who can affect, or is affected by the actions, decisions, policies, practices or goals of the organisation" (Freeman 1984, p. 25). The stakeholders in a university include students, teachers, administrators, parents, employers, the government, and the wider society in which the university operates (Sahney et al. 2004). Depending on the range of information and transactions being offered, the stakeholders in a university website or web portal are a similarly diverse group. In practice, university websites and web portals are mainly aimed at three groups: current students, current staff (Sahney et al. 2004) and potential students (Owlia and Aspinwall 1996). For the purposes of this study, we chose to focus on these three groups.

4.2.2 Online Service Quality

Advances in information and communication technology (ICT) have facilitated the evolution of customer service through telephone, mobile and Internet solutions. Coincidentally, the global shift from a manufacturing-based to an information-based economy has also contributed towards organisations from all sectors to gradually increase the channels of customer service they provide.

Encounters between customers and frontline employees have become a focal point in marketing, as the provision of customer services is now critical to all organisations. Being an intangible concept, the evaluation of online service quality became based upon perceptions gathered from comparing consumer expectations of the quality of physical services (Gronroos 1978). Through the measurement and monitoring of quality, service providers can gain an insight to how consumers perceive services and service quality, and are thus able to formulate provision strategies to influence perceived service quality in a desired direction (Gronroos 1978).

4.2.3 Internet Portals

Strategies in conventional service provision embarked on a new direction with advances of ICT. Portals appeared in the late 1990s as a new type of Internet website architecture specifically designed to provide personalised online services. The success of portals can be attributed to the ability to provide content and services that are tailored to individual users based on their specifications and requirements. In technical terms, portals allow consolidation and distribution of information stored on disparate sources, and facilitate collaboration and interaction between users (Aneja et al. 2001; Brabston & McNamara 1998). Recently, a taxonomy of portal types has assisted in providing a definition of the range of available portals (Dias 2001; Winkler 2001) as shown in Fig. 4.1.

Using this classification scheme, the majority of portals are defined by the audience they intend to serve, providing varying degrees of functionality, security and data sources (Winkler 2001).

- Specialised portals (e.g. Application Service Provider portals) are designed to simply provide their users with access to applications via an extranet or over the Internet. Providing access over the Internet to specialised applications that

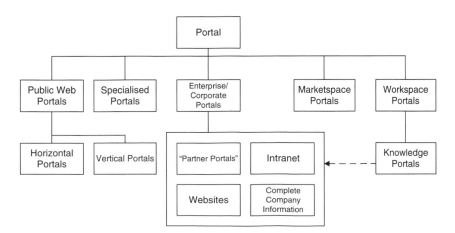

Fig. 4.1 Taxonomy of portals and their hierarchy (Dias 2001; Winkler 2001)

are available to subscribers only; for example, the clients of a software company and a stock-broking firm are examples of this type of portal.

- Marketspace portals are websites that facilitate business-to-business or business-to-consumer interaction through electronic commerce, for example, electronic shopping malls.
- Public web portals exist to provide convenient access to general users. These portals can be further defined based on their audience:

  - Horizontal portals do not have a specific theme and provide a broad range of information and services to attract a wide array of users. Popular public portals such as Yahoo exemplify this type of portal.
  - Vertical portals provide in-depth information and services to support a specific audience group. An online community of practice is an example of a vertical portal, where users can benefit from sharing knowledge and gaining support from like-minded peers on that portal website.

- Enterprise or corporate portals aim to provide authenticated users with personalised information and services they are authorised to access. Corporate intranets are an example of this type of portal.
- Workspace portals are single, coherent and integrated portals that present users with integrated, single-point access to a range of services; for example, tools for communication, collaboration, searching, office applications, and management of online workspace "hygiene" such as security and back-up.
- Knowledge portals increase the effectiveness of knowledge workers by providing easy access to essential or helpful information to their specific roles. Knowledge portals may be a subset of enterprise portals. They might include information feeds or access to research databases, and access to job-related applications. For example, call centre staff may have access to a dedicated knowledge portal that integrates the information and services they need to do their job.

Increasingly, university websites are beginning to act as enterprise portals, offering a single point of access to a range of services aimed at different stakeholder groups. The portal that is the subject of our study is the enterprise portal of a New Zealand university.

4.3 Measuring Online Service Quality

Measurement of customer-perceived service quality has been traditionally dominated by the ServQual instrument, developed prior to the widespread availability of self-service technologies. This identified five dimensions of face-to-face service quality (Parasuraman et al. 1985, 1991): reliability, assurance, trust, empathy and responsiveness. The meaning of service quality has been re-examined in the context of various waves of computing technology, including information technology departments (Pitt et al. 1995, 1997), end user computing (Doll et al. 1998) and the Internet (Alzola and Robaina 2005; Barnes 2001; Barnes and Vigden 2000; Barnes and Vidgen 2002; Sandhu and Corbitt 2003; Zeithaml et al. 2002).

Online service quality has also been the subject of previous studies. For the purposes of this research, we adopted the E-Qual (formerly WebQual) stream of research (Barnes 2001; Barnes and Vigden 2000; Barnes and Vidgen 2002) as a starting point, since it had been extensively informed by previous research, and was based on both qualitative and quantitative studies in multiple business domains

The dimensions included in E-Qual (v4.0) are *usability*, which encompasses aspects such as navigation, appearance and general case of use; *information quality*, which encompasses accuracy, timeliness, relevance, granularity and general "believability" of the information; and *service interaction quality*, which encompasses service quality constructs such as security, trust, personalisation and access to the organization.

4.3.1 Measuring Portal Quality

There have been relatively few studies of perceived service quality in web portals. However, the few that exist suggest that perceived service quality in web portals is an extension of perceived service quality in other websites, rather than a radical new departure. Two recent studies on perceived portal quality (Gounaris & Dimitiadis 2003; Kuo et al. 2005) are both based on previous research in service quality and web service quality. The factors that were confirmed in those studies are similar to those of previous studies, with slight differences in terminology and emphasis. An empirical study on organisational portals (Kuo et al. 2005) identified four factors of service quality: empathy (similar to service interaction quality in E-Qual); ease of use (usability); information quality (content quality); and accessibility (similar to aspects of usability and service interaction quality). A study on business-to-consumer portals in Greece (Gounaris & Dimitiadis 2003) identified three service quality factors: customer care and risk reduction benefit (similar to service interaction quality); information benefit (content quality); and interaction facilitation benefit (usability, extended by adding consideration of technical design and speed). This gives confidence in the use of the E-Qual dimensions and items as a starting point for the current research.

4.3.2 Measuring e-Service Quality in the Public Sector

Many universities are public sector organisations, and it might be expected that e-service quality issues associated with e-government would also apply to universities. However, in our view, there is a limited degree of generalisability between university and other e-government websites and web portals. Although the university user community is potentially quite diverse, it is more homogeneous in many respects than the community of users of other e-government services. Firstly, much of the user community can be expected to have a high level of educational attainment and literacy because they will have attained the minimum requirements for university admission. Secondly, many universities bundle access to computing resources along with access to a range of other services as part of the cluster of benefits available to all students. This means that e-government service quality considerations such as availability, equity, access and language (Tiecher et al. 2002) are not likely to be as important in a university context. An exception to this could be the stakeholder group of potential students.

Qualities valued by users of e-government websites include a sense of control, convenience, and time and cost saving (Gilbert et al. 2004). We expect that these issues will also be important considerations for users of university websites.

4.3.3 Measuring Service Quality in Higher Education

Although we were not able to identify any studies that specifically considered service quality in university websites or web portals, there have been a number of previous studies on service quality in higher education. Once again, these give confidence that user perceptions of service quality in higher education are similar to those in other domains (Lagrosen et al. 2004). However, the dimensions "concretised" differently; for example, library resources and computer facilities were instances of "tangibles" (Lagrosen et al. 2004). Factor analysis identified three dimensions of service quality in higher education: process (including prompt, willing and error-free service); empathy (including convenience and attentiveness); and tangibles. This study also suggests that perceived service quality in universities is similar to that in other business domains, and by implication, perceived e-service quality is also likely to be similar (Lagrosen et al. 2004).

4.3.4 Evolving Functionality: Transaction Processing in Online Services

Website functionality has evolved from static "brochure-ware", through increased interactivity, such as online calculators, to full transaction processing (McKay et al. 2000). Early studies of web service quality (Barnes 2001) had a strong focus on content, reflecting the static nature of early websites. As the functionality of websites continues to advance and organisations implement a range of online transactions, the transaction, rather than the content becomes the central object of electronic commerce (Alzola & Robaina 2005; Zumpe & Madberger 2007). Consequently, we expect that the richness and usefulness of available online transactions will emerge as a new dimension of online service quality . Our expectations are supported by previous studies of online self-service (Bitner et al. 2002) that have found usefulness in solving difficult problems, and increased convenience over alternatives to be components of positive self-service experiences for users.

The increasing transactional focus of websites also comes with increased risks. Online transactions and fulfilment require a higher degree of trust, and incur higher opportunity costs and penalties in the event of a service breakdown (Zumpe & Madberger 2007). We expect that this will also influence customer expectations.

4.3.5 Evolving Understanding: Additional Constructs from Research Literature

Although we initially based our candidate coding categories on E-Qual (v4.0), our literature review revealed some omissions that we believed might be significant for users. For example, rapid response time, or minimal waiting time has been identified as an important aspect of quality in online self-service (Dabholkar 1996; Palmer 2002). A sense of being in control of the experience has also been identified as a factor that users value (Dabholkar 1996; Sandhu & Corbitt 2003). Overall we suggest that perceived service quality in university web portals will have similar dimensions to those identified in other e-service quality studies. However, we propose to extend our understanding of user-perceived e-service quality to include transaction quality, and some additional items hypothesised from the literature.

4.4 Gathering User Perceptions

Focus groups have been found to be a useful way to generate candidate survey items for marketing research in areas such as service quality (Churchill 1979). From listening to people share and compare their different perspectives and experiences with a portal system, a wealth of in-depth insight can be uncovered regarding perceptions, opinions and attitudes about the system and its quality (Morgan & Stinson 1997).

To analyse the focus group data, we apply candidate coding categories, derived from previous studies, to the collected data. Basing our initial coding categories on previous literature creates a link to existing theory and ensures comparability of the results of this study (Yin 1993). This is also important given that there is a significant body of existing literature, and we expect to largely confirm existing scales, albeit for use in a new domain. At the same time, it allows us to identify new items and factors. Finally, applying these coding categories also allows us to assess alternatives, i.e. that the existing and hypothesised items and factors were not important to the participants.

A subsequent literature review, and a scan of practitioner and industry commentaries provide nomological validity (Straub et al. 2004) for the additional items. Following this, the E-Qual instrument was revised and pre-tested for face validity with volunteers from the Victoria University of Wellington community.

4.4.1 Participant Selection

Identification of key stakeholder groups was carried out in consultation with the university's marketing department. Website usage figures confirm that prospective students, undergraduate students and staff make up 95% of all users of the web portal, supporting our above argument to focus on these stakeholders . While it is important that the sample is representative of the community of users of the university web portal , it does not need to be large. Each group consisted of five participants, chosen to represent a wide range of characteristics. Volunteer participants were sought by advertising widely in the university community (online and physical notice-boards, word-of-mouth, announcements to classes by university staff members, and approaches to secondary schools in the university catchment). We reviewed our group of volunteers to ensure that a representative range of roles, ethnicities, study programs, and ages were included. The final composition of the participant groups was as follows:

Group 1: School leavers and prospective university students. We selected five students in their final year at high school who intended to proceed to university the following year. Intended courses of study included sport science, teaching, design and information technology. Participants were aged between 17 and 19, and included two females and three males. One participant was an international student.

Group 2: Current undergraduate students. Five undergraduate students were selected. Students ranged between first year and third year, and were aged between 18 and 22. Courses of study included geography, law, computer science and information systems. Participants included three males and two females. Two participants were international students.

Group 3: Post-graduate and staff. This group consisted of five participants: one full-time staff member, two research students who were also part-time staff members, and two people working full-time outside the university and carrying out post-graduate study. Courses of study included masterates and PhDs. Participants were aged between 22 and 58, and included one female and four males. Two participants were international students.

4.4.2 Focus Group Design

Focus groups ran for between 90 and 120 minutes, and were divided into two main areas of discussion. First, participants were invited to introduce themselves and describe the university web services they had used, why they used them, and how they felt about the experience, and what online service quality meant for them. Then, a semi-structured discussion was led by the facilitator. The facilitator introduced each high-level factor and invited participants to discuss whether that factor had relevance, and what it represented for them. Following this open discussion of each factor, the facilitator introduced each item associated with that factor with a brief definition. Participants were asked whether the item was significant to them, and had an opportunity to discuss the significance of the item.

At this point, the facilitator did not enter the discussion with any further prompting or clarification until the discussion of that item was concluded. Discussion was not confined by the facilitator only to the prompted items. However, the facilitator exercised some judgment to determine when the discussion had ended or ventured into unrelated areas, and another prompt was required.

4.4.3 Analysing Focus Group Responses

The primary researcher initially coded the transcripts. Approximately 20% of the data was coded independently by a second researcher, with an inter-rater agreement of 85% over 20 categories, which indicates sufficient reliability.

We used the "intermediate" approach to coding (Pare 2004, p. 249), where initial codes are adopted based on previous research, and others are added during the analysis process. The initial coding scheme was based on the E-Qual instrument, and additional codes were generated as required.

Since the semi-structured section of the discussion included existing items, where participants were prompted by the facilitator to confirm or disconfirm their relevance, we chose the frequency of codes from the discussion transcript as an indication of the level of interest in, and relevance of each item. Observations that were reasserted by the same participant were not counted as a separate occurrence. Counting has been found to be a useful moderator of researcher bias in qualitative data analysis (Cresswell 1994; Huberman & Miles 1998). The unit of analysis for the coding was a speaker's sentence.

4.4.4 Instrument Revision

Following the analysis of the focus group data, the E-Qual instrument was modified. New questions were developed in the style of the existing instrument and existing items adapted to fit the domain of university web portals. The initial wording of each question was then tested with six volunteers from the stakeholder community. These included staff, graduate and undergraduate students, approximately half of whom were male and half female, and aged from early 1920s to late 1960s. The questions were read to the participants, who were asked to explain the meaning of the question in their own words. Based on this, further modifications were made to the wording.

4.5 Data Analysis and Results

All the items and factors included as anchor concepts based on previous studies, or hypothesised from our literature search or industry scanning were confirmed as relevant items by this research. This included both factors and items from previous versions of E-Qual. No existing factors or items were considered by the focus group participants to be entirely irrelevant or unimportant. However, some items attracted no further discussion, beyond an initial assent, when prompted by the facilitator. Some new items emerged during the coding phase. A summary of the item frequency for each code, by group, is included as Table 4.1. New codes (factors or items) that were added during this study are italicised in the table. As initial assent was universal from all participants for all items, these initial assent expressions were not included in the code count when analysing the data and therefore do not appear in our further analysis.

4.5.1 User Perceptions of Portal Service Quality (from Focus Groups)

Content quality has been one of the most stable dimensions of online service quality and was re-confirmed in this study. In particular, timeliness and relevance attracted considerable discussion, with some participants commenting unfavourably on out-of-date information on some university websites they had visited. There were some differences in the perceived importance of some items between the various focus groups. For example, prospective students were more concerned with information being presented at an appropriate level of detail than current students or staff. In particular, prospective students were interested in overview information with the ability to drill down, "simple, and straight-forward, to the point, [with] the option to go in more depth". Prospective students were also more concerned with the ease with which the content could be understood. Several participants commented that many university websites assume a level of knowledge of their products and services and use internal course codes that have little meaning to people who are not current students or staff. "They need to point out what the numbers mean. I know now what they mean, but I didn't at the time" or "that's an idea – a little question

Table 4.1 Item frequency by group—perceived online service quality

Item	1 Prospective students	2 Current students	3 Post-graduate and staff	Total
Content quality				
Accuracy	–	3	–	**3**
Believability	–	–	–	–
Timeliness	5	4	5	**14**
Relevance	1	6	8	**15**
Ease of understanding	4	–	–	**4**
Appropriate level of detail	8	–	2	**11**
Appropriate format	–	–	–	–
Usability				
Easy to learn to operate	–	1	1	2
Clear and understandable	–	–	2	2
Easy to navigate	5	1	8	14
Easy to use	2	2	4	8
Attractive appearance	3	7	–	10
Design appropriate for site	2	2	9	13
Sense of competency	–	–	–	–
Positive experience	–	–	–	–
Feel in control	–	1	–	1
Response time acceptable	–	4	5	9
Service interaction quality				
Good reputation	1	1	1	3
Security of personal information	–	1	6	7
Sense of community	4	1	3	8
Easy to communicate with the organization	9	2	6	17
Confident that goods or services will be delivered as promised	–	–	–	–
Enjoyability or entertainment	3	3	3	9
Managing and integrating roles and relationships	–	7	9	16
Modify and update content	–	–	3	3
Multi-lingual capability	1	3	–	4
Push notifications	–	–	2	2
Transaction quality and safety				
Transaction safety	–	–	2	2
Transactions that are useful	2	5	8	15
Transactions that save time or money	3	3	5	11
Range of transactions	–	1	2	3
More convenient than alternatives	4	2	4	10
Platform-infrastructure reliability	–	6	6	12
Technical security (e.g. virus protection)	–	2	1	3

Italics: New item or factor added based on literature and/or data analysis mark on the page. . .you click on it, and it goes 'in plain English, this means. . .'". However, despite the differences in perceived importance, this factor was valued across all stakeholder groups, and the items identified were consistent with previous studies.

Usability (ease of use) has also been a stable and consistent dimension of e-service quality. This dimension was also found relevant by all stakeholder groups. Once again there were some differences in the relative importance of items between groups. The ease of navigation item attracted the most discussion of any of the items associated with this factor. A new item hypothesised from literature, "acceptable response time", also attracted considerable interest. Two groups (staff and current students), who used the website regularly to access applications for teaching, learning and research activities were very concerned with response times. Several participants commented unfavourably on the speed of off-campus access, and noted that they preferred to use on-campus facilities because of the superior response times. "It's really good to download something in the computing lab, because it's fast. When I download at home I feel it's like a snail." Interestingly, our hypothesised item based on flow theory, "sense of being in control" did not appear to be a strong priority for focus group participants. Participants also suggested that they were willing to trade off appearance for performance in this business domain "if there's a choice between something that looks really flashy but takes hours to download, you always pick the simpler site". The importance of an attractive appearance generated considerable discussion. Several participants commented that this was a "serious" website, where information quality and general performance were essential, but they appeared to be seeking a happy medium with regard to appearance. The appearance should be "chirpy" and "attractive-ish" and "not boring", but "so long as its got all the information you need, no-one really cares too much". Interestingly, a sense of being in control, which was identified as a benefit in previous e-government studies, did not appear to be a strong priority for our focus group participants.

Service interaction quality is a less well-defined dimension, which relates to the broader experience of interacting with the organisation via its website or web portal. This dimension showed the most diversity in importance across the stakeholder groups. Prospective students were less concerned about security of information than current students and staff, perhaps because their interaction with the website does not involve personal or sensitive information until they make a decision to proceed with enrolment.

Undergraduate students were least concerned about using the website as a means to contact the organisation, with several commenting that they are on campus anyway so they will be more inclined to use face-to-face contact. Postgraduate and post-experience students who were not on campus all the time would have liked the opportunity to augment information searching on the website with a personal enquiry, but expressed little confidence in the fate of their e-mail enquiries. "I didn't feel comfortable, I didn't feel safe, I didn't feel like I'd made a contact." Prospective students did not have a network of existing relationships with the organisation, and were relying on the website to mediate these relationships. They were also aware of the difficulties of presenting information online in a form that would be appropriate for the diversity of enquiries generated by prospective students, and felt that the ability to access personal assistance would likely result in a more adaptive and helpful response "You can always e-mail them, so long as there is someone to contact. . .you can't put everyone's particular circumstances on a website so its important to have the opportunity to ask."

Several new candidate items emerged for this dimension. International students noted that some multi-lingual facilities would be helpful, especially for their family members who did not necessarily speak English fluently. This suggests that although a level of English fluency can be assumed amongst current students, other stakeholders such as intending international students and parents may require access to information and services in other languages.

Many participants identified managing and integrating existing relationships between peers, and between staff and students as a priority. Where participants held multiple roles within the university, they expected integrated access to all the content and applications relevant for them. Several commented unfavourably on the limitations of the current service in this respect "You don't want to go through all those different navigation instructions....the university has about 20,000 WebPages. . .a huge amount of data. You're not being presented with a consistent face." Post-experience and post-graduate students expressed interest in "push" notification for items of interest to them. This could be because this group was more time poor than the others, and the lack of integration within the website meant that they needed to navigate to different parts of the site in order to collect all the items relevant to their multiple roles. This group also expressed interest in the ability to easily modify and update content that they are responsible for.

Transaction quality and safety. The focus group data suggested that evolution in the functionality of university web portals, to include access to a wider range of content and applications, is being reflected in changing perceptions of online service quality . Our focus group data supported our hypothesised a new factor, which we have called transaction quality and safety. This factor was of most interest to current students and staff although prospective students also commented on the usefulness, time saving and convenience of being able to transact online.

Participants that were using the web portal to access essential day-to-day content and applications were concerned about the security of transactions and the reliability of the infrastructure. While more casual users might be prepared to accept occasional outages, users who depend on portal services had higher expectations of technical service quality. "There is a common theme that the information tools are sitting on top of systems that are very good, but we are constantly let down by woeful infrastructure" and "I think more people would use [the services] if you could count on the availability." This extended to not being exposed to technology risks as a result of using university online systems.

Several people said they had got viruses from the university "Viruses! I got [one] from school. I got it in my laptop and it's a trouble to get rid of it."

In summary, there was broad consensus across all three groups about the importance of content quality and usability, which reflected the importance of these dimensions in previous studies. Two new items for the usability dimension, hypothesised from literature, were supported. The item "acceptable response time" was strongly supported, while the item "feel in control" was supported but did not attract much discussion.

Service interaction quality was also valued, and showed more variation from the findings of previous studies. In particular, items emerged that are specific to portal, rather than website, functionality, such as the ability to manage and integrate multiple roles and relationships. We also identified an expectation that portal users would be notified about things they needed to know, rather than needing to continuously check for them.

Group 1 (prospective students) were using the website mainly to obtain information about courses of study. This group was the least demanding overall. They tended to find the online information somewhat cryptic, with an overuse of internal course codes. This group were most concerned with timeliness (currency), ease of understanding, and not getting too bogged down in detail. They were also most interested in being able to move easily between online and offline support, and expected the web portal to assist them in identifying people within the organisation who could help them. They were aware of the limitations of online services when dealing with a diverse stakeholder group, and expected complementary online and personal services. This group were less concerned with security and reliability issues, suggesting that they were not using the web portal for essential activities, and were more prepared to return later if there was a temporary outage.

There was strong support for our hypothesised new factor, transaction quality and safety, which reflects the fact that university web portals are increasingly offering access to a range of transactions, in addition to the traditional role of websites in providing information. This study suggests that although there is a consensus on some factors and items, there are some significant differences in perceived service quality between stakeholder groups.

4.6 Discussion

4.6.1 Service Expectations of Online Customers

Our research confirms previous studies that suggest that some aspects of user expectations of online services have proved stable across multiple studies in multiple domains. The item sets associated with content quality and usability were comprehensive and stable. This may be because these aspects of online services have been consistent since the very early days of online services, and are still essential components of a quality offering. However, beyond these basic expectations, the picture becomes more complicated.

The importance of reliability, first raised in early studies of face-to-face service quality reappeared, although in an online environment it is represented by technical security and platform and infrastructure reliability. This is valued more highly by people who were using online services for essential, everyday transactions rather than those browsing for information. This group were also more concerned with utility rather than beauty.

Customers would like online services to be better adapted to their needs, rather than requiring them to accommodate to the terminology, processes and structures of the organisation. Prospective students noted that they did not always understand the terminology used, while research students who were part-time staff members complained about having to navigate multiple systems in order to support all their roles.

Increasingly, customers do not view an online service in isolation, but as one part of their total relationship with the organisation. If an online service is to be used, it must offer some advantages over other channels (contact points with the organisation). Customers also expect seamless integration between the portal and other channels, with the ability to move offline to seek further personalised assistance by e-mail or telephone. This supports the findings of previous research that emphasises the importance of an integrated approach to customer service delivery (Tate & Hope 2004; Tate et al. 2006).

4.6.2 The Differing Service Expectations of Multiple Stakeholder Groups

Our research found significant differences in the expectations of our various stakeholder groups. Prospective students were most commonly casual users, and information seekers had different priorities to people using the portal for mission-critical activities. This group had the lowest expectations overall, although they tended to have higher expectations of the visual attractiveness of the website and enjoyability of the experience.

By comparison, people with multiple roles are more interested in portal-style integration, personalisation and customisation. They expected assistance in managing and integrating their multiple roles, and a reliable, trustworthy platform for online transactions. The increased concern expressed by this group about response times, platform and infrastructure reliability and technical security supported previous findings about changing user expectations associated with the potential risks and costs of transacting online (Zumpe & Madberger 2007).

4.6.3 Organisational Expectations of Service Delivery

Although our study has concentrated on user perceptions, the authors have also been involved in aspects of the organisational strategy for developing the portal, so we are able to offer some organisational insights in relation to some of our findings. In our selected organisation, management of information technology and the web presence is heavily decentralised. The portal offers access to a range of different applications with different interfaces and in some cases, different access controls. Different organisational units manage their own web presence. Much of the content is structured in a way that mirrors internal organisational structures and processes. The business objectives for delivering a service online via the portal frequently include controlling costs.

It was not surprising under these circumstances, that customers commented on the use of jargon and an inconsistent experience. The lesson is that organisations need to design their online service offerings from a customer's perspective. An anecdote that illustrated the extent of this gap was provided at a recent meeting. The Dean of Commerce had suggested to a secondary school student that perhaps he should consider a "Dean's Blog" on the website. The student asked "What is a Dean?"

4.6.4 Expectations Resulting from Changes in Technology

New technical capabilities, for example, the ability to push out notifications that are relevant to the user using SMS (short message system) technology also generated new service quality expectations. As users become aware that it is possible to receive just-in-time notification of information and events that affect them, they will come to expect it.

The increasing adoption by organisations of web portals and customer service technologies such as customer management systems all tend to raise customer expectations, and organisations that are slow to incorporate new technologies, or that adopt them somewhat half-heartedly can create negative customer perceptions. It was clear from our study that more sophisticated portal users were frustrated with the fact that the web portal mainly provided a top-level veneer, while the information and applications beneath it were still not very well-integrated.

4.6.5 Changing relationships

The expectations and perceptions of customers in our study suggested that portal technologies are affecting the nature of the relationship between the university and its stakeholders . There appears to be some convergence of formal and informal peer relationships. Many students were using the same software applications accessed via the web portal to receive formal communications from staff and to engage in peer-to-peer communication with other students.

The web portal has the potential to bring new stakeholder groups into the university community. Parents of international students at one time would have relied on education agents in their home country, and word of mouth, for information about educational institutions overseas. Now, many are web literate. Many of the international students in our focus groups mentioned that their parents would like to browse information, and be able access services such as enrolment or accommodation booking, but were prevented from doing so by poor English. Multi-lingual capability, aimed at the extended families of international students, was considered to be a reasonable expectation.

4.7 Implications for Practice

The utility of the concept of perceived service quality for businesses, evidenced by the ongoing popularity of service quality measurement instruments, cannot be doubted. Organisations need to ensure that they are measuring perceptions and expectations that are rigorous and informed by theory, relevant to their own business domain, reflect the diversity of their stakeholder groups, and are updated to reflect the possibilities offered by advances in technology. This requires continuous qualitative communication with stakeholder groups.

4.8 Conclusion

University enterprise portals are typically aimed at a wide range of stakeholder groups, many holding multiple roles concurrently. A clear understanding of the differing service expectations of these groups must be obtained if these are to be met. This understanding must be continuously updated to reflect evolutions in the levels of service enabled by new technologies. Historically, we know that people expect the staff of an organisation to be trustworthy, reliable and to fulfil their promises. In the days of online self-service, they expect the same from technology, and a little more. Customers expect that organisations will adopt new technologies, use them to improve customer service and advance internal objectives. Increasingly, customers are aware of the possibility of integrated customer management across multiple channels, and come to expect that it will occur. More sophisticated users increasingly expect active support in managing their multiple roles and responsibilities, a robust environment for online transactions that minimises risk and cost, and just-in-time notifications of events that are relevant to them.

Organisations need to be able to measure and benchmark their success in meeting customer expectations. To this end, we supply a revised instrument in Appendix, based on the outcomes of this focus group research.

Acknowledgments We gratefully acknowledge the assistance of Chicky Pang for her contributions to the literature review.

Appendix: E-Qual Instrument for a University Web Portal

1 The site provides accurate information

Score | Strongly agree | 1 | 2 | 3 | 4 | 5 | 6 | 7 | N/A | Strongly disagree

Importance | Very important | 1 | 2 | 3 | 4 | 5 | 6 | 7 | N/A | Not important

2 The site provides believable information

Score | Strongly agree | 1 | 2 | 3 | 4 | 5 | 6 | 7 | N/A | Strongly disagree

Importance | Very important | 1 | 2 | 3 | 4 | 5 | 6 | 7 | N/A | Not important

3 The site provides timely information

Score | Strongly agree | 1 | 2 | 3 | 4 | 5 | 6 | 7 | N/A | Strongly disagree

Importance | Very important | 1 | 2 | 3 | 4 | 5 | 6 | 7 | N/A | Not important

4 The site provides relevant information

Score | Strongly agree | 1 | 2 | 3 | 4 | 5 | 6 | 7 | N/A | Strongly disagree

Importance | Very important | 1 | 2 | 3 | 4 | 5 | 6 | 7 | N/A | Not important

5 The site provides easy to understand information

Score | Strongly agree | 1 | 2 | 3 | 4 | 5 | 6 | 7 | N/A | Strongly disagree

Importance | Very important | 1 | 2 | 3 | 4 | 5 | 6 | 7 | N/A | Not important

6 The site provides information at the right level of detail

Score | Strongly agree | 1 | 2 | 3 | 4 | 5 | 6 | 7 | N/A | Strongly disagree

Importance | Very important | 1 | 2 | 3 | 4 | 5 | 6 | 7 | N/A | Not important

7 The site presents the information in an appropriate format

Score | Strongly agree | 1 | 2 | 3 | 4 | 5 | 6 | 7 | N/A | Strongly disagree

Importance | Very important | 1 | 2 | 3 | 4 | 5 | 6 | 7 | N/A | Not important

8 I believe I would be able to complete transactions that are useful to me

Score | Strongly agree | 1 | 2 | 3 | 4 | 5 | 6 | 7 | N/A | Strongly disagree

Importance | Very important | 1 | 2 | 3 | 4 | 5 | 6 | 7 | N/A | Not important

9 Completing transactions on this site will save me time or money

Score | Strongly agree | 1 | 2 | 3 | 4 | 5 | 6 | 7 | N/A | Strongly disagree

Importance | Very important | 1 | 2 | 3 | 4 | 5 | 6 | 7 | N/A | Not important

10 This site offered the range of on-line transactions I expected

Score | Strongly agree | 1 | 2 | 3 | 4 | 5 | 6 | 7 | N/A | Strongly disagree

Importance | Very important | 1 | 2 | 3 | 4 | 5 | 6 | 7 | N/A | Not important

11 It feels safe to complete transactions on this site

Score | Strongly agree | 1 | 2 | 3 | 4 | 5 | 6 | 7 | N/A | Strongly disagree

Importance | Very important | 1 | 2 | 3 | 4 | 5 | 6 | 7 | N/A | Not important

12 My personal information feels secure

Score | Strongly agree | 1 | 2 | 3 | 4 | 5 | 6 | 7 | N/A | Strongly disagree

Importance | Very important | 1 | 2 | 3 | 4 | 5 | 6 | 7 | N/A | Not important

13 Completing transactions using this website is more convenient for me than any other way of doing the same task

Score | Strongly agree | 1 | 2 | 3 | 4 | 5 | 6 | 7 | N/A | Strongly disagree

Importance | Very important | 1 | 2 | 3 | 4 | 5 | 6 | 7 | N/A | Not important

14 I feel confident that goods/services I request will be delivered as promised

Score | Strongly agree | 1 | 2 | 3 | 4 | 5 | 6 | 7 | N/A | Strongly disagree

Importance | Very important | 1 | 2 | 3 | 4 | 5 | 6 | 7 | N/A | Not important

15   **I feel confident about the technical security and reliability of this website**

Score   Strongly agree | 1 | 2 | 3 | 4 | 5 | 6 | 7 | N/A | Strongly disagree

Importance   Very important | 1 | 2 | 3 | 4 | 5 | 6 | 7 | N/A | Not important

16   **I find the site easy to learn to operate**

Score   Strongly agree | 1 | 2 | 3 | 4 | 5 | 6 | 7 | N/A | Strongly disagree

Importance   Very important | 1 | 2 | 3 | 4 | 5 | 6 | 7 | N/A | Not important

17   **My interaction with the site is clear and understandable**

Score   Strongly agree | 1 | 2 | 3 | 4 | 5 | 6 | 7 | N/A | Strongly disagree

Importance Very important | 1 | 2 | 3 | 4 | 5 | 6 | 7 | N/A | Not important

18   **I find the site easy to navigate**

Score   Strongly agree | 1 | 2 | 3 | 4 | 5 | 6 | 7 | N/A | Strongly disagree

Importance   Very important | 1 | 2 | 3 | 4 | 5 | 6 | 7 | N/A | Not important

19   **I find the site easy to use**

Score   Strongly agree | 1 | 2 | 3 | 4 | 5 | 6 | 7 | N/A | Strongly disagree

Importance   Very important | 1 | 2 | 3 | 4 | 5 | 6 | 7 | N/A | Not important

20   **The design is appropriate to the type of site**

Score   Strongly agree | 1 | 2 | 3 | 4 | 5 | 6 | 7 | N/A | Strongly disagree

Importance   Very important | 1 | 2 | 3 | 4 | 5 | 6 | 7 | N/A | Not important

21   **Overall, the response time was acceptable to me**

Score   Strongly agree | 1 | 2 | 3 | 4 | 5 | 6 | 7 | N/A | Strongly disagree

Importance   Very important | 1 | 2 | 3 | 4 | 5 | 6 | 7 | N/A | Not important

22   **I feel in control on this site**

Score   Strongly agree | 1 | 2 | 3 | 4 | 5 | 6 | 7 | N/A | Strongly disagree

Importance   Very important | 1 | 2 | 3 | 4 | 5 | 6 | 7 | N/A | Not important

23   **This site has a good reputation**

Score   Strongly agree | 1 | 2 | 3 | 4 | 5 | 6 | 7 | N/A | Strongly disagree

Importance   Very important | 1 | 2 | 3 | 4 | 5 | 6 | 7 | N/A | Not important

24   **This site creates a sense of personalization**

Score   Strongly agree | 1 | 2 | 3 | 4 | 5 | 6 | 7 | N/A | Strongly disagree

Importance   Very important | 1 | 2 | 3 | 4 | 5 | 6 | 7 | N/A | Not important

25   **The site conveys a sense of competency**

Score   Strongly agree | 1 | 2 | 3 | 4 | 5 | 6 | 7 | N/A | Strongly disagree

Importance   Very important | 1 | 2 | 3 | 4 | 5 | 6 | 7 | N/A | Not important

26   **This site conveys a sense of enjoyability or entertainment**

Score   Strongly agree | 1 | 2 | 3 | 4 | 5 | 6 | 7 | N/A | Strongly disagree

Importance   Very important | 1 | 2 | 3 | 4 | 5 | 6 | 7 | N/A | Not important

27   **The site creates a positive experience for me**

Score   Strongly agree | 1 | 2 | 3 | 4 | 5 | 6 | 7 | N/A | Strongly disagree

Importance   Very important | 1 | 2 | 3 | 4 | 5 | 6 | 7 | N/A | Not important

28   **This site makes it easy to communicate with the organization**

Score   Strongly agree | 1 | 2 | 3 | 4 | 5 | 6 | 7 | N/A | Strongly disagree

Importance   Very important | 1 | 2 | 3 | 4 | 5 | 6 | 7 | N/A | Not important

29   **This website helps me manage and integrate the roles and relationships I have with the organisation**

Score   Strongly agree | 1 | 2 | 3 | 4 | 5 | 6 | 7 | N/A | Strongly disagree

Importance   Very important | 1 | 2 | 3 | 4 | 5 | 6 | 7 | N/A | Not important

30   **This site advises me of things I need to know**

Score   Strongly agree | 1 | 2 | 3 | 4 | 5 | 6 | 7 | N/A | Strongly disagree

Importance   Very important | 1 | 2 | 3 | 4 | 5 | 6 | 7 | N/A | Not important

31	The site has an attractive appearance	
Score	Strongly agree I 1 I 2 I 3 I 4 I 5 I 6 I 7 I N/A I	Strongly disagree
Importance	Very important I 1 I 2 I 3 I 4 I 5 I 6 I 7 I N/A I	Not important
32	This website creates a sense of community	
Score	Strongly agree I 1 I 2 I 3 I 4 I 5 I 6 I 7 I N/A I	Strongly disagree
Importance	Very important I 1 I 2 I 3 I 4 I 5 I 6 I 7 I N/A I	Not important
33	What is your overall view of the quality of this website	
Score	Highest quality I 1 I 2 I 3 I 4 I 5 I 6 I 7 I N/A I	Lowest quality
34	Comments: Please add any comments you would like to make about any aspect of this site	

References

Alzola LM, Robaina VC (2005) SERVQUAL: Its applicability in electronic commerce B2C. The Quality Management Journal 12:46

Aneja A, Brooksby B, Rowan C (2001) Corporate portal framework for transforming content chaos on intranets. Intel Technology Journal 11:21–28

Barnes S (2001) An evaluation of cyber-bookshops: The webqual method. International Journal of Electronic Commerce 6:11–30

Barnes S, Vigden R (2000) Assessing the quality of auction web sites. In: Hawaii Conference on System Sciences, Hawaii

Barnes S, Vidgen R (2002) An integrative approach to the assessment of e-commerce quality. Journal of Electronic Commerce Research 3:114–127

Bitner MJ, Ostrom AL, Meuter ML (2002) Implementing successful self-service technologies. Academy of Management Executive 16:96–109

Brabston ME, McNamara G (1998) The Internet as a competitive knowledge tool for top managers. Industrial Management and Data Systems 98:158

Churchill Jr. GA (1979) A paradigm for developing better measures of marketing constructs. Journal of Marketing Research 16:64–73

Cresswell J (1994) Research Design: Qualitative & Quantitative Approaches. Sage Publications, Thousand Oaks, California

Dabholkar P (1996) Consumer evaluations of new technology-based self-service options: an investigation of alternative models of service quality. International Journal of research in Marketing 13:29–51

Dias C (2001) Corporate portals: A literature review of a new concept in Information Manage-ment. International Journal of Information Management 21:269

Doll W, Hendrickson A, Deng X (1998) Using Davis's Perceived Usefulness and Ease-of-Use Instruments for Decision Making: A Confirmatory and Multigroup Invariance Analysis. Decision Sciences 29:839–869

Freeman RE (1984) Strategic Management: A Stakeholder Approach. Pitman, Boston, MA

Gilbert D, Balestrini P, Littleboy D (2004) Barriers and benefits in the adoption of e-government. The International Journal of Public Sector Management 17:286–301

Gounaris S, Dimitiadis S (2003) Assessing service quality on the web: Evidence from business to consumer portals. The Journal of Services Marketing 17:529

Gronroos C (1978) A service-orientated approach to marketing of services. European Journal of Marketing 12:588–601

Hind P (2005) New Zealand Directions 2005 for Victoria University of Wellington. IDC Re-search, Sydney, Australia

Huberman AM, Miles MB (1998) Data Management and Analysis Methods. In: Denzin NK, Lincoln YS (eds) Collecting and Interpreting Qualitative Materials. Sage, Thousand Oaks

Kuo T, Lu I, Huang C et al. (2005) Measuring user's perceived portal service quality: An empirical study. Total Quality Management and Business Excellence 16:309

Lagrosen S, Seyyed-Hashemi R, Leitner M (2004) Examination of the dimensions of quality in higher education. Quality Assurance in Education 12:61

McKay J, Pranato A, Marshall P (2000) E-business maturity and the SOGe model. In: Austral-asian Conference in Information Systems (ACIS), Brisbane, Australia

Morgan D, Stinson L (1997) What are Focus Groups? A report by the American Statistical Association, Alexandra, VA

Owlia MS, Aspinwall EM (1996) A Framework for the Dimensions of Quality in Higher Educa-tion. Quality Assurance in Education 4:12

Palmer J (2002) Website usability, design and performance metrics. Information Systems research 13:151–167

Parasuraman V, Zeithaml V, Berry L (1985) A conceptual model of service quality and its implications for future research. Journal of Marketing 49:41–50

Parasuraman V, Berry L, Zeithaml V (1991) Understanding customer expectations of service. Sloan Management Review 32(3):39–48

Pare G (2004) Investigating Information Systems with Positivist Case Study Research. Communications of the AIS 13:233–264

Pitt L, Watson R, Kavan B (1995) Service Quality: A Measure of Information Systems Effectiveness. MIS Quarterly 19

Pitt L, Watson R, Kavan B (1997) Measuring Information Systems Service Quality: Concerns for a Complete Canvas. MIS Quarterly 21

Sahney S, Banwet DK, Karunes S (2004) Conceptualising total quality management in higher education. The TQM Magazine 16:145–159

Sandhu K, Corbitt BJ (2003) Web-based Electronic Service Adoption Model (E-SAM). In Pa-cific-Asian Conference in Information Systems (PACIS), Adelaide, South Australia

Straub D, Boudreau M-C, Gefen D (2004) Validation guidelines for IS positivist research. Communications of the ACM 13, article 24:1–79

Tate M, Hope B (2004) The Importance of Service Branding in Multi-Channel E-Commerce Success: Towards a Research Framework. In: Australasian Conference in Information Sys-tems (ACIS), Hobart, Australia

Tate M, Hope B, Johnstone D (2006) ICT, Multi-channels and the Changing Line of Visibility: an Empirical Study. In: HICSS 39, Kauai, Hawaii

Tiecher J, Hughes O, Dow N (2002) E-government: A new route to public sector quality. Managing Service Quality 12:384–393

Winkler RE (2001) Portals – The All-In-One Web Supersites: Features, Functions, Definitions, Taxonomy, in SAP Design Guild Publications Series.

Yin RK (1993) Applications of case study research. Sage Publications, Thousand Oaks, CA

Zeithaml V, Parusaman A, Berry L (1990) Delivering Quality Service: balancing customer per-ceptions and expectations. The Free Press, New York

Zeithaml V, Parasuraman A, Malhorta Y (2002) Service quality delivery through websites: A critical review of extant knowledge. Journal of the Academy of Marketing Science 30:262–375

Zumpe S, Madberger M (2007) A transaction-based Framework for Business Models in Electronic Commerce. In: Pacific-Asia Conference in Information Systems (PACIS), Auckland, New Zealand

Chapter 5
Cybermediation in the Tourism and Travel Industries

Les Killion

Abstract Travel and tourism are second only to pornography in adopting Internet-based technologies to intermediate between those supplying the total travel experience, and those seeking to satisfy leisure needs by engaging in tourism. From Thomas Cook in the 1800s, traditional 'travel trade networks' have provided the components of the travel experience: transport, accommodation and attractions. However, the Internet has encouraged customer self-service, and on-going debate regarding the future of traditional travel trade intermediaries. The intermediation debate suggests the emergence of 'hybrid' intermediation systems combining customer self-service with face-to-face customer contacts characteristic of traditional travel agents. A focus group investigation identified profiles and motives of customers using the Internet to make holiday arrangements. Potential cost savings are a primary motivation for customer self-service. Using the Internet for travel and tourism is becoming commonplace among older travellers as well as younger people. In gathering information before making holiday decisions, potential tourists also engage in a Web 2.0 environment where family and friends, not established intermediaries, provide reliable and authentic information via their individual blogs.

5.1 Introduction

The tourism and travel industries aim to create satisfying travel experiences providing leisure tourists and business travellers with positive recollections of a destination. Positive memories may differentiate one location from the numerous alternative places that compete for the tourist dollar and the direct and indirect economic impetus associated with tourism development. Providing satisfying travel experiences demands effective synergies between all elements of the destination mix : available transport, accommodation, attractions,

L. Killion (✉)
School of Arts and Creative Enterprise, Faculty of Arts, Humanities and Education,
Central Queensland University, Rockhampton QLD 4702 Australia
e-mail: l.killion@cqu.edu.au

D. Oliver et al. (eds.), *Self-Service in the Internet Age*,
DOI 10.1007/978-1-84800-207-4_5, © Springer-Verlag London Limited 2009

facilities and hospitality services. As service industries, the success of travel and tourism has depended upon operators and providers to assemble packages of tourism products and services. These packages are sold to the tourist market through industry distribution channels and intermediaries including travel agents, tour organisers and conference planners. Traditionally, these intermediaries have linked those seeking a holiday destination (reflecting their motivations, wants, needs and demands), with tourism operators able to provide transport, accommodation and attractions. The expanded availability on the Internet of a full range of travel related resources, from destination information through to reservations and payment services, has seen a growing number of travellers develop their own links and employ their own self-service strategies in preference to the services provided by travel agents and other industry intermediaries.

This chapter provides an initial discussion of the role of Thomas Cook in the genesis of travel agencies and tour organisers. It was the now legendary 'Cooks Tour' that began the pattern of having intermediary agents and others organise holiday travel, as opposed to individuals making their own arrangements. The roles of intermediaries in marketing in general, and in the marketing of tourism and services and products in particular, are then considered. As tourism and travel have embraced the world of e-commerce, and customer self-service has become more popular, the impacts of the Internet are viewed from two perspectives. Firstly, the chapter directs attention to the on-going debate prompted by online destination marketing and promotion concerning the future of travel trade intermediaries and the issues of disintermediation, reintermediation and hybrid forms of cybermediation. Secondly, the chapter considers the deeper question of the inversion of control as users increasingly determine and take control of Web-based information encouraged by the Web 2.0 environment (Lew 2007a,b). The Web 2.0 environment comprises that part of the Web on which individuals are able to create their own Web spaces for the purposes of sharing information and communicating with others including family, friends and colleagues. It is within the Web 2.0 environment that more of us are sharing our travel experiences and memoirs through individualised blogs. In turn, these are becoming significant sources of influence over the travel decisions and destination choices of others.

5.2 Thomas Cook: The First Travel Trade Intermediary

The idea that people would pay for someone else to organise their leisure travel and holiday arrangements and creating a role for intermediaries in a travel trade network, was the brainchild of Thomas Cook. In the social chaos of the Industrial Revolution, Cook, a Baptist pastor, conceived the rudiments of the package tour when he formed the idea of chartering trains to transport workers into the countryside to attend temperance meetings and bible camps. The first of these excursions was a day trip on 5 July 1841 from Leicester to Loughborough. The excursions grew both in terms of numbers of participants and the destinations visited, and sightseeing and pleasure travel overtook the initial spiritual reasons for these journeys. Regular tours were conducted between Leicester and London, and in 1851 a package tour was conducted to the Great Exhibition in London. By 1863 Cook had organised the first international tour to the Swiss Alps, followed in 1872 by the first round-the-world excursion, the itinerary including the colonies of Australia and New Zealand (Withey 1997).

The business opportunity Cook perceived, resulted in the emergence of extensive networks of travel agencies to whom individuals increasingly turned to make arrangements for holiday travel, rather than undertaking such arrangements for themselves. Through Cook's initiatives, inclusive pre-paid single price structures including transport, accommodation, tour guides, food and other services became commonplace. With them also came organised itineraries, affordable prices associated with economies of scale, and standardisation of tourism services and products in terms of both quality and value for money. Tourism was emerging as an industry essentially following the same production techniques and market distribution channels that were the foundations of the Industrial Revolution. Significantly, these approaches persisted and individuals remained increasingly dependent on market intermediaries, rather than serving themselves in the tourism and travel markets. Moreover, operators and providers in the tourism and travel industries reciprocated and the travel agent became their major link to the market of consumers seeking satisfaction from their travel experience. With the growth of customer self-service through the Internet, the fundamental question is: for how much longer?

5.3 Intermediaries and Distribution Channels

Tourism and travel are not unique in having intermediaries occupying distribution channels. The provision of all goods and services is characterised by intermediaries who establish and facilitate exchange relationships between producers and suppliers, and consumers who demand their goods and services.

5.3.1 Distribution Channels, Value and Supply Chains

The exchange relationship between producers and consumers rests on the concept of 'value'. The notion of value exchange is a general concept on which the profession of marketing is based. In simple terms, a transfer of value occurs between those who supply goods and services and those who consume them. Except in situations where there is an immediate or direct transaction between supplier and consumer, the relationship between them is facilitated through distribution channel intermediaries. Differences are found in the nature of distribution channels. How goods and services are distributed to consumers reflects the nature of the particular good or service. In the case of some manufactured goods, for example, the exchange relationship may require little more than arranging transport from the factory to the consumer.

The distribution channels typically used in marketing comprise interdependent organisations involved in the process of making a product or service available to the consumer or business user. Kotler et al. (1996) emphasise that distribution channels are also marketing channels . At each point of exchange, opportunities exist for marketing to facilitate the exchange relationship and hence the value exchange. This is especially obvious when we consider the exchange of goods and services through multiple channels of wholesalers and retailers existing between the supplier and the final consumer.

Intermediaries are usually individual business organisations arrayed along the distribution or marketing channel between the supplier and the final consumer of the service or product. The number of intermediaries corresponds with the number of points of value exchange along the distribution channel. In a single (or direct) distribution channel there are no intermediaries. In the absence of 'middlemen' the supplier is responsible for promoting the service or product and also delivering the service or product to customers. However, small operators often lack the financial resources to carry out such direct marketing. They find that intermediaries provide a more efficient way to make their goods and services available to target markets. As Kotler et al. (2001, p. 287) observe, 'through their contacts, experience, specialization and scale of operation, intermediaries usually offer the firm more than it can achieve on its own'.

Through intermediaries and their associated distribution channels the product or service provided to the customer '... is the end result of the work of a chain of different organizations. Each organization adds extra value. Each depends on the others and all impact on the quality of the end product' (Morgan 1996, p. 188). This view of distribution is the basis for the notion of a value chain . Kim (2005 pp. 3–4) emphasises that the value chain is 'a model that describes a series of activities connecting a company's supply side (raw materials, inbound logistics and production processes) with its demand side (outbound logistics, marketing and sales).' Value can be thought of as the difference between the value of the product or service and the costs involved in its production. In their interpretation of the price of a product or service, consumers make their evaluation of the product or service, and decide whether or not to make a purchase if they conclude that it represents value for money. Clearly, the different stakeholders and intermediaries involved in a transaction aim to add further value to the product or service.

To achieve this requires the careful management and coordination of value chains and their 'marketing logistics networks' (Kotler et al. 2001, p. 284). The coordination and management required extends to all stakeholders including suppliers of services and products, agents, marketers, businesses within related distribution channels, including government and not-for-profit organisations, and, of course, customers and their expectations. The distribution of services and products requires a military-style organisation from which, of course, the term 'logistics' is derived. Such logistical organisation, coordination and collaboration occur through market intermediaries.

5.4 Intermediaries in the Travel and Tourism Industries

In the travel and tourism industries, the number of distribution channels, and the numbers of intermediaries within them, is made more complex by the diverse elements comprising the destination mix. The term 'destination mix' refers to the combinations of facilities, attractions, transport and hospitality services found at a particular location. Each element of the destination mix is itself a segment of larger industry sectors. For example, the various forms of transport used by travellers are also components of the more general transport sector. That sector has diverse channels for distributing information between those operating transport systems and those who use them. The railway network in Queensland, Australia, for instance, certainly transports tourists to and from destinations. The same network also carries commuters to and from work as well as transporting a variety of freight, livestock and minerals. Not surprisingly, in such a network there will be multiple intermediaries and multiple distribution channels each targeting specific markets for, and forms of, rail transport.

5.4.1 The Travel Trade Network

Intermediaries and the related distribution channels in travel and tourism are generally referred to as the 'travel trade network' or more simply, 'the travel trade'. At least until recent times, the travel trade intermediaries have performed functions that both directly and indirectly linked suppliers of tourism services and products with those tourists seeking to travel to a destination to consume the same services and products. The exchange between suppliers and tourists in turn creates the basis of the travel experience.

Retail travel agencies have occupied a prime position among the travel trade intermediaries. The travel trade network also includes tour wholesalers and operators assembling tour packages for on-sale by retail travel agents , conference and convention organisers, and events managers. Retail travel agencies have, however, represented the largest group in the travel trade network, creating holiday packages and earning income through commissions paid by carriers, accommodation operators and other suppliers of tourism services and products. The numbers of traditional shop-front travel agents grew dramatically until the mid-1990s. At that time the first impacts of customer self-service via the Internet began to be felt causing some agencies to close or reorganise their operations. However, at least in the United States, the decline in the numbers of travel agents cannot be solely attributed to the impacts of Internet usage for customer self-service. Around the same time, travel agents in that country experienced reductions in the payment of commissions (Morrison 2002), forcing some agents out of the market.

5.4.2 Roles and Functions of Travel Trade Intermediaries

Intermediaries in the tourism and travel markets function to establish and facilitate exchange relationships between producers and suppliers of tourism services and products, and tourists who are motivated to travel to diverse tourist destinations to consume the services and products on offer. Until the advent of Internet-facilitated customer self-service, the exchange relationships in travel and tourism typically occurred through multiple forms of distribution involving a wide range of travel agencies and other intermediaries in the marketplace. The exchange and value relationships between suppliers of tourism services and products and the tourists who consume them are complex.

Each element of the destination mix (transport, accommodation, hospitality services and attractions) is likely to be distributed in different channels and may occur through multiple forms of distribution. In these terms, Morrison (2002) suggests that when it comes to distribution it is appropriate to talk of a distribution mix. The distribution mix will reflect the 'combination of the direct and indirect distribution channels that a hospitality and travel organisation uses to make customers aware of its services and to reserve and deliver them' (Morrison 2002, p. 339). On this point, Pearce and Schott (2005) highlighted some interesting findings from their study of how visitors perceive various distribution channels. In their study these researchers observed that tourists use distribution channels for three key functions: searching for destination information, making bookings and reservations, and making payments for these. Some tourists may use the Internet for only one of these purposes (often the initial search for destination information). Others, however, expect to use the Internet for all three functions. This has important implications for the contemporary travel and tourism industries as they move increasingly into the electronic era. It would be incongruous for a supplier of a tourism service or product to rely upon the distribution of information about the offering through a Web site, but then not make provision on that site for consumers to take the next step and actually make a booking or reservation. On the other hand, it would be equally incongruous for a supplier to use the Internet for any of these functions if the market segment that is being targeted is known not to be regular Web users.

As well as facilitating exchange relationships with tourists, intermediaries in the tourism and travel industries also facilitate exchange relationships between one business and another. For example, an exchange relationship (and therefore a developed distribution channel) may exist between a company supplying transport for tourists and companies providing accommodation and attractions as components of the total tourism service product. Traditionally, travel agents have been the usual intermediaries in their exchange relationships with all elements of the destination mix. More recently, increasing use of the Internet in the travel and tourism industries has encouraged the development of single direct distribution channels between suppliers and consumers who are increasingly intent on serving themselves in the travel trade market. However, at least for the present, many tourism operators continue to participate in the indirect distribution channels provided through travel agencies.

5.4.3 Travel Trade Intermediaries and the Travel Experience

The travel experiences that tourists either enjoy or endure are the end results of travel trade intermediaries and their associated distribution channels. As emphasised earlier, each stakeholder and intermediary involved in providing services and products to the tourist aims to add to the travel experience by adding value to the product or service. This is the general nature of any value or supply chain as observed previously. Value chains in the travel and tourism industries are potentially global in their extent. While the Internet ensures the global reach of travel and tourism value chains, it tends to reduce the number of channels and intermediaries, thereby shortening the chain.

The successful delivery of a packaged travel product requires that the multiple components of the destination mix are working effectively. This requires close collaboration within the shared distribution channels that comprise the tourism and travel industries. However, as tourists make increasing use of the Internet, they are finding their own logistical solutions in their search for satisfying travel experiences. That is, without relying on the services of travel trade intermediaries, tourists have rapidly discovered that by using the Internet they are able to make their own holiday arrangements.

5.5 'Dub, Dub, Dub' and Self-Service in Travel and Tourism

The World Wide Web has extended the opportunities for marketers to inform the market about available travel and tourism services and products. This has resulted in a related shortening of value chains and the number of marketing distribution channels. The travel and tourism industries are among the leading users of this communications technology. As yet not all tourists are drawn to the Web as self-service customers for the purposes of making reservations for travel and accommodation. However, they are certainly making use of Web-based resources to discover new travel opportunities, acquire knowledge of new destinations, and to make travel decisions.

5.5.1   The Internet as a Tourism and Travel Distribution Channel

Operators in the tourism industry increasingly recognise that their first contact with a potential visitor comes via the Web. With this comes an immediate opportunity to build relationships with potential tourists in order to strengthen their motivation to visit the destination.

Individual tourism and travel operators are now making increasing use of the Internet to provide information about their products and services to would-be tourists. An increasing number of destination-marketing organisations now also figure prominently on the Web. Destination marketing organisations market entire locations and what they have to offer to tourists. As opposed to individual travel operators and tourism enterprises, such organisations aim to present an aggregate view of the destination's tourism services, products and attractions. In Australia as elsewhere, destination marketing organisations are found at a number of levels from regional organisations through to national tourism offices . These levels of operation largely reflect the nature of government funding allocations. Not unexpectedly, the Internet presence of such organisations mirrors their levels of operation. Some Web sites are those of regional tourism authorities such as the Capricorn Tourism Organisation that markets and promotes the Central Queensland region (www.capricorntourism.com.au). Others are the Web sites of state-based organisations exemplified by Tourism Queensland (www.tq.com.au). Still others are the sites of national tourism offices such as that of Malaysia (www.tourism.gov.my), Hong Kong (www.tourism.gov.hk/english/welcome/welcome.html) and New Zealand (www.newzealand.com/Australia). Tourism Australia is the country's national tourism office with a major Web presence directed principally at international markets. The Tourism Australia Web site has undergone a number of innovative changes over time. The most recent of these occurred in July 2007 with the launch of www.PleaseTakeMeTo.com together with a Web-linked DVD-ROM. This has been heralded as Australia's major breakthrough in electronic destination marketing.

Every invention or innovation has the potential to exert fundamental change in human culture and society, and to redefine human behaviour, preferences and established ways of doing things. Distribution channels in marketing are used strategically to inform the market of available goods and services. The general aim of all marketing activities is to convert prospects into customers to whom the particular good or service can be sold. Whether in the form of the printing press, radio or television, changes in communications technologies have always exerted far-reaching effects on the ways that marketers go about this task. From its inception in the 1990s, the Internet now stands as a further addition in the development of communications technologies through which users are able to retrieve and share information, exchange messages, display audio and video files, interact with others through discussion groups, and sell products and services (Reid and Bojanic (2006, p. 342)). The Internet has fostered channels of communication, and hence distribution, within global e-commerce networks which has had profound impacts and consequences for tourism marketing. Lumsdon (1997, p. 193) observed that the Internet '... has enabled timely information to be made available to all levels of the distribution system regarding availability and occupancy of facilities at any given time. This is vital when the offering is both perishable and intangible. Furthermore, it has enabled thousands of suppliers from around the globe to connect into computerized reservation systems.' Interestingly, at the time that he was writing (and that was only a decade ago), Lumsdon (1997) made the statement that 'the Internet is as yet an untried marketing tool, but commentators suggest that it will become more important in future years.' Given more recent developments and applications of the Internet, clearly the future is now!

5.5.2 *Tourism and Travel and the Internet*

Law et al. (2004, p. 100) observed that the rapid growth of the travel industry and the need to manage the increasing volume of tourism traffic requires sophisticated information technologies. So popular has it become for this purpose that, apart from the number of sites related to pornography, the next largest users of the Internet are those that relate to the travel and tourism industries. There are some very good reasons that explain the burgeoning adoption of the Internet by tourism operators and tourists. Based on the earlier research of Buhalis and Licata, Law et al. (2004, p. 101) have pointed to the '... direct fit of the Internet and travel and tourism products.' In particular, relevant information can be provided rapidly at low cost and in a timely fashion when the tourist most wants to receive it. Furthermore, the ready association between the Internet and the travel and tourism industries reflects the fact that, like all services, tourism products and services are highly perishable. This creates a need for operators to respond rapidly to changes in tourist demand patterns. The tourism industry is characterised by a large number of different suppliers with varying scales of operation, operating independently. Tourists, on the other hand, expect travelling to be a complete and coordinated experience. The Internet offers the means of resolving this mismatch. Law et al. (2004, p. 101), for instance, suggest that the single, sustainable electronic infrastructure provided by the Internet provides the basis for information gathering and business transactions for both travellers and tourism suppliers. The Internet also offers the opportunity for operators and suppliers of tourism services and products to engage in one-to-one marketing and mass customisation (Law et al. 2004, p. 101). With the opportunities that it provides for both tourists and operators in the travel and tourism industries, the growth of Internet usage is not unexpected. Sales data provided by Jetset Travelworld chairman, John King, demonstrated the increases in online sales for both domestic and international holidays. For example, making bookings online is now the preferred method for arranging a domestic trip over three nights or more. Over the period 2001–2005 online domestic travel sales increased from 1.7% to 20.4% of all sales (Jones 2007a, p. 1).

5.5.3 Advantages and Disadvantages of Internet-based Intermediation

In the more general context of Internet marketing, and acknowledging the continued use of other offline media, Hsu et al. (2001) have highlighted six major advantages associated with Internet marketing in the travel and tourism industries including:

- The ability to target specific market segments
- The ability to collect information on individual users as a basis for future planning and development
- The capacity to target the individual who is accessing the information and through further tracking, to construct customer profile data
- The ability to deliver on a global and 24/7 basis when the customer is seeking information, so ensuring the synchronous delivery of information
- The flexibility and speed with which online campaigns can be implemented
- The level of interactivity involving the customer in the promotional process.

Connolly et al. (1998) have noted that in extending global distribution systems, the Internet offers the advantage of reducing costs by bypassing traditional distribution channels in the form of travel agencies and other intermediaries to whom commissions and transaction fees must be paid. As the Internet extends a company's reach into global markets, it has also become an important means of enhancing customer service through the provision of more and better information with multimedia.

When it comes to Internet applications in travel and tourism, there are, however, some disadvantages. At least for the time being, these disadvantages suggest that traditional intermediaries such as travel agents will remain in the distribution mix used by operators and providers. Some disadvantages are cost-related and it is important to recognise that especially for the numerous small and medium enterprises, in tourism the costs associated with developing a Web presence may seem prohibitive. There is also the question of the extent to which the same small and medium operators may be marginalised. They may be reduced to little more than a pop-up window hosted on the Web site of a corporate or destination marketing Web site.

Questions associated with security and computer hacking need to be considered both in terms of their realities, and also the perceptions of some market segments when it comes to making online reservations and especially payments that require the provision of personal and financial information.

Travel and tourism are service industries . In contrast to industries that produce and sell tangible products, in the ultimate sense, travel and tourism offer tourists intangible holiday experiences. In common with other communications media, the Internet does not, and cannot, resolve the fundamental dilemma that confronts the marketing of services that customers cannot touch, but only experience. Representations loaded onto the Internet attempt to make the intangible more tangible, by depicting hotel rooms, landscape vistas and available activities. In seeking to attract the interest of potential customers, such images tend to be selected from already existing iconic stereotypes that might be seen as a 'brand' or at least a label for the destination. According to a study undertaken by Killion and McGehee (2007), the iconic images come to dominate the destination imagery established in the minds of would-be visitors. This carries the risk of other attractions being overlooked, and the possibility of visitors gaining false impressions of the destination.

There are, then, both advantages and disadvantages associated with the applications of the Internet in travel and tourism. In the final analysis, in deciding to participate in Internet-based distribution channels operators in these industries need to acknowledge the importance of other forms of distributing information about their products and services to the marketplace. The most effective approach to marketing tourism services and products may be found in a mix of distribution channels that is appropriate to those market segments being targeted by the overall marketing strategy.

5.5.4 Who Are the Self-Serving Customers in Travel and Tourism?

As might be anticipated, when it comes to using the Internet as a basis for self-service in travel and tourism, there are differences between market segments. Some tourists express a preference for on-going personal contact and service provision from established travel agents and other intermediaries. Through their use of the Internet, others have become almost entirely self-sufficient, self-serving customers. These patterns almost certainly reflect more general differences in uptake of any changes and innovations. Simply, some people are early adopters. Others remain to be convinced. The influences of early adopters over the decisions of others to take up innovations and participate in change processes, is a basic principle of Roger's (2003) explanation of how innovations are diffused. As will be noted later, in discussing the findings from the small focus group study that was undertaken, when early adopters are close friends and associates, other people whom they influence are more likely to take up the innovation. Moreover, the differences reflect a wide range of variables related to the nature and purpose of the trip, the perceived importance (to the individual customer) of cost savings, and the question of who actually pays for the travel and accommodation.

In their research, Law et al. (2004, p. 104) demonstrated that those most likely to make online travel and travel-related purchases were males, in the age group 26–45, with a university education, with incomes above $100,000 and in full employment. People over 65 years were least likely to make such purchases. If these data are generalised more widely, there are implications for the future of customer self-service via the Internet. For instance, it would seem that traditional travel agencies may continue to meet the information and reservation needs of older tourists whose numbers, mobility and participation in travel will all increase in the future.

5.5.5 *Some Findings from a Focus Group Study*

A more limited investigation into Internet-based customer self-service in tourism and travel was carried out with focus groups in Central Queensland. Informants participated in one of two focus groups, each comprised of 10 individuals. Table 5.1 illustrates demographic details for each group.

Focus group 1 comprised students studying tourism courses at Central Queensland University. With an average age of 20 years, this group included seven females and three males. Focus group 2 was made up of individuals ranging in age from 28 to 71 years, with an equal number of men and women. While supporting some aspects of the Law et al. (2004) study, information provided by members of the two focus groups pointed to some interesting differences. Regardless of age, all participants used the Internet to make travel reservations because of the cost-savings available through online bookings especially with airline companies. Such savings, for individuals residing outside major metropolitan centres are not inconsiderable, especially if the traveller is able to plan the trip well ahead of the proposed travel date, with the possibility of also taking advantage of a range of special offers made by competing airline companies.

Table 5.1 Demographic details of focus group participants

Group 1 students		Group 2 general population	
Gender	Age (years)	Gender	Age (years)
F	18	F	28
F	19	F	55
F	21	F	56
F	19	F	71
F	22	F	62
F	24	M	60
F	18	M	32
M	20	M	47
M	19	M	64
M	20	M	69
N = 10	Mean = 20	N = 10	Mean = 54.4

Interestingly, in the case of both focus groups, women were as likely as men to use the Internet to make their own travel arrangements. Even more interesting, although possibly reflecting the age distribution in the second focus group, older women (that is, aged over 55 years) were equally motivated to go online to make cost-saving travel arrangements. Some of these women had also recently undertaken a preliminary computer training course that had involved Internet usage as well as instruction in e-mailing and other functions.

It is worth noting that the self-service activity displayed by participants in both focus groups was almost entirely confined to domestic travel arrangements. Of the five older focus group participants (that is, aged 60 years or older) who had planned international travel, the use of Internet sites was limited largely to the information search stage of planning their trips. Armed with information extracted from multiple Web sites detailing travel, accommodation and attractions, the next step for them was to visit a travel agent for advice and assistance, sometimes drawing from the experiences the travel agent had gained from familiarisation tours . It was also interesting to note that while all focus group participants were comfortable with making travel reservations in the form of domestic airline tickets, some were less enthusiastic about booking accommodation online. When it came to booking accommodation at domestic destinations they often preferred to telephone a particular hotel or motel. For international reservations, accommodation was often booked through the chosen travel agent. When this was discussed further, participants reported bad past experiences as their reason. For example, some had attempted to reserve accommodation but had become confused with the systems used on the selected Web site. For instance, in one case the calendar function for indicating arrival and departure dates had been the source of some difficulty. Another focus group participant who had attempted self-service in booking accommodation reported that the particular site required payment in American dollars with no provision for modifying the international currency unit for payment.

Among those who participated in the two focus groups, the overwhelming reason given for serving themselves when making travel purchases related directly to cost savings. One participant had gone so far as to plan out an entire 12 months travel to visit family and friends in various locations. She commented that on her limited income this was the only way to make best use of her tourist dollar. Several participants noted their awareness of the fact (noted from the relevant Web site) that it would cost more to make a reservation over the phone or in person. Mention was also made of the convenience of being able to make arrangements outside of regular business hours. This had been important to one informant who needed to travel, sometimes at short notice, to medical appointments in the metropolitan centre. It might be debated whether this is, in fact, a form of tourism. What this participant emphasised was the fact that had she had a longer lead time to make the arrangements she would have been better placed to find a cheaper fare.

Among the older focus group participants (those 60 years or older) one further interesting phenomenon emerged. This involved introducing friends and associates to self-service for tourism and travel products and services via the Internet. As happens in the diffusion of other innovations, it was often a matter of a friend recommending Internet bookings and reservations. In the context of Rogers' diffusion of innovation theory (2003), these friends could be regarded as early adopters who have influenced the adoption of Internet usage by others as they discovered the cost advantages of making online bookings, and became familiar and more confident with navigating the particular Web site. Once this had been achieved, the use of the Internet then became a preferred option. While acknowledging that more recent developments have occurred since they completed their analysis of Australian-based tourism and hospitality Web sites, Weeks and Crouch (1999) noted that while there was consistently high usage of tourism and travel sites for promotion and advertising, the functionality of the sites they examined was extremely low. These authors also urged Web designers to be more mindful of the fact that not everyone who seeks to take advantage of the self-service possibilities offered by the Internet necessarily has state-of-the-art computers. Wilson (2007, p. 1) is also critical of some travel and tourism Web sites noting that 'while most tourism organisations are by now familiar with the Internet, far fewer have really gained an understanding of the technologies, new resources, new communication opportunities, and the requirements that they represent.'

5.5.6 Future Usage Trends, Patterns and Potential

Using the Internet to search for information regarding destinations and their attractions, at least in the view of the focus group participants, has become commonplace in the preliminary planning stages of the travel experience. Regardless of their age differences, most focus group participants now use the Internet for this purpose. It was also apparent that when it comes to making arrangements for domestic travel, focus group participants had become quite accustomed to using the Internet, as self-serving customers taking advantage of cost savings. However, when it came to what were seen to be more complex activities such as reserving accommodation or making international travel arrangements, these participants were more inclined to visit traditional travel agencies or to make reservations over the telephone. All of this provides some insights into the extent to which self-service through the Internet has become a major form of intermediation and distribution in the marketing of tourism services and products in developed nations. Travel and tourism operators and providers have responded to such trends with increasingly sophisticated Web sites with enhanced functionality. Frequently, these Web sites include details of the multiple elements of the destination mix. Hence, the would-be tourist is able to take advantage of packaged products and services that typically include transport, accommodation, entry to attractions, or tickets to a theatre production.

As we contemplate the future of self-service in travel and tourism using the Internet and related communications technologies, and aside from applications in business operations and academic research, their widespread adoption and usage among the population at large in contrasting cultural contexts is stunning.

The global diffusion of Internet technologies and the magnitude of their adoption are testimony of the increasing role the Internet will play within distribution channels of various types in the future. Table 5.2 lists the top 15 countries ranked by Internet usage and charts the percentage changes in use between 2006 and 2007. Even allowing for per capita population differences, this information depicts significant penetration of Internet use within populations of those countries listed.

This table contains several points that are worthy of further note:

- Developed nations such as the United States, Germany, the Netherlands and the UK continue to experience varying increases in Internet usage. Arguably, and possibly reflecting a point of near saturation within these populations, the rate of increase has seemingly slowed. For example, each of these nations experienced a percentage increase in Internet usage of less than 5% from 2006 to 2007.
- In contrast to most of the developed nations listed, the rate of increase in Internet usage in developing nations has been dramatic. It can be noted, for instance, that nations such as China (with a 20% increase) and India (exhibiting a 33% increase) have experienced the highest rates of growth.

Table 5.2 Top 15 countries worldwide ranked by internet users, January 2006 and January 2007 (thousands of unique visitors and % change)

Country	January 2006	January 2007	% change
1. US	150,897	153,447	2
2. China	72,408	86,757	20
3. Japan	51,450	53,670	4
4. Germany	31,209	32,192	3
5. UK	29,773	30,072	1
6. South Korea	24,297	26,350	8
7. France	23,712	24,560	4
8. India	15,867	21,107	33
9. Canada	18,332	20,392	11
10. Italy	15,987	18,106	13
11. Brazil	12,845	14,964	16
12. Spain	12,206	12,710	4
13. Russia	10,471	12,707	21
14. Netherlands	10,772	11,077	3
15. Mexico	8,624	10,149	18
Total Worldwide	676,878	746,934	10

Source: The eMarketer Daily (7 March 2007).

It is this second point that contains a powerful message for those who market tourism services and products. On the basis of their population sizes alone, it is widely acknowledged that China and India are significant and growing international export markets for a wide range of goods and services. Importantly, for tourism and travel operators, and again bearing in mind the sheer magnitude of their populations, China and India are among those nations that are currently undergoing the wider and deeper social, cultural, political and economic changes that will contribute to the emergence of huge and growing mass tourism markets both for domestic and outbound destinations. It is, for example, now an established fact that economic change and development is producing significant middle classes in both nations. These have steadily increasing amounts of disposable income and leisure time that can be devoted to tourism and travel. Relatedly, in the case of mainland China, the easing of government restrictions has stimulated travel to destinations such as Hong Kong for the purposes of family reunions. The real point here is that a potent combination is emerging as the forces that drive mass tourism and travel by people in developing nations are juxtaposed alongside their increasing usage of the Internet. In the future of tourism and travel marketing, the potential for tourists from developing nations to engage in customer self-service for a full range of tourism services and products via the Internet is unbounded.

5.6 Impacts of Internet Usage on Intermediaries: Disintermediation or Reintermediation ?

The widespread uptake of the Internet by travel and tourism providers has been the catalyst for on-going debate concerning the effects and impacts on traditional intermediaries, and the emergence of new intermediaries within travel and tourism's marketing distribution channels. Given expanding Internet usage, the persistent question raised by Giaglis et al. (2002), Law et al. (2004) and Kim (2005) is as follows: will intermediaries continue to exist within the travel and tourism industries in the future? The search for an informed answer to this question has given rise to three possible scenarios, which are discussed in the following sections.

5.6.1 Disintermediation

As providers of tourism services and products use the Internet to enter into more direct marketing relationships with customers, the disintermediation scenario suggests the demise of intermediaries, or the 'middlemen'. This will result in ever shorter value chains. This possibility has already fostered significant and on-going organisational change in tourism distribution channels. However, as Giaglis et al. (2002) emphasise, the disintermediation view has been founded almost entirely on the analysis of costs associated with intermediation. The Internet certainly has the capacity to lower costs (to suppliers and subsequently to customers) and to enhance profit levels. In reporting the responses made by Qantas, Jones (2007b), for example, notes that traditional travel agents are regarded as the most expensive distribution channel and that the most expensive cost per sale was directly associated with leisure travel agents. As Qantas continues its search for cheaper ways to market its tourism and travel services and products, the corporation is aiming to drive more sales through the lowest cost channels. Currently for Qantas that means Qantas.com (Jones 2007b). In supporting the disintermediation side of the debate, Jones (2007b p. 1) cites the view of Qantas' general manager of distribution and planning that 'there are changing business dynamics, and business that is transacted through certain channels now might not be at a future date.'

However, we should not be too hasty in consigning traditional travel agents to the scrapheap. Other 'non-cost' functions that intermediaries such as travel agents perform within distribution channels must be considered. These include the needs of some customers for personalised service delivery, the facilitation of information searches and provision of advice based upon the direct experiences gathered from familiarisation tours of a destination. In addition, travel agents provide advice to operators concerning customer responses to tourism product and service developments. All of this reflects the nature of tourism as a service industry. In itself this might be sufficient reason for intermediaries to continue within the industry, albeit in new guises. Others such as Cowley (cited in Jones 2007c p. 1) have urged agents to become retailers, and to 'get rid of the term travel agent once and for all.' As Jones (2007d) observes from the views expressed by the Brisbane-based travel retailer, Suncity Travel, in this scenario traditional travel agencies face the challenge of reduced commissions. The loss of experienced agents from the industry poses a further challenge. To whom can tourists turn for advice and assistance to supplement their own search for information on the Internet? This question comes at a time when, at least as Lew (2007a) has reported, some users, particularly within the family travel market, have become somewhat disillusioned with Web-based intermediaries, whom some see as less reliable than traditional travel agents.

5.6.2 Reintermediation

The reintermediation scenario directly challenges the disintermediation perspective. While the disintermediation scenario argues that intermediaries are disappearing, the reintermediation view is that intermediaries have re-emerged in the distribution channels of the travel and tourism industries. Those who favour the reintermediation argument point to an increased number of intermediaries motivated by lower barriers to entering the market as well as new opportunities (Giaglis et al. 2002). In part, Law et al. (2004) and Giaglis et al. (2002) argue, it is conceivable that in the significant changes brought about by the Internet, traditional travel trade intermediaries may find opportunities to leverage their expertise as well as taking advantage of economies of scale. In particular, argues the reintermediation case, traditional travel agents may play an important role in facilitating transactions within specific niche markets as travel agents seek to differentiate themselves from competitors. There would also appear to be an ongoing role for intermediaries able to provide 'the human touch and professional services' (Law et al. 2004, p. 103), at least when it comes to some segments within the tourism and travel marketplace such as the elderly, those who are less computer 'savvy', or those less trusting of the new style technology. According to this view of future tourism and travel distribution channels, there may well be room for both traditional intermediaries and those who function within the electronic environment of the Internet. At least for the present, it appears that intermediaries of both types supplement each other in terms of customer service and satisfaction. This situation is exemplified in the development of the new Travelscene Amex Tourabout distribution system. As Jones (2007e) explains, this system searches and compares the numerous packages and prices from over 40 suppliers. It also includes details of departure dates and destinations. Using the system a traditional travel agency is able to synchronously match available products with customer needs, thereby shortening the sales cycle.

5.6.3 Cybermediation

The integration of online and offline distribution channels may well be the way of the future for tourism and travel marketing. Intermediaries, according to this third scenario, will utilise hybrid forms of distribution channels to target specific market segments. These hybrid forms of intermediation will combine some of the perceived advantages of the Internet with the expectations of some existing market segments that the traditional services of travel agents and other intermediaries will continue to be available.

According to Giaglis et al. (2002, p. 231) there will be opportunities for new style cyber-intermediaries who can 'provide the necessary infrastructure support for those market functions that will be fundamentally restructured in the electronic commerce world.' In responding to changing customer needs and expectations in the world of e-commerce, large-scale agency mergers are likely to create the basis for larger distribution networks as tourism and travel intermediaries extend their penetration of niche market segments.

Paul Scurrah, managing director of AOT Holidays (cited in Jones 2007f p. 1) argues that the wealth of information on the Internet is playing into the hands of traditional travel wholesalers and retailers. Scurrah's view is that while the Web is a growing distribution channel used by an increasing number of better educated travellers, it could not replace 'credible and educated advice' from travel trade intermediaries equipped with direct product knowledge and experience.

The knowledge and experience of travel agents continues to be valued by consumers especially with regard to international tourism products and services. It is for this reason, that Carroll (2007) anticipates online intermediaries will continue to face stiff competition from traditional travel agencies. The mix of online and traditional travel intermediaries in the context of cybermediation is likely to continue in the foreseeable future. For example, the report prepared by PhoCusWright cited by Carroll (2007) indicated that in 2006 travel agents generated US \$189 million of online sales, the equivalent of around 5% of the total online market. The same report forecasts that by 2009 that figure would more than double to US \$488 million as 'major groups used their financial, marketing and retail muscle to roll out a hybrid (online/offline) model'. In the context of the Australian and New Zealand leisure and unmanaged business travel markets, the PhoCusWright report (as cited by Carroll 2007) indicated these markets will increase by 48% from US \$4.1 million in 2006 to an estimated US \$6.1 million in 2009. By that time online travel bookings will account for an estimated 24% of the total Australian and New Zealand travel market. Given that the travel experience is derived from the combined effects of all elements of the destination mix, the airline and hotel industries will continue to dominate. However, it is anticipated that other elements such as car rentals and tour packaging will increase.

5.7 Tourism, Travel and the Web 2.0 Environment

Customer self-service is a growing trend in travel and tourism. However, it would seem that intermediaries will continue to be found in the marketing distribution channels of these industries although almost certainly in a form that is different from the traditional travel agency of the past. New-style intermediaries will have a continuing role once the would-be tourist has identified a possible destination and is intent on making the necessary reservations and arrangements. Before this, in the preliminary stages of gathering information about possible destinations and before the idea of taking a trip is acted upon, the environment created by Web 2.0 is exerting significant influences over customer choices.

The participation of consumers in the Web 2.0 environment reflects some of the perceived deficiencies in the Web sites of established enterprises and organisations when it comes to providing up-to-date and credible information. The Internet offers individual operators and destination marketing organisations enormous potential in marketing tourism services and products. However, Web sites require very careful design. To achieve visual impact, destination Web sites generally feature iconic images associated with particular destinations. There is, though, a limit to the number and complexity of Web site images. According to Killion and McGehee (2007), tourists relate more readily to iconic images. However, they may dominate other destination attractions to their detriment, and may even be misleading. Consider, for example, some of the images appearing on Australian travel Web sites that convey the impression that this destination offers rugged bushland and coastal locations, but little else.

Additionally, such Web sites require efficient functionality in balancing content, images and download time. Those taking too long to download encourage potential visitors to browse other sites as they search for possible holiday destinations. Destination Web sites that some users consider to be among the best also provide up-to-date information, language translations and a local news service and weather details. Operators and marketing organisations must allocate sufficient time and resources to carry out regular updates and upgrades of their Web sites. A cursory browse of some Web sites currently on the Internet reveals that many have not been updated, much less upgraded, for several months and in some cases, years. Where this is the case, it is hardly surprising to find that would-be tourists turning to the growing number of individually developed blogs in the Web 2.0 environment to satisfy their quest for current information.

5.7.1 Inversion of Control

As a consequence of the widespread use of the Web, Hinchcliffe (2006, p. 1) has suggested we are witnessing the 'inversion of control'. In relation to consumers who are increasingly able to create their own blogs, podcasts and Web sites, Hinchcliffe comments that 'the interesting parts of the Web are increasingly contributed by its users directly, or indirectly, apparently establishing that the sheer mass of innovation is in control of the greater Web community rather than by a few centrally controlled outlets. The implications for business seem to be that control over a lot of things is moving from top-down to bottom-up, or at least heading in one particular direction instead of the other.' Hinchcliffe (2006, p. 1) has coined the term 'disintermediation in public' to describe this phenomenon. Characteristically, '... people are increasingly conducting business amongst themselves, without even much of an enterprise in the way.'

If this is indeed the case, the future implications for intermediaries in the tourism and travel industries are quite profound. Leary (2007) has recommended the use of blogs and podcasts as new marketing and distribution channels for providing information to potential customers. With their relatively low costs and prerequisite skill requirements, these forms of Internet usage are of particular interest to the legion of small and medium enterprises within the tourism industry. It can be anticipated that using the tools of Web 2.0 will again revolutionise the ways in which travel and tourism companies relate to customers and do business.

Apart from time for regular tracking and updating, such information communication technologies have relatively few barriers to effective use. The reality is that even before their wider adoption by business operators, they are already used by the population at large to satisfy demands for information. In the early adoption stages, the Web 2.0 environment has been particularly attractive to the Generation Y market. Much of the initial development of instant messaging, blogs (Web logs), wikis , RSS and social networks had an almost instant appeal to Gen Y users. In tourism and travel marketing, word-of-mouth is a powerful influence. The Web 2.0 environment provides a ready channel through which travellers to a particular destination or attraction can communicate their negative, as well as positive, travel experiences to others, often in real-time. This presents a major challenge to any tourism operator aiming to compete against other destinations and attractions on what has always been an intensely competitive battlefield.

The level of sophistication found in individualised blogs is limited only by the user's time and imagination. The most casual Web search provides numerous examples that illustrate the extent to which blogging was, in effect, the birth of Web 2.0 as well as its impacts on individual travel. It is not intended to provide an extensive list of such examples here. One interesting blog is that maintained by Alan Lew, Travel Geographer, which can be accessed at the following site: web20travel.blogspot.com/2006/02/podcasts-about-tourism-and-travel.html. Demonstrating the levels of sophistication that can be found on some blogs are the following sites: golden-triangle.blogspot.com/ and seasiatourism.blogspot.com/.

As Lew (2007a) notes the related information communication technology of podcasting is, in essence, a form of audio blogging; he suggests there are three forms of travel and tourism podcasts:

- Destination podcasts that describe and sell destinations
- Travel experience podcasts
- Travel and tourism industry and education podcasts

Both business and individual blogs can be found within these three categories.

Of growing interest in a world of customer self-service, is the growing number of sometimes less sophisticated blogs and blog derivatives of individual travellers. These are often used to inform family and friends of their travels and tourist experiences. Inevitably, this information about the particular destination and its tourism services and products is spread to others. Among some travellers, YouTube , MySpace and FaceBook have become popular ways of communicating in a fashion that in an earlier time was achieved by sending postcards from the holiday destination. While obviously not designed to assist the would-be tourist to make reservations and travel arrangements, given their source, such sites contain destination information that is regarded as more authentic, credible and timely than could be achieved by the most trusted and time efficient travel agent. The possible influences over the subsequent travel decisions of others can be far-reaching.

Among the participants in the focus group study were two individuals who were quite familiar with the Web 2.0 environment as a result of the travels of family members. In one case, a 60-year-old man had a nephew travelling through the United Kingdom and Scandinavia. The nephew had created a

FaceBook blog on which he regularly posted images and comments about his experiences at the locations he had visited. This focus group participant, who had been contemplating an overseas holiday, decided that his trip would follow in the footsteps that his nephew's FaceBook album had so graphically illustrated. The second focus group participant had a daughter travelling in Japan, while also studying at a Japanese university as part of her undergraduate degree program. Initially, contacts between the two had been via e-mail and the mother was quite confident in using that technology following a short course in computing that she had undertaken at the local technical college. Following a brief return visit to Australia, the daughter established her own blog using MySpace and registered her mother as a contact. Images and comments of Japanese cherry blossom festivals, travels on the bullet train and so on prompted this focus group participant to make arrangements to visit Japan while her daughter was there. Interestingly, in this case and prior to logging onto her daughter's MySpace, the mother held unfounded negative perceptions of Japan as a possible holiday destination. She had been especially concerned about the nature and quality of available facilities and accommodation. She had previously spoken with a travel agent about this destination, but had remained unconvinced until able to view the information contained in her daughter's MySpace entries. These two examples demonstrate several important points about the Web 2.0 environment and its potential to influence travel behaviours and decisions. The most important of these is that Web 2.0 has become the new form of word-of-mouth. Users regard the information provided and exchanged as more authentic and reliable than can be obtained from traditional travel agents. Some users consider the information more reliable than can be obtained from the Web sites of other travel trade intermediaries.

The uptake of Web 2.0 tools has been somewhat slow at this time. This pattern of innovation adoption may, though, vary with access to the requisite technology and the skills of users. What is remarkable is that already a Web 3.0 environment (Lew 2007b), for which Web 2.0 is merely a forerunner, is emerging. When it comes to acquiring preliminary travel information, it can be expected that the extent of customer self-service will become even more pronounced. Web 3.0 will be characterised as a total immersion in a Web-based environment or, as it is described by some commentators, 'Web all round'. As Lew (2007b p. 1) observes, 'Travel 3.0 is clearly not here, yet. However, because we can conceptualise it – imagine what it will be like – it is an important force shaping the visions of today's Travel 2.0 engineers and entrepreneurs.'

5.8 Conclusion

Tourism and travel have become significant stakeholders in the global electronic business environment. In promoting a growing level of customer self-service, the Internet has provided what is perhaps the most exciting development in distribution channel construction and functioning in the travel and tourism industries. Travel and tourism are service industries. They will continue to provide the human contact sought by many tourists, especially when arranging complex international travel. However, in the future this will occur within a hybrid cyber-mediated distribution network. In this hybrid network, traditional travel intermediaries like travel agents will function as travel retailers. In meeting the needs of their customers, they will combine human contact with Web-based services regarding destinations and attractions.

Those who travel to domestic destinations have rapidly discovered and take advantage of cost-savings available through the Web sites of travel and tourism providers. Cost savings are a primary motivation for customer self-service activity in travel and tourism. As illustrated by the participants in the focus group study, regardless of their age and their experience of computer technologies, people are drawn to the advantages provided by the Internet when making their holiday travel arrangements. Largely, because of their previous poor experiences and concerns regarding the provision of financial details on the Internet, some people feel less confident in using the Internet for related tourism services and products such as booking accommodation. When it comes to arranging international travel, there is a continuing customer preference to use the advice and expertise of traditional travel agents. However, those who have decided to travel internationally may well have used the Internet sites of tourism operators and destination marketing organisations to research potential destinations prior to having a travel agent arrange their trip.

While engagement with Web-based booking and reservation systems is now widespread, some tourists gather information about possible holiday destinations through the features of the Web 2.0 environment. Through their individual blogs, family and friends provide their 'cyber postcards' seen to more authentically convey destination details and experiences that potential travellers might use in making their own holiday decisions.

As a basis for customer self-service, the Internet has revolutionised the way in which large numbers of people in developed nations now plan and organise their leisure and business travel. While the percentage increase in the numbers of users shows some signs of plateauing, the numbers using the Internet in developed nations are significant. Based upon these trends alone, arguably, travel and tourism Web sites will continue to retain their prominent second place in the sites visited by self-serving Internet users. In terms of the future of Internet-based customer self-service for travel and tourism, more breathtaking implications are emerging in the context of developing nations. Nations such as China and India are experiencing the coincidence of two causal factors that will contribute to the emergence of mass tourism facilitated by the Internet. On the one hand, these nations, with their extremely large populations, exhibit dramatic increases in the uptake of information communications technologies. On the other, these are also the nations currently experiencing the economic and social advances that are fundamental to the emergence of mass tourism markets – the increases in leisure time and disposable incomes among emerging middle classes, together with the relaxation of previous political restrictions on travel.

Travel and tourism are global industries. Traditionally, customers have relied upon travel trade intermediaries to arrange their holidays and business trips. In a relatively short period of time, the Internet has provided new distribution channels in which tourists are able to engage more directly with providers of tourism services and products. Travel agents and other intermediaries have not been made redundant. They will continue to have a role in service delivery. As with any innovation, customer self-service in travel and tourism on a global scale will be at the heart of significant changes in the organisation and functioning of intermediaries and distribution channels.

Appendix: Glossary of Key Terms

Destination mix	The destination mix comprises all the elements found at a tourist destination, including facilities, attractions, infrastructure, transport and hospitality services.
Distribution	In the traditional 4Ps of the marketing mix, distribution refers to place. That is the distribution, or placement in the market, of information about goods and services and their availability.
Distribution channel	A distribution channel refers to the linkages between the producers of goods and services and the consumers of those goods and services. Some distribution channels are single and direct from producer to consumer. Others, especially in tourism involve multiple linkages between the providers of tourism services and products and the tourists who seek them.
Intermediary	Intermediaries are individuals and businesses that function in distribution channels to make the links between producers and consumers. Travel agents are examples of intermediaries.
Distribution network	Where several distribution channels are involved in distributing goods and services between producers and consumers, a network of distribution channels may exist. The logistical management of such networks is essential that goods and services are provided where and when required.
Marketing channels	Distribution channels also provide opportunities for marketing goods and services and so are sometimes referred to as marketing channels. Marketing channels may exist between producers and consumers. Marketing channels may also be found between producers where one business is the customer of another.
Web 2.0	Web 2.0 refers to those parts of the World Wide Web where individuals are able to create their own Web spaces for the purposes of sharing information and communicating with others including family, friends and colleagues.
Web 3.0	Web 3.0 is seen by some as signifying the third evolutionary stage in the development of Web-based technologies and capabilities. Web 1.0 comprised the first stage and featured 'read only'

	content generated by organisations; Web 2.0 extended this to a 'read–write' situation which, as noted in the chapter gave users an active role in creating their own Web spaces; Web 3.0 is considered to have the potential to allow users to actually modify the site itself and create databases.
Blogs	The term 'blog' is a contraction of 'Web log'. That is, a space on the Web where individuals, companies and organisations are able to maintain a log or diary of their activities.
Wiki	Now used in popular jargon, this term is derived from the name of server software that allows users to freely create and openly edit the content of Web pages using any Web browser. Wiki facilitates group communication, supports hyperlinks, and in its relative simplicity allows nontechnical users to create Web content.
RSS	This acronym stands for Really Simple Syndication. RSS is an XML-based format for content distribution. RSS feeds can be used for a variety of purposes to distribute news items, report summaries and blogs.
Social network	Social networks (in this context) refer to networks of Web users sharing common interests and able to communicate with each other using the Web. One such network in travel and tourism is TravBuddy.com.
Generation Y Gen Y Millenials	Succeeding Generation X, Gen Y individuals, of whom there are some 60 million, were born in the 1979–1994 baby boom. Some suggest that Generation Y heralds a fundamental shift in consumer values among a generation that responds to marketing differently and expects to find products and services advertised where they congregate, often on the Internet. Gen Y questions established brands, and are either intensely loyal consumers or, just as readily, totally, 'switched off'.

References

Carroll D (2007) Retailers set for online bonanza. Travel Today. traveltoday@travelweekly. com.au. Accessed 8 August 2007

Connolly DJ, Olsen MD, Moore RG (1998) The Internet as a Distribution Channel. Cornell Hotel and Restaurant Administration Quarterly 39(4):42–54

Giaglis GM, Klein S, O'Keefe RM (2002) The Role of Intermediaries in Electronic Market-places: Developing a Contingency Model. Information Systems Journal 231(12):231–246

Hinchcliffe D (2006) Consumers as producers: Disintermediation without a net. http://blogs. zdnet.com/Hinchcliffe/?p = 55. Accessed 8 March 2007

Hsu T-W, Murphy J, Purchase S (2001) Australian and Taiwanese Advertiser's Perceptions of Internet Marketing. Australasian Marketing Journal 9(1):33–45

Jones S (2007a) King Spells Out Online Challenge. Travel Today. traveltoday@travelweekly. com.au. Accessed 13 March 2007

Jones S (2007b) Qantas warning for travel agents. Travel Today. traveltoday@travelweekly. com.au. Accessed 19 July 2007

Jones S (2007c) Agents Must Become Retailers, says Sabre. Travel Today. traveltoday@tra-velweekly.com.au. Accessed 13 March 2007

Jones S (2007d) Industry losing experienced agents. Travel Today. traveltoday@travel-weekly.com.au. Accessed 7 February 2007

Jones S (2007e) Travelscene Amex in system launch. Travel Today. traveltoday@travel-weekly.com.au. Accessed 7 August 2007

Jones S (2007f) Internet confusion helping agents: Wholesaler pledges not to go direct. Travel Today. traveltoday@travelweekly.com.au. Accessed 8 February 2007

Killion L, McGehee N (2007) Collaborative Cross-Cultural Curriculum Development in Cyber-space. Working Paper Council of University Tourism and Hospitality Education (CAUTHE) Conference Proceedings 11–14 February 2007, Sydney Australia

Kim Chul-won (2005) Enhancing the Role of Tourism SME's in Global Value Chain: A Case Analysis on Travel Agencies and Tour Operators in Korea. Proceedings of Global Tourism Growth: A Challenge for SMEs. Conference Organisation for Economic Co-operation and Development Centre for Entrepreneurship SMEs & Local Development and Ministry of Culture and Tourism Republic of Korea, 6–7 September,Gwangju, Korea

Kotler P, Bowen J, Makens J (1996) Marketing for hospitality and tourism. Prentice Hall, Upper Saddle River, NJ

Kotler P, Adam S, Brown L, Armstrong G (2001) Principles of Marketing. Prentice Hall Pearson Education Australia Pty Ltd, Frenchs Forest, NSW

Law R, Leung K, Wong RJ (2004) The Impact of the Internet on Travel Agencies International Journal of Contemporary Hospitality Management 16(2):100–107

Leary B (February 27 2007) SMBs Looking To Raise Their Profiles Need To Examine Their Own Experience. www.CRMguru.com/. Accessed 28 February 2007

Lew AA (2007a) Travelography for July 21, 2007 Return of the Travel Agent, Family Travel, and Gladiators. podcasternews.com/programs/35/travelography/4375/return-of-the-travel-agent-family-travel-and-gladiators/. Accessed 24 August 2007

Lew AA (2007b) What is Travel 3.0? web20travel.blogspot.com/2007/08/what-is-travel-30.html. 14 August. Accessed 24 August 2007

Lumsdon L (1997) Tourism marketing. International Thomson Business Press, Oxford.

Morgan M (1996) Marketing for Leisure and Tourism. Prentice Hall, Herfordshire

Morrison AM (2002) Hospitality and Travel Marketing, 3rd edn. Delmar Thomson Learning, Albany NY

Reid RD, Bojanic DC (2006) Hospitality Marketing and Management, 4th edn. John Wiley and Sons Inc, Hoboken NJ

Pearce DG, Schott C (2005) Tourism Distribution Channels: The Visitors' Perspective. Journal of Travel Research 44(1):50–63

Rogers EM (2003) Diffusion of Innovations, 5th edn. Free Press, New York

The eMarketer Daily (7 March 2007) www.emarketer.com/Newsletter/emarketer_daily.html. Accessed 8 March 2007

Weeks P, Crouch I (1999) Sites for Sore Eyes: An Analysis of Australian Tourism and Hospitality Web Sites. Information Technology and Tourism 2:153–172. www.cognizant-communication.com/filecabinet/Info_Tech/ittabs.htm. Accessed 8 March 2007

Wilson B (2007) Marketing Tourism Online: Part One The Basics. www.strteetdirectory.com/travel_guide/4923/marketing/marketing_tourism_online-Part-one-the-basics.html. Accessed 8 March 2007

Withey L (1997) Grand Tours and Cook's Tours: A History of Leisure Travel 1750–1915. Autumn Press, London

Chapter 6
Tricks and Clicks: How Low-Cost Carriers Ply Their Trade Through Self-Service Websites

Chris Barry and Ann M. Torres

Abstract Ethics on the Internet has been a widely debated topic in recent years covering issues that range from privacy to security to fraud. Little, however, has been written on more subtle ethical questions, such as the exploitation of web technologies to inhibit or avoid customer service. Increasingly some firms are using websites to create distance between them and their customer base in specific areas of their operations, while simultaneously developing excellence in sales transaction committal via self-service. This chapter takes a magnifying glass with an ethical lens to one sector – the low-cost, web-based, self-service airline industry, specifically in Ireland. It is noted that the teaching of information systems development (ISD) and, for the most part its practice, assumes ethicality. Similarly, marketing courses focus on satisfying customer needs more effectively and efficiently within the confines of an acceptable ethos. This chapter observes that while these business disciplines are central to the success of self-service websites, there is a disconnect between the normative view and the actuality of practice.

6.1 The Success of Low-Cost Carriers (LCCs)

Historically, legacy airlines were noted for offering a premium service, and through the protection of government regulation, cartels of these established airlines flourished and easily drove out competition (de Neufville 2006). The advent of economic deregulation of the US airline industry in 1978 followed by the United Kingdom (1987), Canada (1988), Australia (1990), the European Union (1992) and Japan (2000) meant legacy airlines had to consider carefully their cost of operations. The most important consequences associated with the progressive deregulation of markets are lower fares and higher productivity (Kahn 2002). Although the average yields per passenger mile (i.e. the average of

C. Barry (✉)
Department of Accountancy and Finance, National University of Ireland, Galway,
Ireland
email: chris.barry@nuigalway.ie

D. Oliver et al. (eds.), *Self-Service in the Internet Age,*
DOI 10.1007/978-1-84800-207-4_6, © Springer-Verlag London Limited 2009

the fares that passengers actually paid) were falling prior to deregulation, between 1976 and 1990, average yields declined 30% in real, inflation-adjusted terms, which translated into an estimated savings to travellers of $5–$10 billion per year (Kahn 2002). Deregulation also fostered higher levels of productivity by removing the airlines' restriction on pricing and destinations. Without these restrictions, intense price competition ensued, which spurred airlines to seek improvements in efficiency (Kahn 2002).

The low-cost operation has been a highly successful model in the airline industry over the last decade (Alamdari & Fagan 2005). In Europe, LCCs are growing 20–40% annually (Alamdari & Fagan 2005) and currently hold 33% of the overall market (de Neufville 2006). Although there are variations in strategy among carriers, the basic LCC model is to achieve cost leadership to allow for flexibility in pricing and achieve higher operating margins. Typically, this strategy requires the carrier to examine every function and service they perform and either to eliminate those considered as superfluous frills or to charge for them separately as an addition to the basic fare. The sophisticated information systems (IS) LCCs employ for dynamic pricing and revenue management have contributed substantially to their healthy profit margins. However, in their focused pursuit to eliminate frills, customer service is one function that appears to have declined in importance. Among some LCCs, the justification given for neglecting meaningful customer service (such as managing complaints and concerns) are the low air fares they offer customers (Alamdari & Fagan 2005; de Neufville 2006).

6.2 Ideals for IS Developers and Marketers

Information systems have for many years been developed and implemented using structured or object-oriented methods. Both methods are based on a system's development life cycle that contains a number of stages, checkpoints and tasks. ISD involves systems analysis, systems design, construction and implementation as major stages that are facilitated with a range of techniques from process modelling to data modelling to object-oriented modelling (Constantine & Yourdon 1979; DeMarco 1979; Martin & Finkelstein 1981; OMG 1998). The critical importance of the users and their interaction with the computer system has been recognised and great effort has been expended to ensure the experience is engaging and productive. This area, known as human computer interaction (HCI), has a long held goal to improve the interaction between users and computer systems by making systems more usable and amenable to the users' needs.

The fields of ISD and HCI are taught to students with the aid of popular texts on virtually every IS/IT college programme with a universal supposition that a central objective of systems development is to maximise usability and deliver a satisfying user experience (Shneiderman 1998). An examination of widely used texts on the principles of web design (Nielsen 1999; Krug 2000; Nielsen & Tahir 2001; Sklar 2006) supports the hypothesis that IS professionals adopt a benign and moral posture in designing and developing IS. No advice or guidance was discovered that there exist design strategies or instructions that set out to inhibit customer response or impede interaction. The authors would argue that amongst some practitioners, the supposition that they adopt a considerate and user-centred approach is no longer a central tenet.

The essential premise of marketing is to develop ways to satisfy customer needs and wants more effectively and efficiently than the competition, as a means to achieving organisational success (Kotler & Levy 1969; Hunt 1976; Houston 1986; Trustrum 1989). This marketing management philosophy, also know as the marketing concept, clearly distinguishes between those firms that merely have forms of marketing, such as the presence of a marketing or customer service department, from those firms which are market-focused and customer-driven in implementing their strategies. Firms successfully employing the marketing concept pursue a delicate balance between satisfying customers' needs by creating more value, while simultaneously achieving organisational objectives by accruing profits.

An effective interaction between a buyer and seller may result in a satisfied customer, but to retain customers over the long term means managing customer relationships consistently. In today's technology rich environment, marketers facilitate their individual interactions with customers through customer relationship management (CRM) processes (Payne & Frow 2005; Jayachandran et al. 2005; Srinivasan and Moorman 2005). Other terms for CRM are relationship marketing, real-time marketing and customer intimacy; all of these terms reflect CRM's strategic intent – focusing on satisfying individual customers meaningfully as well as profitably for the firm (Wagner & Zubey 2007; Antón et al. 2007). Through the systematic combination of people, process and technology, CRM techniques facilitate in enabling firms to acquire and retain customers. Finding and acquiring customers cost firms money, but retaining existing customers is substantially more profitable than seeking fresh customers for new transactions. On average, the cost of acquiring new customers is five times more than servicing existing customers (Keaveney 1995). Furthermore, the marginal cost of servicing existing clients declines over time, whereas the cost of attracting new customers typically increases over time.

In CRM, *meaningfully satisfying customers* refers to facilitating the full spectrum of customer interactions, including complaints and concerns. Marketers view customer complaints as opportunities for service recovery that can turn angry, disgruntled customers into loyal, vocal advocates for the firm. Indeed, good service recovery typically translates into higher sales than if all had gone well in the first place (Smith et al. 1999). Poor service recovery is an indication that a firm lacks commitment and diligence, which along with trust and earned reputation, are indispensable to establishing enduring relationships in service and dotcom businesses (Murphy et al. 2007). Ultimately, service failures and poor service recovery translate into lost customers that migrate, often permanently, to competing firms (Keaveney 1995). Because many firms handle customer complaints poorly, those firms that do succeed in offering excellent service recovery may secure an unrivalled source of competitive advantage (Antón et al. 2007).

6.3 *Gummy* Practices and Social Responsibility

LCCs offer value to customers through their low fares, and achieve profits by calibrating costs carefully to achieve attractive margins. However, a number of LCCs use their information systems in a conflicting manner when managing customer interactions. The websites for these LCCs smoothly engage and facilitate customers through the self-service process to commit users to purchase tickets and ancillary products, such as insurance, accommodation and car rental. However, once users move beyond the *committal* point (when they have chosen where and when they wish to travel and received an initial quote) the websites appear *gummy*. It becomes problematic in navigating towards a *real* final price, necessitating the users to side-step a series of options. Moreover, the websites seem awkward, sluggish and opaque in facilitating customer complaints and concerns, and make it challenging for the users to contact the airlines. These difficulties and omissions are contrary to the ethos of designing a *good system* to facilitate the full spectrum of customer service.

Increasingly, social responsibility is viewed not just as a good idea, but rather as good business practice, which increases efficiency and ultimately translates into positive financial performance. A recent study conducted by the investment bank Goldman Sachs (Rominger 2007) found socially responsible firms outperformed a global stock index by 25%, indicating a positive correlation between social responsibility and earnings. Consequently, socially responsible investing (SRI), also known as environmental, social and governance (ESG), is gaining in momentum (Cohen 2006). Investors are seeking firms, which express core values beyond financial objectives, such as environmental responsibility, fair employment practices, and robust corporate governance that incorporate codes of conduct that espouse principles of transparency, integrity and ethical behaviour.

A key question is to what extent could gummy practices be considered unethical and thus indicative of a firm's diminished social responsibility? In employing gummy practices in their websites, it could reasonably be suggested that LCCs are displaying a conflict in values, where the pursuit of strong institutional performance conflicts with addressing meaningful customer complaints and concerns in a transparent and responsive manner. At its most basic level, ethics are meant to "support justice, rights, and duties. [One wants] others to keep their promises and agreements, to obey the law and to fulfill their duties" (Tavani 2007, p. 64). Thus, if an airline carrier fails to provide a reliable and transparent service by knowingly designing gummy features into their websites, in the absence of contravening considerations, it is acting unethically.

Certain gummy features may not be accidental in design, but neither are they grossly offensive or subject to serious regulatory sanctions, yet. Ireland's

National Consumer Agency (NCA) requires firms trading online to comply with the EC Distance Communication Regulations, 2001 and the European Communities E-Commerce Regulations, 2000. The NCA states "web traders are required under both sets of regulations to provide certain information to the consumer prior to an order being placed. The on-site requirements include information on the geographical address of the retailer, how the consumer may correct errors while making an order, the tax inclusive price of the product, arrangements for payment and delivery, the right to cancel the order, etc." (ODCA 2006, p. 13). However, many LCCs operating out of Ireland do not comply substantially with these requirements, in particular the requirement for displaying a tax inclusive price. For example, while Aer Lingus displays air fares inclusive of taxes and charges on the website homepage for Germany, Netherlands, Portugal, Spain and Switzerland, for the other 19 countries in which Aer Lingus operates (including Ireland), the air fares displayed on the homepage do not include taxes and charges.

Other jurisdictions are beginning to regulate as well. The UK's Office of Fair Trading (OFT) threatened to take legal action against airlines in an attempt to tackle misleading pricing practices. In February 2007, the OFT gave airline "carriers and travel agencies three months to include all fixed non-optional costs, [such as fuel charges and passenger taxes] in their basic advertised prices" throughout all media, including websites (BBC News 2007). In response to the OFT, Easyjet promised by the end of the summer that all prices on its website would include taxes and charges, while Ryanair claims to have changed the prices on the homepage for its UK website and would include all extra costs on the rest of the site by the end of the year (BBC News 2007).

6.4 Research Approach: Heuristic Evaluation

The purpose of this study is to assess the proposition that certain features of LCCs websites are gummy by assessing their usability. In this case, the key interaction issues in question are navigation, achieving functionality, consistency, ease of effort and being able to communicate with web-based operators who primarily have an online rather than a high-street presence. A study was conducted to evaluate the usability and functional design of four LCC websites operating out of the Republic of Ireland: Aer Arann, Aer Lingus, bmibaby and Ryanair. The methodology was based on heuristic evaluation, which is well established within the HCI field. It is a usability inspection technique that systematically assesses a user interface design for usability (Nielsen 1994). Heuristic evaluation is guided by recognised usability principles (i.e. heuristics) that examine if interface elements conform in practice to those principles. They were empirically compiled from an analysis of a large number of usability issues and were customised to consider web-specific problems (Sharp et al. 2007) for the low-cost airline industry – based partly on Nielsen's set and the authors'

Table 6. 1 Analysis of functionality

Functionality: Finding and booking flights.

Sub-function 1: You have decided on a brief holiday return trip in August to anywhere in Europe. You have some flexibility on dates (get as far as the final screen at credit card entry.)

Sub-function 2: You want to identify a cheap flight later this year since you are on a very tight budget. You are very flexible on dates and destination. You just want details to discuss it with your friend or partner.

Functionality: Contacting the airline.

Sub-function 1: Find and establish the nature of contacting the airline (For example: How can the LCC be contacted? What is the nature of customer feedback details?)

Sub-function 2: You had an unpleasant experience with an airline and wish to report it to them (For example: on-board toilet hygiene on a recent flight was very poor or you received a very unsatisfactory response from cabin staff.)

knowledge of relevant issues, as well as ethical problems emerging from the sector (Alter 2003; Clark 2006; ECC Network 2006). The study involved using a group of six usability experts to evaluate the interfaces and judge their compliance with usability principles. The work goes beyond the assessment of the *goodness* or otherwise of usability and makes judgements on the concordance of website features with broader expectations of IS design and marketing principles. The heuristics and the guidelines for evaluating them are shown in Table 6.2. To gauge the effectiveness of each of the LCC websites, the heuristics were evaluated against typical functionality users would expect to use as part of an online, self-service website (see Table 6.1). They constitute representative pre-sale, sale and post-sale functionality.

6.5 Analysis of the Heuristic Evaluations

The analysis is presented on the basis of each aspect of functionality that was evaluated by the experts. Evaluations were comprehensive and extensive, and the presentation below represents a distillation in general and the highlighting of features that are of particular interest.

6.5.1 Booking Flights

6.5.1.1 Destinations

One of the main functions a LCC website needs to facilitate is providing a quote for a specified flight and leading the user through to sales completion. Where

Table 6. 2 Evaluation Heuristics

Heuristic	Description
Aesthetic and minimalist design	The website should not contain unnecessary or rarely needed clutter.
Navigation design	The means by which users navigate their way around the information structure should be clear.
Internal consistency	Users should not have to ponder whether different terms or actions have the same meaning.
	The language should be that of the user where possible and information should appear in a natural and logical order.
Depth of navigation menu	The website should be designed so that it is shallow rather than deep.
Completion of tasks	The system should be designed so that users are able to efficiently and effectively complete a task to their expectations.
	Are there features that accelerate functionality for expert users while remaining flexible enough for novice users?
Clarity of feature functionality	A feature should fulfil the function implied by the dialog.
	Dialog should be simple with no irrelevant or unnecessary information.
Minimizing the user's memory load	The interface should not require users to remember information between one part of the system and the next.
Help users recognize, diagnose and recover from errors or unintended actions	Careful design that prevents a problem from ever happening is better than good error or warning messages.

the user begins the process of identifying the destinations the carrier serves, all of the LCCs afford advanced design features such as *hub and spoke* route maps that superbly assist users in visualising what would otherwise be complex flat information. What is also interesting is that each airline made it easy to find the map and used consistent language; the button was called either *Where We Fly* or *Destinations*. Figure 6.1 illustrates the similarity of this feature in each LCC's website. It demonstrates how an industry can gravitate towards conformity when a product feature is deemed to be of high quality and preferred by customers.

6.5.1.2 Initial Pricing of Flights

Pricing is achieved by using the booking systems of all airlines, rather than a separate quote facility. For this purpose, the LCC websites afford a high level of usability, assisting the user to complete the activity effectively. Initial price

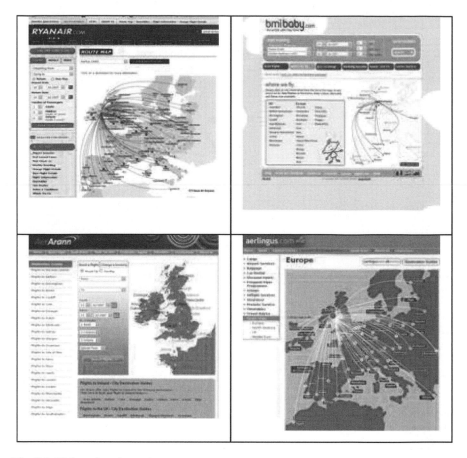

Fig. 6.1 Hub and spoke route maps

completion is achieved quickly and with a minimum effort. There are many design features that accelerate the process, from giving users available flights around the preferred date to retaining user details during an interaction. All airlines use extraordinarily similar features and functionality for pricing flights. For example, list boxes for *from* and *to* airports, date selection using list boxes and calendars, choosing the number of passengers, and *Return/One Way* choice are all presented in a similar manner. The depth of navigation is low for all LCCs, reducing the memory load and achieving rapid completion of tasks. The list boxes do not, however, operate in identical ways. Some features that are of the highest standard warrant special mention:

- The visibility of systems status for Aer Lingus is excellent, achieved by using breadcrumb-like indicators.
- Aer Lingus allows a user with flexible dates to play with all available flights for a 2-week period at a glance around the preferred date. The flights, all

priced, can be seen for outbound and inbound flight segments on consecutive screens.

- Regarding flexible dates of travel, bmibaby goes one step further by showing the information on just one screen and providing clearly visible tabs to display the option of a 3- or 7-day view around the preferred date, whilst still highlighting that date.
- Internal consistency for this functionality was excellent for Aer Lingus, bmibaby and Ryanair.

A number of features on Aer Arann's website were identified by experts as problematic, but were not a major hindrance to the essential task of completing a quote. Since the airline is small compared to others, many flights are not daily. Thus, where a user selects a flight on days for which there is none, a variety of explanations are proffered (see Fig. 6.2). They have chosen to supply *Prev Day* and *Next Day* buttons for users to manually find the closest available flights instead of finding them on their behalf. Ryanair uses a similar design feature but because of flight frequency.

Another problematic feature on Aer Arann's website is that some important links, such as *Terms & Conditions*, *Baggage Policy*, *Id Policy* and *Passenger Liability* are at the bottom of the page, almost out of sight. Being unable to get back to the homepage was another common problem experienced by experts and was considered a hindrance to usability on their website.

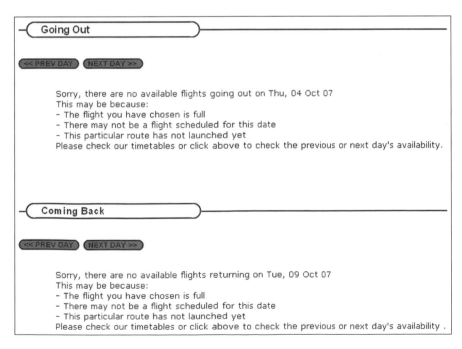

Fig. 6.2 Aer Arann's screen on unavailable flights

While the problems identified above did not impinge on users' quickly getting an initial price quote, far more serious problems emerged when experts sought to conclude transactions. These problems are discussed in the following sections.

6.5.1.3 Getting to a Final Price: Handling Fees, Taxes and Charges

Apart from entering personal information required to complete a transaction, the main difference between pricing a flight and booking a flight is navigating the imposition of additional charges and negotiating a series of opt-in and opt-out services. All LCCs play with the currency of language in respect of what constitutes a quoted price and other charges. Many of these charges are unavoidable and revealed progressively as the user completes the transaction. Hence, there is significant uncertainty as to what constitutes a *final price* due to baggage fees, taxes and a plethora of *services* for which extra charges are levied. All airlines quote a price that suggests it is either *Final* or *Total* whereas, in fact, it is neither. Consequently, these design features with respect to reaching a final price adversely affect usability and trust. Some airlines are more transparent than others; bmibaby is the only airline that claims to include taxes and charges, but they appear high and are not broken down and explained to the user during the booking process. Nonetheless, despite repeating the claim on six consecutive screens that *all prices now include taxes, fees and charges*, at the final screen bmibaby applies a charge of •5 for credit card payment (see Fig. 6.3(a) and (b)).

The language that is used to describe charges is quite inventive. LCCs describe unavoidable charges that most other sectors would consider a cost of doing business as, for example, taxes, charges, levies, fees, handling fees, airport charges and even *September 11th security fee for each enplanement at a U.S. airport*. The expressions used by particular LCCs to describe the final price of a flight (when it is not) are listed below:

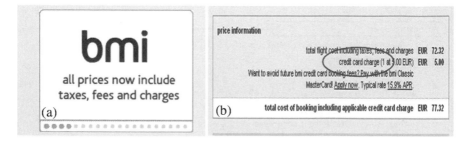

Fig. 6.3 (**a**) and (**b**) bmibaby's taxes and charges

- Aer Arann chooses to display flights quoting a *regular fare*, but upon flight selection, hefty *taxes and fees* are added that then make up the *total cost of flight*.
- Aer Lingus, under *Booking Help*, explains what *price* means by stating: "Price Total includes all relevant taxes and charges." However, on the page after a flight is selected a *TOTAL* price is given that includes a specified *handling fee* for credit card processing. In this respect, it is reasonably visible.
- bmibaby, once a selection of flights appears for chosen dates, a message states (as noted above) the calculated price to be *total price now including taxes, fees and charges*, but neglects to mention handling charges, which are added later.
- Ryanair displays available flight for each segment priced as *reg fare*, which are then appended with *taxes, fees & charges* to arrive at the *total cost of flight*.

Aer Lingus and Aer Arann do not provide clear information on the nature of taxes and charges during the reservation process. As an illustration, Fig. 6.4 reveals how a •2.00 Aer Lingus return flight becomes •75.44 with the addition of

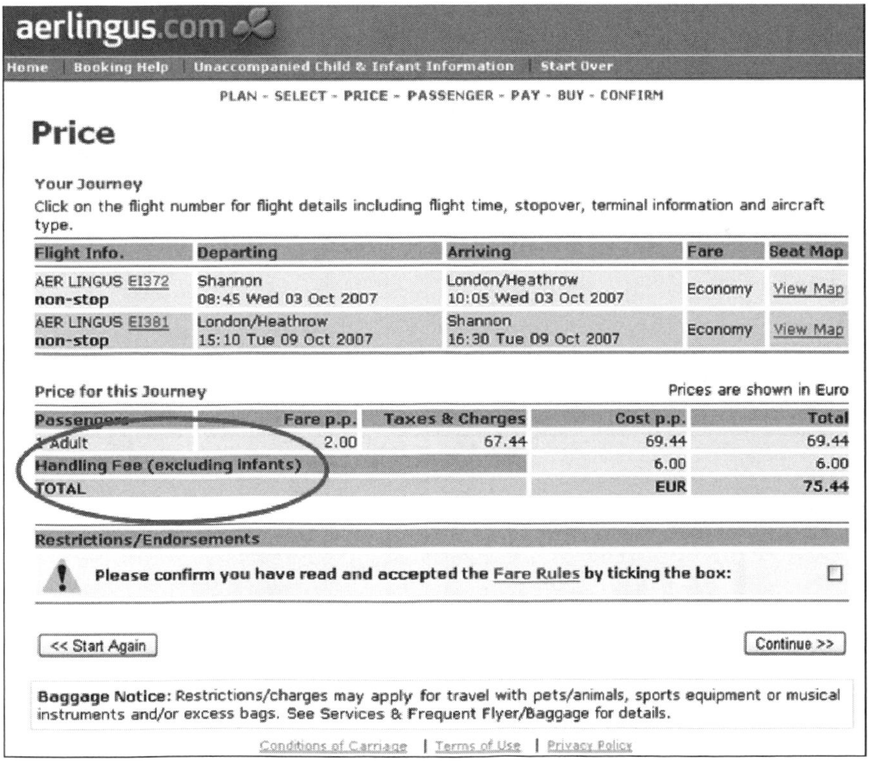

Fig. 6.4 Aer Lingus's taxes and charges

taxes and charges. On top of the *taxes and charges*, there is a *handling fee* with the useful addendum that it is applied *excluding infants*. One might be forgiven for thinking that this might be a seat charge if an infant is carried on one's lap, but how could Aer Lingus be charging •6.00 for the seat? Does it refer to a credit or debit card charge? The user is not informed and *booking help* sheds no light on the construction of these charges. But it does not end here: choosing to bring a piece of luggage costs •5.00 per segment. Users are also automatically charged •12.00 for travel insurance. If this is declined by opting-out, then the apparently nearly free flights costing •2.00 becomes •85.44. While the final cost is still reasonable in this case, the user is left utterly misled about the real cost of the flight.

To their credit, Ryanair has a clear message on the screen that displays the available flights for the chosen journey, informing users that "... unless you are taking advantage of one of our advertised flight offers, which are free of taxes and charges, the below flight costs do not include taxes and charges." No other airline is as explicit. bmibaby offers a *tiny tip* delivered by an angelic figure that first says "fly cheaper" followed by a wholly opposite message: "the total price per person includes taxes and charges and is shown at the bottom of the page." Ryanair also provides some degree of explanation of its charges. However, it is accessed via a *details* link that reveals a pop-up alert box displaying a partial explanation of charges as a graphics image rather than text, illustrated in Fig. 6.5(a) and (b). This last point is quite troubling; the design feature means a customer cannot print or even highlight and copy the charges. In effect, if one wishes to closely examine such charges one either reads them while the box is open or writes them down on paper. Can this feature be anything other than deliberate?

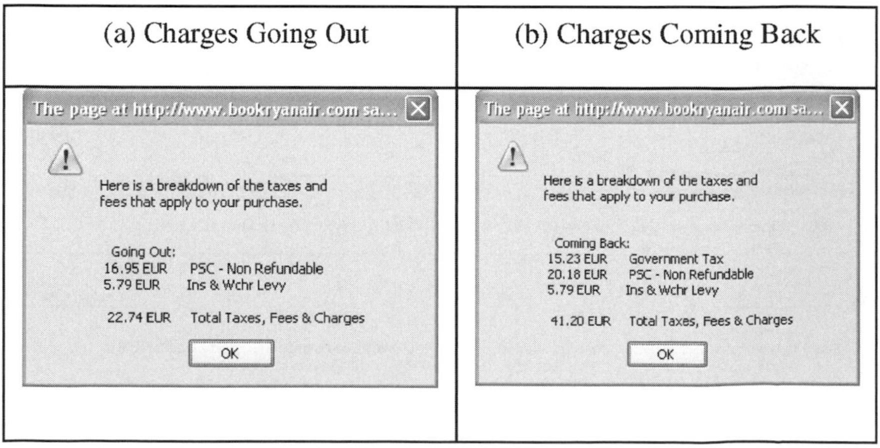

Fig. 6.5 (**a**) and (**b**) Ryanair's taxes and charges

It is also worth noting the charges going out and coming back are, in this case, significantly different for each segment and little effort is made to explain the differential. To reveal, as far as is possible, what these charges are composed of, it is necessary to burrow deep into Ryanair's website. The strangest charge is the *passenger service charge/airport tax* denoted *PSC* in Fig. 6.5(a) and (b), which is "a charge made by the airport authority to an airline for the use of the terminal, runway, emergency services, security facilities etc." One would speculate on the motives for publishing prices for flights that do not include the use of an airport terminal and other essential services for flight operations.

Similar to Ryanair, Aer Arann uses pop-up alert boxes to display different fare types denoted as *E, K, O, V, W* and so on. Figure. 6.6(a) and (b) demonstrate the incomprehensible nature of these fare types. The crammed information cannot be printed, copied or stored, and disappears when a user wants to check a different fare type. Spotting the differences between the various fares is not for the poor sighted, since they are extremely difficult to distinguish from each other. Indeed, in one interaction it was discovered the conditions for *E, S, T, V* and *W* fares were exactly the same. Such a scenario makes it hard to square the phenomenon with one particular condition found to be common to all fares: "changes allowed in the same fare class". Once a fare is selected the fare type conditions appear more clearly on the next screen, but a user would not know this in advance. Aer Arann's logic for designing such a wholly confusing mechanism for communicating the fare conditions to users is difficult to understand. The evaluation found no explanation on the website of what differentiates these fare types. Such lack of clarity in design camouflages the real nature of the flight for users.

6.5.1.4 Card Charges Policies

Amongst all the airlines evaluated, there is substantial gumminess in respect of charging for card processing. If LCCs are treated similarly by card processors, it

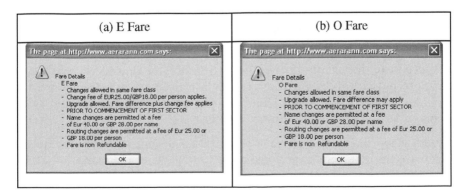

Fig. 6.6 (a) and **(b)** Aer Arann's fare types

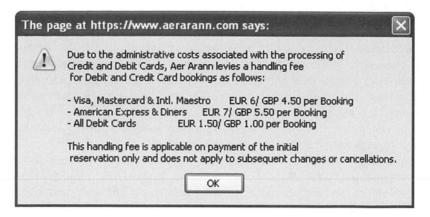

Fig. 6.7 Aer Arann's transaction charges

might be expected that the charges incurred would be passed on in a uniform manner. However, this study shows considerable variation in the way card charges are handled. For example, Aer Arann charges per booking (see Fig. 6.7), Aer Lingus charges per passenger, while bmibaby charges a percentage of the total payable and Ryanair charges for each passenger for each flight segment. Although difficult to find, Ryanair's explanation of card charges is located on the site map under *frequently asked questions* where a link to *why is there a handling charge when I reserve my flights?* are explained in the following way. Ryanair claim they incur "substantial administration costs ... when processing credit and debit cards or ELV [i.e. *Elektronisches Lastschriftverfahren* or electronic debit procedure] direct debits" and must therefore apply a handling fee for each passenger per flight segment. Thus, it would appear internal administration costs have been disaggregated from the price and cited separately.

6.5.1.5 Frills or No Frills: Opt-in and Opt-out Fee-Based Services

Another gummy feature is the series of fee-based services, which customers must negotiate throughout the websites. Typically, the onus is placed on customers to opt-out of fee-based services. Most airlines have a preference for using this feature, which is well-known among commercial websites and by no means exclusive to the LCC industry. To illustrate:

- Aer Lingus, bmibaby and Ryanair make users opt-out of travel insurance.
- Aer Lingus and Aer Arann force users to opt-out of the receipt of "occasional – emails about our services..." and to "receive news, new route announcements and special offers...".
- Ryanair requires passengers without luggage to opt-out of priority boarding.

This last example violated the most heuristics during the analysis: the process of trying to choose the number of bags with Ryanair and whether the user wished them checked-in online or not. When the user enters passenger details, the number of bags is chosen from the drop down box, which quite clearly advises that should a user select *0* bags, they are automatically choosing *Online Check-in/Priority Boarding* (see the circle in Fig. 6.8a). Thus, it would appear a charge is unavoidable even if one is travelling with only hand luggage. This feature is not just misleading or vague; it is an intentional design feature to propel users into paid-for, online check-in. Once a bag-less user has pondered their options, they will find there is no way to progress unless *0 Bags – Online Check-in/Priority Boarding* is selected. What happens next is quite remarkable; text instantaneously appears beneath the drop down box that allows the user to *remove* the choice the system has led them to select (see the smaller circle in Fig. 6.8b and the text below).

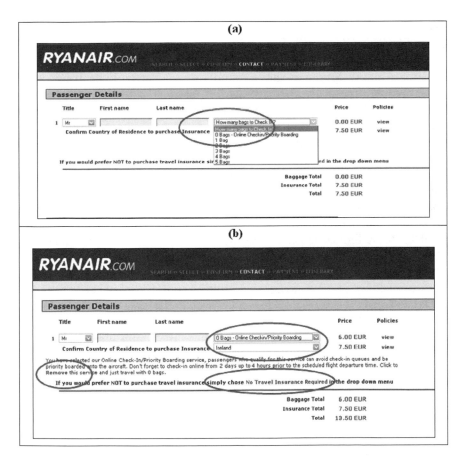

Fig. 6.8 (a) and (b) Ryanair's gummy baggage selection process

You have selected our Online Check-In/Priority Boarding service, passengers who qualify for this service can avoid check-in queues and be priority boarded onto the aircraft. Don't forget to check-in online from 2 days up to 4 hours prior to the scheduled flight departure time. Click to Remove this service and just travel with 0 bags.

However, the user would need to be quick-sighted to catch the manoeuvre since it happens so swiftly and the *remove* option (in blue) is embedded deep within the text (in blue) so the unwary customer could easily miss the presentation of an opt-out choice. The sequences of messages that relate to the purchase of insurance are less explicit than they could be. The same screen (see Fig. 6.8b) applies a •7.50 insurance charge and, beneath a drop down box that defaults to *Ireland*, asks users to "Confirm Country of Residence to purchase Insurance". It would appear from this message that insurance is unavoidable. However, further down the screen it states "If you would prefer NOT to purchase travel insurance simply chose No Travel Insurance Required in the drop down menu".

6.5.2 *Finding Cheap Flights*

In the past, many consumers have found some advertised cheap fare to be *elusive* (Whitehouse 2001). This evaluation discovered that some advertised *cheap* flights can be found. However, the process may involve considerable time as well as a great deal of trial and error. All LCCs have headline offers, some inclusive of charges and others with the charges added on, although it is unclear if card charges are included.

Aer Lingus did not appear to have any cheap flights departing Ireland. There were plenty of advertised offers on the homepage, but they were from the US cities. To secure a last minute offer of US $199 from New York to Shannon, the applicable travel period (10/9/07–30/9/07) was clearly displayed, but a strap line stated "seats are limited and fares may not be available on all flights and dates." When choosing a break of 1 week within those date limits, only nine departing dates and eight return dates were priced at US $199. Taxes and charges brought this fare to US $482.65. The process was quite easy and Aer Lingus did make the advertised flights accessible to users. They even had a page that tells users how to secure the flight (see Fig. 6.9).

Aer Arann display on its homepage that there are "Daily Specials: Dublin to Cork from •25 inc tax", but when users click on the link it brings them to the usual price selection screen except that Dublin and Cork are pre-entered. However, there is absolutely no indication of how the advertised cheap flight can be bought. No expert evaluator was able to determine a mechanism to qualify for this fare. The homepage also provides a list of destinations, so it looks like flights from Galway to Edinburgh are •50, but once again, no way can be found to secure this price. Furthermore, the word *from* is quite a distance away at the top of the panel and it would be easy to overlook.

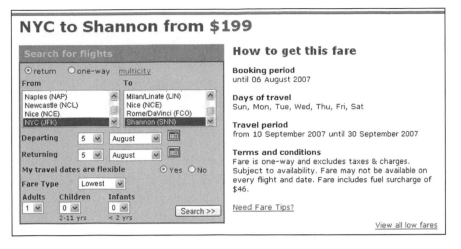

Fig. 6.9 Aer Lingus's cheap flights

Fig. 6.10 Ryanair's cheap flights

Ryanair's homepage appears full of cheap flights (see Fig. 6.10). Flying "...
cheaper to the UK" does make the terms of booking clear to the user. However,
some experts found actually pinning down one of these offers impossible. Since
the departing airport from Ireland was not specified, not only did it require trial
and error with dates, but also with airports. Nonetheless, one evaluator did find
a return flight inclusive of taxes and charges for •20.

With bmibaby, users are asked to *click here to view our cheap flights*. Upon
doing so a page appears advertising all flights have 40% off from some UK
airports only. However, on the homepage it clearly states there is a sale of up to
40% off all flights with some date restrictions (see Fig. 6.11). Choosing a return
flight from Birmingham to Cork did show a free flight priced at £0.00 plus taxes
and charges of £32.40, and presumably card charges. Reversing the flight from
Cork to Birmingham returned one segment free and the other priced at •12.74,
while taxes and charges came to a sizeable •48.61, totalling •61.35. An operational incongruity detected here is that sometimes, for example with the Dublin
to Heathrow flight, one is transferred onto British Midland's main website

Fig. 6.11 bmibaby's cheap
flights

www.flybmi.com with no way back to bmibaby, a serious violation of the
heuristic that promotes the internal locus of control for users.

6.5.3 Contacting the Airline

6.5.3.1 Making an Enquiry or Giving Feedback

Contacting the airline directly can be for a variety of reasons, such as general
enquiries, resolving post-sales issues, complimenting the airline, or complaining. For the most part, engaging with this functionality was highly problematic.
For three of the LCCs (Aer Arann, Aer Lingus and bmibaby), there is a contact
link at the homepage, usually requiring scrolling down depending on the size of
your screen. Aer Lingus have two links – one through *About Us* at the top of the
homepage's navigation bar, and *Contact Aer Lingus* in a lower sidebar navigation panel.

Ryanair proved to be the most challenging in locating contact information
since there is no *Contact Us* or equivalent link on the homepage. The experts
reported great difficulty in their attempts to find relevant contact information –
as one observed "the user is forced to navigate blindly". Interestingly, the
evaluators each navigated unique paths to try to find Ryanair's contact details.
The most direct way is through the site map, where *Contact Us* is listed under
About Us. However, from the homepage where users would ordinarily begin the
expedition to find such information, if a customer clicks on the *About Us* link on
the horizontal navigation bar at the top of the page (see Fig. 6.12(a) and (b)), the
same navigation bar changes to include a *Contact Us* link. After some consideration, the experts believe this feature is an attempt to build a contextualised
sub-menu of links relevant to the four main left-handed links, a wholly confusing technique since the same colour text and background is used. The page itself
displays the history of Ryanair and its growth in passenger numbers.

What happens next is exceptional. When the *Contact Us* link is clicked it
displays a series of *Reservation Contact Numbers* that list telephone numbers for
different countries. However, the left-hand panel changes to include another,

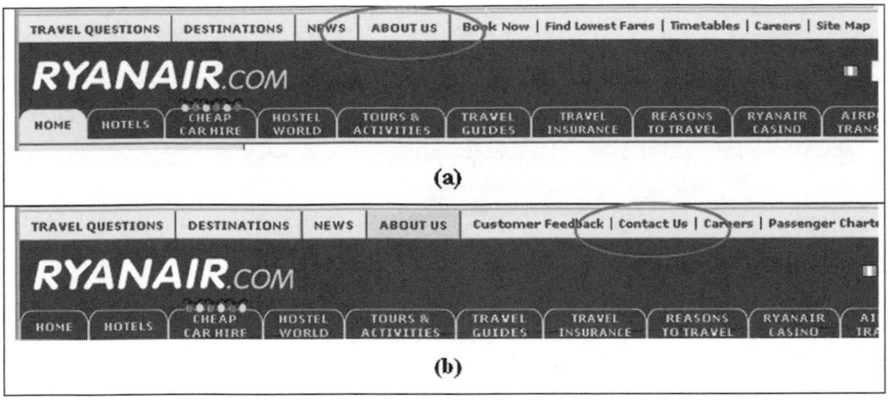

Fig. 6.12 (**a**) and (**b**) Ryanair's menu structure for contact information

different, *Contact Us* link (see Fig. 6.13). The manner in which the modified panel changes is extremely difficult to spot as one is naturally drawn to the central panel content.

Selecting the *Contact Us* in the left-hand panel in Fig. 6.13 displays a series of questions and links, shown in Fig. 6.14. Some of these links in the central panel (titled *Contact Us*), are related to communicating with the airline on certain matters. Other links are meaningless in respect of contacting the airline, such as "Can you help me book a hotel, organise car hire, arrange car parking, get travel insurance etc?" or "I am interested in your financial reports, company

Fig. 6.13 Contacting Ryanair

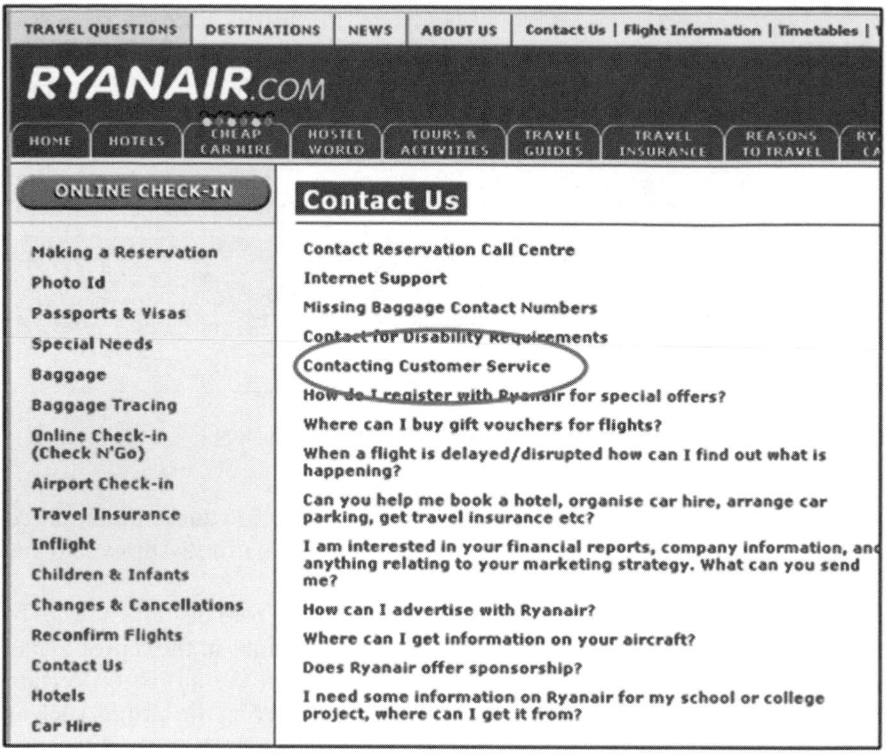

Fig. 6.14 Ryanair's contact information link

information, and anything relating to your marketing strategy. What can you send me?" One link titled *Contacting Customer Service,* nestled in-between *Contact for Disability Requirements* and *How do I register with Ryanair for special offers?,* actually provides *real* contact information. Thus, two links on the same page with the same name, lead to completely different pages with different information.

Only two of the six experts actually found Ryanair's contact information within an acceptable timeframe of a few minutes. There is no order or apparent logic to this design and it makes no sense if Ryanair wishes users to find contact details; it is either exceptionally poor design or deliberately gummy. The heuristic that websites should be designed so they are shallow rather than deep (Larson & Czerwinski 1998; Shneiderman & Plaisant 2004) is clearly violated in this instance.

6.5.3.2 Nature of Contact Information

It is expected (ODCA 2006) that online businesses provide comprehensive contact information on a variety of pre-sales, sales and post-sales topics like

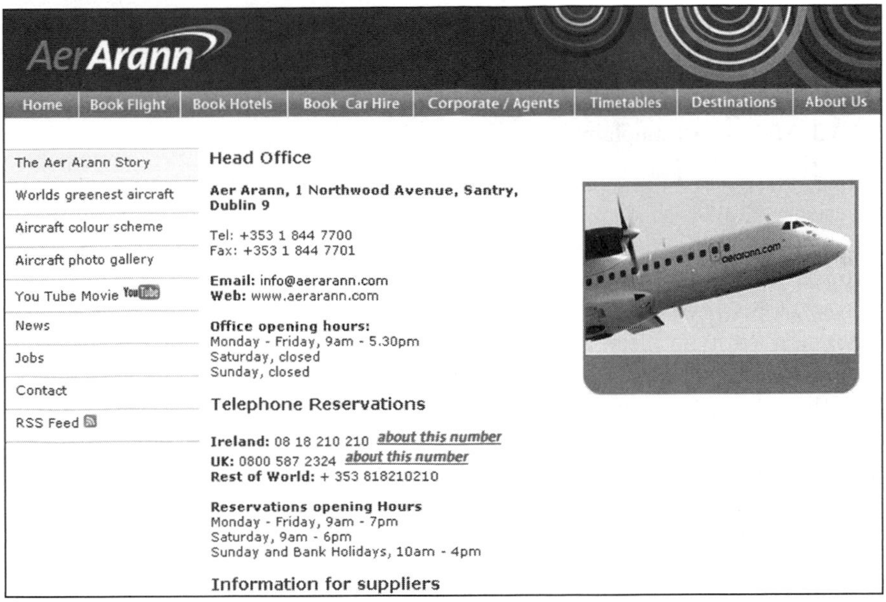

Fig. 6.15 Aer Arann's contact details

reservations, technical support and customer relations. The LCCs presented this sort of information in distinctly different ways.

For Irish reservation enquiries, Aer Arann, Aer Lingus and bmibaby provide a low cost number, while Ryanair refer users to premium-rated numbers charging •1.75 per minute. Depending on the country, the kind of contact details Aer Lingus offers can vary substantially – some countries offer an array of contact details by providing an address, telephone number, fax number and email address; while other countries may offer only one or two forms of contact details. Technical support is not visible for Aer Arann or Aer Lingus, while bmibaby offers FAQs and Ryanair refers users to the same premium-rated numbers.

Among the four airlines reviewed, Aer Arann commendably provide the most complete contact information (see Fig. 6.15). Not only were there full contact details for the head office in Dublin airport, but also contact information for Aer Arann's reservations desks across Europe, where in each instance, an address, phone number, fax number and email address were included. Moreover, Aer Arann uniquely facilitated post-flight assistance by offering email addresses for feedback, customer relations and refund queries.

For baggage handling, Aer Lingus offers low-cost phone support and, oddly on a different page, an email address. In the case of bmibaby, there are phone numbers and postal addresses for damaged and lost bags. Despite Aer Arann's otherwise excellent contacts page, no reference was found to a specific contact point for baggage enquiries. Ryanair supplies telephone numbers for missing baggage enquiries at local rates. On a different page altogether, Ryanair provides a postal address and a fax number to which claims are made.

6.5.3.3 Making a Complaint

Experts were asked to examine how the LCCs websites dealt with an unpleasant experience they wished to report. Experts were largely unanimous that Aer Arann provided the best mechanism if they wished to make a specific complaint through the contacts page. However, they confusingly have *Feedback* and *Customer Relations* with email addresses for each and a phone number for the latter, but with no clear explanation as to what distinguishes them. When customers want to complain about (or compliment) an Aer Lingus flight (i.e. post-flight assistance), they are asked to write to the nearest Aer Lingus office and to include a copy of their ticket or boarding card (see Fig. 6.16). No telephone numbers or email addresses are provided for post-flight assistance, which would appear to be an unhelpful manner in which to process a complaint, or indeed a compliment.

Similar to Aer Lingus, bmibaby follows the same policy when it comes to pre-flight assistance, which is sales-related inquiries and post-flight assistance, which relates to complaints. However, even though bmibaby has an Irish presence in several airports, they only advise customers using the UK airports to contact them.

The Ryanair website provides a list of FAQ links. Thus, for pre-flight assistance, customers may find the relevant information through the *Reservation*

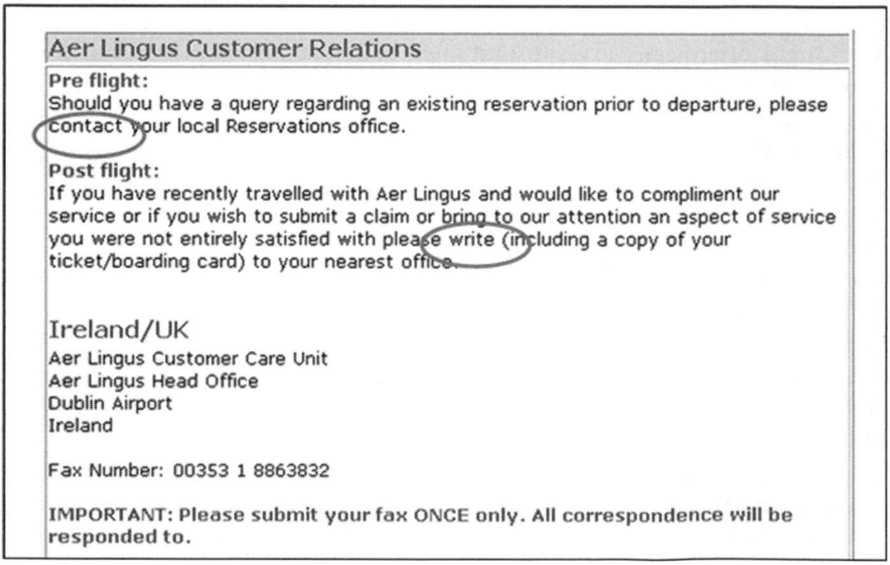

Fig. 6.16 Aer Lingus' customer relation contact details

Contact Numbers and the *Internet Support* links, which list premium telephone numbers by country. For *Contacting Customer Service*, the link directs users to a series of postal addresses according to the nature of the issue. Complaints are to be written in English and provide full flight details (i.e. dates and routes) and passenger names. A key word search on the website for customer service returns another link for *How can I contact Ryanair* where a fax number is given for post-flight assistance. Again, faxed letters should be written in English and full flight and passenger details provided. According to *Ryanair's Passenger Service and Lowest Fares Charter*, the airline will respond to written complaints (to the email address provided at the time of reservation) within 7 days. It is baffling that Ryanair can respond to complaints by email, but it cannot receive complaints by email. Also, their claim on its website to have the fewest complaints in the industry rings somewhat hollow when the process of complaining is extremely difficult.

Although it is common sense that making websites gummy when customers have complaints or concerns will increase the level of customer dissatisfaction, some LCCs appear prepared to take such risks.

6.6 Discussion

For LCCs, it appears many non-sales related activities are simply removed or distanced from the operations of the organisation. This deconstructed, *no-frills* business model is reflected in the design of the supporting IS. That the IS should reflect the business model is precisely how a *good* IS should be designed. LCC self-service websites are thus primarily aimed at capturing revenues and appear highly effective, as they focus on sales committal and minimising effort on the part of the customer. However, there remains a gap between the functionality one would expect to find in sophisticated, web-based IS and what they actually offer. Similarly, some of the features are unorthodox in their design. The differential cannot be explained by Ogburn's cultural lag thesis, which proposes material culture generally advances more rapidly than non-material culture. Thus, physical and operational systems first appear while ethics, philosophy and belief systems surface much later (Marshall 1999). Certain questions arise from this analysis.

How is one to interpret these gummy design strategies? They are not accidental; the clear focus on assisting users in committing to sales contrasts radically with strangely ineffective, poorly accessible or completely missing functionality in other operational areas. It is evident that some firms are quite deliberately using web technologies to design out features one might expect in *traditional* information systems and to obfuscate or complicate others. To cite the most obvious examples: why, for the most part, do LCCs not provide email or web forms to facilitate customer communications; do they really expect customers to have a fax; why is it so difficult to quickly find contact details; and why are the structures of additional charges so unclear or fragmented?

What is it about self-service websites that lend themselves to this type of customer service? Such websites have certain unique characteristics that are different to bricks and mortar operations. The channel is indirect and features can be designed in (or out) in a way that would not be tolerated with face-to-face or telephone-based models. It is possible to de-market the business model far more effectively when direct contact is avoided. Self-service websites also devolve tasks to customers – delegating responsibility for accurate data entry and the initiation and cost of remedial procedures when things go wrong. A key consideration here is how endemic the problem is? Is it common to all forms of self-service websites or primarily prevalent among the websites of LCCs?

Are customers inured to the gumminess of LCCs? Can it be that LCCs have succeeded in convincing customers that they must expect some level of pain and suffering in exchange for cheap flights? Do users believe that somewhere along the road to their reservation destination they are going to get *mugged*? If desensitised users are expectant of poor customer service, devaluation of the currency of language, little transparency, hidden costs, considerable effort and intense wariness, then LCCs have achieved a remarkable relationship with their customers – all of it enabled without the exchange of conversation.

Is the web any less ethical than business practices elsewhere? Probably not, the virtual world reflects the real one. To help, corporate codes of ethics have been widely adopted in ways that range from moderating business practices to guaranteeing the principles of fair trade in the supply chain. However, new web technologies allow firms to develop obstacles and barriers that a bricks and mortar model would not facilitate.

Are ethics of IS and marketing professionals of any relevance? In a highly competitive industry that thrives on a low-cost strategy, simplicity and limited functionality are natural consequences for the design of IS. However, some IS/IT practitioners must be acutely aware that they are guilty of, at the very least, sins of omission in IS design practice. Furthermore it is, without evidence to the contrary, reasonable to assume there is a congruence of values between managers, marketers and IS practitioners. Specifications must have been designed that incorporated management policies that would undoubtedly violate the first principle of the Software Engineering Code of Ethics and Professional Practice that "software engineers shall act consistently with the public interest" (Quinn 2006). While there are well-established, if dissimilar, professional codes of ethics in the IS/IT field (Oz 1993), the notion of emancipatory ideals (Hirschheim & Klein 1994), once feted in the IS literature, finding a role in the design of low-cost airline websites appears to have found little resonance in this area of practice.

LCCs employing gummy features in their websites are exhibiting the classic strategic flaw of having the trappings of marketing without offering substantive marketing practices (Ames 1970; Trustrum 1989; Peattie 1999). That is, LCCs offer superficial customer service on their websites, by discouraging customers to lodge complaints and concerns, resulting in service failures, poor service recovery, and ultimately, the potential loss of future revenue from these disappointed customers. In doing so, LCCs are pursing a transactional rather than a relational model of marketing behaviour. They are seeking a high volume of discrete, profitable transactions rather than a high volume of profitable customer relationships enduring over time. The loss of existing customers does not appear to be a concern for many LCCs; they would appear to believe their low fares compensate for poor service or justify the lack of service recovery efforts. Ultimately, these LCCs may be increasing their operating costs in the search for new customers. Moreover, they appear to manage their business as if there were an infinite supply of new customers. In time, perhaps the more successful LCCs will be those who offer customers competitive pricing policies as well as high levels of service recovery.

6.7 Conclusions

There are a number of implications of this study. While many business ethics issues are not manifestly new in web-based IS, it is "becoming apparent that the ethical dimensions of IS-related business decisions cannot be safely ignored" (Smith & Hasnas 1999, p. 111). It is necessary to renew the articulation of ethics in view of the capacity of new technologies to affect dubious practice. Ethical guidelines and frameworks in IS design and marketing; corporate and professional codes of ethics; and ethics in the IS and marketing curricula, also need to be re-visited.

There is assumed ethicality in how IS are designed and how marketing practice is conducted; such assumptions need to be challenged. Writers have advised practitioners and teachers to be worried if there is a *complete absence* of contact information (Kassler 2002). This concern is largely focussed on the potential for deceit and fraud. It is not normally directed at *reputable* firms who obscure contact details to reduce interaction and dialogue. This oversight demands some revision in how information systems and marketing are taught to students of IT and business programmes. But how should teachers approach this issue – as an advocate of entrepreneurs or of consumers? Do teachers make students critically aware of gummy practices or should they demonstrate how they can be achieved to match the demands of business practice? Conversely, should educators more fully teach students how to develop systems so that they are *ethically* acceptable?

Social responsibility in corporate governance has become an imperative for many firms. Do LCCs using self-service delivery demand different standards because they are low-cost? Is there a layer of insulation that such operators enjoy because, to many non-technical observers, the nuances of intentional design practices remain unclear? The lowering of customer expectations that de-marketing has brought about, has lowered the threshold of systems design.

Is this benchmark acceptable or is it a tolerable outcome of a Faustian-like bargain? While all of these questions involve a much broader social discourse, it is timely to debate them.

References

Alamdari F, Fagan S (2005) Impact of the adherence to the original low-cost model on the profitability of low-cost airlines. Transport Reviews 25(3):377–392

Alter S (2003) Customer service, responsibility, and systems in international e-commerce: should a major airline reissue a stolen ticket? Communications of the Association for Information Systems 12(10):146–154

Ames C (1970) Trappings vs. substance in industrial marketing. Harvard Business Review 48(4):93–102

Antón C, Camarero C, Carrero M (2007) Analysing firms' failures as determinants of consumer switching intentions: the effect of moderating factors. European Journal of Marketing 41(1/2):135–158

BBC News (2007) Action threatened over air fares. BBC News. news.bbc.co.uk/1/hi/uk/6759197.stm. Accessed 5 August 2007

Clark A (2006) Ryanair . . . the low-fare airline with the sky-high insurance levy. Guardian. business.guardian.co.uk/story/0,,1769707,00.html. Accessed 5 April 2007

Cohen AJ (2006) Capital Markets at the Crossroads – Sustainable Investing: Environmental Focus. Goldman Sachs Global Investment Research

Constantine E, Yourdon E (1979) Structured Design. Prentice-Hall, New York

DeMarco T (1979) Structured Analysis and Systems Specification. Yourdon Press, New York

de Neufville R (2006) Planning airport access in an era of low-cost airlines. Journal of American Planning Association 72(3):347–356

ECC Network (2006) Report on Air Passenger Rights: Consumer Complaints 2005. European Consumer Centre Network

Hirschheim R, Klein H (1994) Realizing emancipatory principles in information systems development: the case for ethics. MIS Quarterly 18(1):83–109

Houston FS (1986) The marketing concept: what it is and what it is not. Journal of Marketing 50(2):81–87

Hunt SD (1976) The nature and scope of marketing. Journal of Marketing 40(3):17–28

Jayachandran S, Sharma S, Kaufman P, Raman P (2005) The role of relational information processes and technology use in customer relationship management. Journal of Marketing 69 (4):177–192

Kahn A (2002) Airline Deregulation. The Concise Encyclopedia of Economics. The Library of Economics and Liberty. URL: www.econlib.org/LIBRARY/Enc/AirlineDeregulation.html. accessed 10 April 2007

Kassler H (2002) It's a dangerous world out there: misinformation in the corporate universe. In Mintz A (ed), Web of Deception: Misinformation on the Internet. CyberAge Books, New York

Keaveney S (1995) Customer switching behavior in service industries: an exploratory study. Journal of Marketing 59(2):71–82

Kotler P, Levy SJ (1969) Broadening the concept of marketing. Journal of Marketing 33(1):10–15

Krug S (2000) Don't Make Me Think – A Common Sense Approach to web Usability. New Riders Publishing, San Diego, CA

Larson K, Czerwinski M (1998) web Page Design: Implications of Memory, Structure and Scent for Information Retrieval. ACM CHI 98 Conference on Human Factors in Computing Systems. Los Angeles, USA, April 21–23

Marshall KP (1999) Has technology introduced new ethical problems? Journal of Business Ethics 19(1):81–90

Martin J, Finkelstein C (1981) Information Engineering. Savant Institute, UK

Murphy PE, Laczniak GR, Wood G (2007) An ethical basis for relationship marketing: a virtue ethics perspective. European Journal of Marketing 41(1/2):37–57

Nielsen J (1994) Heuristic Evaluation. In: Nielsen J, Mack R (eds), Usability Inspection Methods. John Wiley and Sons, New York

Nielsen J (1999) Designing web Usability: The Practice of Simplicity. New Riders Publishing, San Diego, CA

Nielsen J, Tahir M (2001) Homepage Usability: 50 websites Deconstructed. New Riders Publishing, San Diego, CA

ODCA (2006) Office of the Director of Consumer Affairs Annual Report 2005. ODCA

OMG (1998) Object Management Group: Unified Modeling Language Specification. Framingham, Mass

Oz E (1993) Ethical standards for computer professionals: a comparative analysis of four major codes. Journal of Business Ethics 12(9):709–726

Payne A, Frow P (2005) A strategic framework for customer relationship management. Journal of Marketing 69(4):167–176

Peattie K (1999) Trappings versus substance in the greening of marketing planning. Journal of Strategic Marketing 7(2):131–148

Quinn M (2006). Ethics in the Information Age. Addison-Wesley Publishing, London

Rominger E (2007) Social Responsible Investing: Here to Stay? Goldman Sachs Global Investment Research

Sharp H, Rogers Y, Preece J (2007) Interaction Design: Beyond Human-computer Interaction. 2nd edn. John Wiley and Sons, New York

Shneiderman B (1998) Relate-create-donate: a teaching/learning philosophy for the cyber-generation. Computers and Education 13(1):25–39

Shneiderman B, Plaisant C (2004) Designing the User Interface: Strategies for Effective Human-Computer Interaction. Addison-Wesley Publishing, London

Sklar J (2006) Principles of web Design. Thomson Learning, London

Smith HJ, Hasnas J (1999) Ethics and information systems: the corporate domain. MIS Quarterly 23(1):109–127

Smith A, Bolton R, Wagner J (1999) A model of customer satisfaction with service encounters involving failure and recovery. Journal of Marketing Research 36(3):356–372

Srinivasan R, Moorman C (2005) Strategic firm commitments and rewards for customer relationship management in online retailing. Journal of Marketing 69(4):193–200

Tavani HT (2007) Ethics and Technology: Ethical Issues in an Age of Information and Communication Technology, 2nd edn. John Wiley & Sons Inc

Trustrum LB (1989) Marketing: concept and function. European Journal of Marketing 23(3):48–56

Wagner W, Zubey M (2007) Customer Relationship Management: A People, Process and Technology Approach. Thomson Course Technology, London

Whitehouse C (2001) Fare and Square. Time Europe 157(10):49. search.ebscohost.com/login.aspx?direct = true&db = aph&AN = 4181067&site = ehost-live. Accessed 5 April 2007

Chapter 7
Experiences of Users from Online Grocery Stores

Mark Freeman

Abstract Grocery shopping, traditionally considered as the pinnacle of the self-service industry, is used as the case study in this chapter. As the Internet has become widely used by many segments of the population, the opportunity to shop online for groceries has been presented to consumers. This chapter considers issues that need to be addressed to make online grocery shopping systems more usable for these consumers, based on feedback from individuals who participated in a study of user interactions with Australian online grocery stores.

7.1 Introduction

The ability to purchase groceries via an online mechanism has the potential to significantly alter the behaviour of consumers. The challenge for online grocery stores is to provide a functional method of self-service item selection and ordering that consumers find more convenient than using a conventional self-service grocery store.Grocery stores appeared in the early twentieth century, and over the past 100 years have adapted to become a weekly part of most individuals' lives. The initial concept behind the grocery store was for a self-service, cash and carry facility for consumers. The three factors that led to the initial success of grocery stores were the growth of cities; an increasing population with a rising demand for food; and the spread of the motor vehicle and refrigerator. With these developments, the grocery store has become an institution in western economies.

It is essential for online grocers to realise that, while the public must shop for groceries, consumers have the choice of using conventional self-service grocery stores or their online counterparts. While, originally, many Internet users purchased goods via e-commerce for the novelty factor, online grocery stores

M. Freeman (✉)
School of Information Systems and Technology, University of Wollongong,
Wollongong, NSW 2522 Australia
e-mail: mfreeman@uow.edu.au

D. Oliver et al. (eds.), *Self-Service in the Internet Age*,
DOI 10.1007/978-1-84800-207-4_7, © Springer-Verlag London Limited 2009

need to provide a strong incentive for consumers to continue to purchase their goods online once the novelty wears off. To date, this incentive has been advertised as the convenience of being able to purchase from home and the reduced stress involved when shopping for groceries online. A number of studies have found that conventional self-service grocery shopping is the most stressful of all types of shopping (Aylott & Mitchell 1998). The decision to purchase groceries online and the users' perceptions of success are affected by many issues, both online and offline. These issues include the selection process, payment process, receipt of goods, returns, customer service, quality of goods, substitutions, price, privacy, security, time and convenience. The importance of each of these issues varies among users, and is likely to be influenced by the structure of the grocery store (i.e. whether the store is 'web only', or has a physical presence). This chapter will focus on issues of usability related to online grocery shopping.

This chapter presents the results of an extensive case study into the usability of one Australian online grocery store, and identifies issues that need to be overcome by online grocery stores in order to be successful. The results presented will discuss the differences between conventional self-service and online grocery stores, and feedback provided by users who completed the usability testing. This information is used to develop recommendations for necessary features of online grocery stores, which may be used to assist online grocery stores (and potentially online stores in other industries) to provide a functional method of self-service item selection and ordering for their users.

7.2 Background

The development of the Internet has introduced a new shopping medium for consumers. The Internet continues to create a great deal of hype and hysteria, and alongside the more sensational aspects, issues of e-commerce have arisen. One of the major issues that has been identified is the usability of e-commerce websites, as shown in previous studies (Raijas 2002; Tilson et al. 1998). If an online store is unusable then customers are unlikely to make a purchase (James 2001). There have been numerous predictions of a dramatic increase in online grocery shopping in the next few years; however, these predictions are only likely to be fulfilled if online grocery stores provide an efficient and logical shopping experience for consumers. Usable systems are paramount in meeting the expectations of consumers using this self-service medium for their groceries. Most e-commerce usability research has focused on the ordering of single products, and the issue of multiple product multiple quantity ordering, such as in a grocery store, has only been addressed in a very limited way.

With usability being a prime concern for online stores, it is playing an increasingly important role in the development of e-commerce systems such as online grocery systems, and with this various techniques for conducting usability testing have emerged. These techniques range from informal processes such as heuristic evaluation to formal techniques such as usability laboratories. If usability testing deems a site to be poor in that respect, there is a need to redesign the site, thus mandating a prompt reaction in order to remain competitive in the marketplace.

A set of ten preliminary guidelines have been established during previous research as a basis for orders that deal with multiple product and varied quantity ordering. The preliminary guidelines established (Freeman 2003; Freeman et al. 2003) were as follows:

1. Informative home page
2. Pages should follow a clear left to right path
3. Searching capabilities visible and usable
4. Searching available across multiple columns
5. Logical ordering of results, with consistent naming
6. A separate column for each part of the description
7. Each row differentiated by different colours
8. Clear method for item and quantity selection
9. Buttons differentiated from text and graphics
10. Simple instructions

It can be argued that grocery shopping is fundamentally different to any other typical shopping experience by its nature, in both conventional self-service and online contexts. A typical grocery shopping trip involves selecting and purchasing multiple products with multiple quantities, while other shopping typically involves purchasing one or a limited number of items. Website designers for grocery shopping should reflect these considerations as they endeavour to support users fulfil these traditional patterns of behaviour.

The emphasis and concerns of this research differ from all previous HCI research because of the inherent complexity of placing multiple product multiple quantity orders, as opposed to purchasing only a few items. The issue of multiple product multiple quantity ordering has been shown to be of significance in previous studies (Heikkila et al. 1998) and is of great significance in self-service, with a grocery order having 54 items on average. Harlam and Lodish (1995) identified a difference in mindset for purchasing multiple products as shoppers 'balance' the contents of their trolley. Research has shown that grocery shopping is the most stressful form of shopping (Aylott & Mitchell 1998) due to a range of factors, many of which are removed by shopping online. Previous research in the field of online shopping has also usually focused on the purchase of a 'hard-good', such as a book, CD or item of clothing. These items are fundamentally different to those that a consumer purchases from a grocery store.

One figure suggests that just over 3% of the total grocery sales in Australia occurred online in 2002 (Hannen 2002). There are a growing number of individuals using the Internet to perform their shopping duties. These users are also gaining greater competence and confidence in using such services. There is therefore a need for the systems to have ever-increasing levels of usability and to ensure that a high level of user satisfaction is maintained.

A study (Raijas 2002) of online grocery shopping in Helsinki, Finland, found that the average user is a woman, 35–46 years old living in a household with children. 73% of customers were women, 88% were under 45 years old and most users had high incomes. A similar situation of the typical online user has been established through this research, with interviews of online stores in Australia indicating that over 80% of their registered customers were women.

Online shopping research has traditionally focused on non-essential items, with the experience designed for enjoyment. Online grocery shopping involves the purchase of essential items, and efficiency is therefore more important than enjoyment. Efficiency is also an issue when it is considered that groceries are usually disposable and therefore need to be repurchased on a regular basis. Groceries are substitutable goods, meaning that if one product is not available then the consumer will usually be able to purchase a similar product as a replacement. Facilities to support the identification of alternate products are currently not available in online grocery stores, but would be of great advantage to consumers. As a result of these issues, online grocery stores are inherently different to other types of online stores.

With the introduction of the Internet and the development of online shopping during the 1990s, individuals were offered the opportunity to purchase their weekly groceries online, releasing the consumer from the stressors associated with conventional self-service shopping. Behavioural and consumer research has proven that the weekly grocery-shopping trip is one of the most stressful shopping experiences that an individual has to undergo (Aylott & Mitchell 1998). By providing access to the grocery shopping process online, consumers are now more able to shop at their convenience and in an environment which is comfortable for them (Kempiak & Fox 2002). With the ubiquitous nature of the Internet providing the possibility of purchasing items in an environment that is familiar to the user, there is scope for reducing shopping-related stress. However, it is still to be determined whether, in reality, online grocery stores are a true alternative to conventional self-service shopping.

When designed well, the basic experience that a user gains from using an online grocery system should be not unlike that of a conventional self-service shop. Browsing allows customers to explore the website and purchase goods in a manner that is similar to a conventional self-service grocery store by viewing virtual aisles to narrow down the products that are available. Online systems also have the advantage of a search facility, which most users associate with the Internet, and this allows a user to locate a product by typing in product descriptors such as the name, brand or type of good. With both methods, lists of results are displayed for the consumer to select from.

Images and explanations are essential to support online browsing and selection, because consumers are unable to touch or see the products they are considering purchasing (Bannister 2002; Consumer Union of U.S. 2000). A limited number of researchers (McGovern 2001; Nielsen 2001) disagree with the use of supporting images, suggesting that 'the web is a literate rather than a visual medium', and is visually constrained, so sites should be based around text due to resolution and screen size limitations. Limited bandwidth also supports this requirement, with users inevitably being impatient and the web being time-sensitive, meaning that information needs to be displayed in a timely manner (McGovern 2001). Lohse and Spiller's (1998) research contradicts these recommendations, stating that the most sophisticated 'list windows' (which combine a description, an ADD button and an image) use both images and extra navigation buttons, such as 'more details'. Hong et al. (2004) corroborate this argument, finding that the design of product listing pages can dramatically influence the users' performance and their attitude to shopping online. By providing a product image on the listing page to support the brand name, the efficiency and effectiveness of finding a product is dramatically increased, and the provision of a vertical list of the products as opposed to that of 'an array' (in a grid) improves performance. Yen and Gwinner (2003) identify four attributes that are of importance for Internet self-service technologies (ISST): perceived control; performance; convenience; and efficiency. These four attributes will be discussed throughout this chapter.

7.3 History of the Grocery Store

Conventional self-service grocery stores have existed in their current form for more than 90 years. The first conventional self-service grocery store, 'Piggly Wiggly Store', was established in the United States by Charles Saunders in 1916. His idea was for a self-service, cash and carry grocery store (Oi 2004). Although this grocery store failed due to the US stock market crash of 1929, the idea for such stores was created. The three factors that led to the initial success of grocery stores were '(i) the growth of cities, (ii) a rising demand for food, and (iii) the spread of the automobile and refrigerator' (Oi 2004). With these developments, the self-service grocery store became a worldwide success.

Over the second half of the twentieth century, grocery stores have established themselves in the Australian retail sector, just like in the rest of the developed world. The first self-service grocery stores in Australia appeared in the 1950s and have since risen to a position of dominance, accounting for 61% of all food and grocery purchases in Australia in 1998–99 (ACNeilson 1998, p37 cited in Pritchard 2000). In 2003–04 'food and non-alcoholic beverages' had the highest average household expenditure of $153 per week, representing 17% of total household expenditure on goods and services (ABS 2003–04). In the United States of America, annual grocery expenditure is around US $540 billion. Australia's largest grocery store group, Coles Myer, had sales in their food and liquor division of AU $19,255 million during 2005 (Coles Myer Ltd 2005). These figures demonstrate that there is an enormous potential market for business to consumer (B2C) e-commerce in the online grocery area.

With expenditure in Australian grocery stores accounting for such a large percentage of household expenditure, numerous grocery stores have established themselves in the market. This provides consumers with the ability to select their preferred supermarket company for regular grocery shopping visits. Since the introduction of the Internet, consumer choices have expanded further and they may now choose to conduct their regular grocery shopping using an online grocery system. In some societies, conventional self-service grocery stores have been incorporated into larger 'supermarkets' over the recent years, with these supermarkets having a wider selection of products. This chapter compares the stressors of using a conventional self-service grocery store with its online counterpart.

7.3.1 Online Grocery Stores

Online grocery stores realise that, while the public must shop for groceries, consumers have the choice of using conventional self-service grocery stores or their online counterparts. While, originally, many Internet users purchased goods via e-commerce out of curiosity, online grocery stores must provide a strong incentive for consumers to continue to purchase their goods online once the novelty wears off (Goldstein 2002). To date, this incentive has been advertised as the convenience and ease of being able to purchase from home. However, this concept of convenience must be extended to the convenience and ease of use of a specific online grocery system, not just the overall idea of online shopping. It is also important to note that the benefits provided by the convenience of shopping online can come at a cost to the user.

Despite predictions of a high take-up rate for online grocery shopping, this has not occurred to date. The slow acceptance of online grocery shopping compared to other types of online shopping has been considered in previous research by analysing the products commonly purchased online (Kempiak & Fox 2002). Products traditionally purchased online are 'hard-good' items such as music and books. In contrast, shoppers are used to inspecting groceries for quality when shopping in a traditional grocery store, and some grocery products such as fruits are considered to be high-touch items (Kempiak & Fox 2002). Shoppers using online grocery stores are not able to 'touch' items to assess quality. Another significant feature of grocery products is their perishable nature, with many products having specific delivery needs, such as refrigeration and a limited life span. The perishable nature of products demands a regular turnover of inventory, often resulting in changing availability of products. This poses an added challenge for online shoppers, as they are forced to vary their purchasing patterns based on limited information. Consumer perceptions regarding the delivery of 'soft-good' items need to be changed to allow for further growth in online grocery shopping (MyWebGrocer 2001).

When designing online grocery systems, a key concept to consider is the aisle layout of conventional self-service grocery stores. Designers of online grocery systems need to understand the 'mental models' that users associate with grocery shopping in the 'real-world' environment (Badre 2002). This notion is based on the idea that users of online grocers are likely to have experience with buying goods in a conventional self-service grocery store, and who are therefore experienced in determining the aisle location of items. It is the categorisation of items that is important for website designers and developers, with users commonly transferring conventional self-service grocery shopping experiences to the online domain.

There are three forms of virtual store layout presented in conventional retailing store layout theory (Vrechopoulos et al. 2004):

- Freeform. It is a free-flowing layout with both displays and aisles in different sizes and shapes (this type of layout is generally used in large clothing stores);
- Grid. It is usually set in a rectangular layout of long aisles running parallel to each other (this type of layout is generally used in grocery stores); and
- Racetrack. It is organised into individual semi-separate retail areas with each area being built around a theme (this type of layout is generally used in large department stores).

In conventional environments, it has been found that 'selling floor layouts are extremely important because they strongly influence in-store traffic patterns, shopping atmosphere, shopping behavior, and operational efficiency' (Lewison 1994, p. 289). The layout of an online grocery website significantly affects online consumer behaviour; however, practical research has found that predictions generated from the literature of conventional retailing about differences in the outcome of layouts do not generally hold in a virtual setting (Vrechopoulos et al. 2004). This is in opposition to the proposal for designing a website based on the users' 'mental model' (Badre 2002). Vrechopoulos et al. (2004) and Nielsen (2000a) claim that some of the research findings, such as users taking what appears to be the 'easiest' path rather than the most logical, can be explained by human–computer interaction theories that suggest users prefer simple online design due to the self-service nature of the Internet.

Interviews conducted with major online grocery stores revealed that for one store, of their 200,000 registered customers, only 100,000 had ever made a purchase. Out of these customers, 30,000 had only ever placed one order (Freeman 2003). Completed orders at online grocery stores have an average order size of 54 items. While a user may struggle with an e-commerce website when placing an order for a single item, it is unlikely that users will be willing to repeat the process 54 times if it is difficult or time-consuming. Although the percentage of registered customers who have made a purchase is high, Hicks (2002) claimed that the registration process was the first hurdle in online ordering, with studies revealing high dropout rates during the registration process. Another possible explanation is that the online grocery stores are not usable, causing users to feel stressed during the registration process and thus discontinue using the system.

Due to the repeated nature of grocery shopping, online grocery systems have the potential to develop time-saving features to enable a consumer to complete repeat purchases easily. Research indicates that convenience is a more important factor than cost savings when users decide to purchase groceries online (Bellman et al. 1999). A significant incentive to use only one vendor and shop online is argued to be the persistent shopping trolley (also referred to as a cart) (Bannister 2002; Consumer Union of U.S. 2000), which allows shoppers to place items in their trolley, and return later to continue shopping. The ability to 'recognise' customers on return visits forms the basis for users being able to customise the site (Consumer Union of U.S. 2000). Product information used to build the shopping trolleys commonly includes availability information for each item. This information allows users to make efficient choices, rather than requiring contact from grocery store staff after the order is placed (Consumer Union of U.S. 2000). The trolley feature aids sales in several ways:

- Users can see that you 'recognise' them, and that they have visited previously (Bannister 2002).
- Users can build their orders gradually before placing it (Consumer Union of U.S. 2000).
- Users can access previous purchases on a repeat visit. The first shopping experience can be time-consuming because users must search for the individual items, with future visits becoming more efficient as users are able to choose from a list of their previous purchases (Consumer Union of U.S. 2000). This is a significant incentive to use only one vendor.
- The e-business can gather customer tracking and behavioural data, used to further tailor the site to increase usability (Bannister 2002).

Claims that grocery shopping is the most stressful form of shopping (Aylott & Mitchell 1998) are based on a range of factors including the need to attend a busy store and the transportation of a large quantity of items, which may be difficult for some groups of the population. Online grocery shopping removes these stressors, as ordering can be completed in the user's home and the transportation is completed by the store. Despite these apparent benefits, only about 3% of the total grocery sales in Australia occurred online in 2002 (Hannen 2002). It has been suggested that poor usability is creating new stresses, and this may be a contributing factor to the low usage.

Compared to other forms of shopping, 'grocery shopping has more negative associations. It is a necessity, and even though some consumers experience it as relaxing, it remains something you cannot avoid, something you have to do' (Geuens et al. 2003, p. 244). A list of positive and negative associations related to conventional self-service grocery shopping was developed by Geuens et al. (2003). Of the 15 negative associations, only 1 (the possibility of out-of-stock products) is apparent when using an online grocery store. The negative factors that are removed when purchasing groceries online are as follows: waiting in lines; decayed products; melting products; crowds of people; elderly people; annoying music; no parking spaces; badly manoeuvrable trolleys; bringing back trolleys on rainy days; narrow aisles; unfriendly personnel; ignorant personnel; and stress before closing hour. An online grocery system may have a different set of negative connotations and/or stressors when users become familiar with the technology, such as the loss of the trolley contents or issues with delivery.

A study conducted in the United States of America (Ahuja et al. 2003) on the current use of the Internet and its future use by both students and non-students presented the following figures about grocery shopping online. The population was classified into students and non-students based on Phelps et al.'s (2000) article, which stated that students were more likely to know how to use the Internet and had less privacy concerns when working online. In 2003, 6.9% of students and 6.8% of non-students were purchasing their groceries online, with 18.6% of students and 9.6% of non-students having future intentions to purchase groceries online. The major reasons that they stated for purchasing products online were convenience, saving time and better prices. The major reasons that they did not purchase products online were privacy/security, customer service, lack of interaction and high prices including high shipping and handling costs. One factor identified by some of the respondents that was especially relevant to the nature of groceries was an inability to touch and feel the product. Online grocery stores have little control over the negative factors identified in the Phelps et al. study (2000). The online stores must therefore work to maximise the advantages of using online grocery shopping, with the focus commonly on usability. With usability being a prime concern for online stores, the field of usability testing has come into prominence. Two clear usability goals have been identified when dealing with e-commerce websites: a clear path to products and transparency of the ordering process (Benbunan-Fich 2001).

7.3.2 Shopping Differences Between User Groups

Links have been identified between user groups (as defined by their online shopping experience) and their behaviour (James 2001). Most online purchases are made by users who have had over 2 years of Internet experience (usually considered 'advanced' or 'expert' users), and have therefore adapted to the medium and the related purchasing arrangements. The typical web customer is one who spends a significant amount of their time on the Internet, indicating that they are an advanced user (Bellman et al. 1999, p. 32). In contrast, only 56% of light Internet users have attempted to make a purchase of any type online (James 2001).

Search facilities must be flexible to be able to cater for different user groups with varying levels of Internet experience, due to the behavioural differences between these groups (Hölscher & Strube 2000). While novice users experienced severe problems when attempting to develop successful queries, advanced users did not experience such problems (Freeman 2006; Freeman et al. 2006). A flexible system that provides support to all users would be likely to reduce the problems experienced by less experienced users; however, it should not impede the interactions of more advanced users.

7.4 Research Method

As previously stated, many issues affect a user's perception of an online shopping experience. The research described in this chapter considers *usability* issues. Fifty-four users selected items in an online grocery store from shopping lists provided by the researcher. The selection and classification of these users into groups was based on their online shopping experience. All users completed their shopping tasks using the same online grocery store, in a laboratory environment to ensure consistency and comparability of results. This store was selected based on extensive heuristic evaluations of 14 online grocery stores internationally, which deemed this store to be highly usable relative to the other stores evaluated. A store with high usability was chosen to ensure that the results from this research informed best practice, rather than addressing issues of poor design.

7.4.1 Usability Testing

While there is no single definition of usability, for the purposes of this chapter, the key elements in usability are ease of use, ease of learning, efficiency, visual pleasure, speed and effectiveness (Bara et al. 2001; Mandel 1997; Preece 2000). Preece (2000) explains that, in a practical sense, 'usability is concerned with developing computer systems to support rapid learning, high skill retention, and low error rates.' According to the ISO 9241-11 (1998) standard, usability is the 'extent to which a product can be used by specified users to achieve specified goals with effectiveness, efficiency and satisfaction in a specified context of use.' If a system is usable then it is believed that a user will be less stressed and their reaction to using it will be more positive.

The term 'usability testing' refers to 'a process that employs users who are representative of the target population to evaluate the degree to which a product meets specific usability criteria' (Rubin 1994). Its use as a research tool is based on traditional experimental methodology, and allows tests to be conducted under a generic title, rather than being required to specify the particular method to be used. Usability testing encompasses a range of methods. Developers are able to gain greater understanding about their website by conducting usability testing, and observing how users interact with it. User interaction is often different to the designer's envisaged flow of interaction, and usability testing is therefore an important tool to employ, as it can provide valuable feedback on unplanned use and areas requiring improvement.

Usability testing involves evaluating users' experiences of a website through carefully prepared tasks. As users perform these tasks, they are observed and their interactions with the system are logged. The performance of the user is commonly measured by task completion time and the number of errors made during each task. The usability testing process is highly controlled and is usually conducted in a laboratory-style environment. This environment eliminates typical distractions such as answering telephone calls, checking emails or discussions with colleagues. This method was used in this research to assess online grocery shopping because it provides a constant environment for all users conducting the evaluations. It provides constant access times due to consistencies in Internet bandwidth.

Usability testing was used in this research to observe the interaction of users with the chosen online grocery shopping website. On completion of the usability testing, users completed a post-test questionnaire, which recorded user perceptions of the online grocery system. The method of usability testing is based on scientific research (Rubin 1994), where controlled experiments are conducted and the outcomes recorded. These results are then examined to identify trends in the data. For this study, *Camtasia Recorder* was used to record the interaction of the users with the online grocery system. The statistical tool SPSS was used to examine the data.

The test comprised two stages that were 1 week apart. In the first stage, users completed two shopping lists one of 10 products and one of 20 products. In the second stage, users completed one shopping list of 50 products. Each user was required to complete a post-test questionnaire at the conclusion of each round of tests on the online grocery system. This information was used to gain overall feedback of users' perceptions of ordering grocery products online and to conduct a comparison of their views across the three shopping lists.

The recommended usability testing group sample size varies amongst the experts in the field, and is dependent on the type of study that is being conducted. Qualitative testing sample size recommendations range from 5 (Nielsen 2000b) to 12 users (Rubin 1994). However, for the use of quantitative tests Nielsen recommends testing be conducted with 20 users. The discrepancies between experts indicate that there is no generally agreed size for usability testing groups.

For this study a sample size of 54 users was chosen, consisting of three types of users: beginner, intermediate and advanced users of e-commerce websites. Advertisements for participants were displayed on public notice boards, and participants received AU $20 gift voucher as remuneration. Each of these groups consisted of 18 users to give statistically significant results (Cochran & Cox 1957, p. 24). Beginner users had never made an online purchase; however, they were familiar with using the Internet. Intermediate users had purchased

'hard-goods' only online, such as books and CDs. Advanced users had purchased 'soft-goods' online, typically food and clothing items. Each user was
required to complete a background/screening questionnaire to determine to
which user group they belonged. This questionnaire is based on previous studies
about users of websites.

7.5 Results – Usability Test Analysis

7.5.1 User Performance

The following sections present the user performance using the online grocery
system based on the average time taken per product when completing the lists
of products. The short test consisted of 10 products, each with a quantity of 1.
The medium test consisted of 20 products, with some products having multiple quantities (30 items in total). The long test consisted of 50 products, with
some products having multiple quantities (75 items in total). The descriptive
statistics for the average time per product for the three tests are shown in
Table 7.1.

In the three tests, the mean for the advanced users was lower than the mean
for the intermediate users, and the mean for the intermediate users was lower
than the mean for the beginner users, i.e. the differences in the means were in the
direction expected.

An analysis of variance was also conducted across the three tests looking for
changes in the average time users spent locating products. The results of the
ANOVA between subject effects of the tests and participants were $F(53,106) =
8.364$, $p < 0.001$, which indicates that there is a statistical significance of the
difference at the 5% significance level.

The results for the Scheffe comparison (see Table 7.2) indicate that there is a
statistical significance at the 5% level between the short and medium tests
(p value of 0.000) and the short and long tests (p value of 0.000). However,
there is no statistical significance between medium and long tests. This result
indicates that the users learnt how to use the online grocery system very quickly,
with a 26% decrease in average time per product between the short and the
medium tests. No difference between the medium and the long test could be

Table 7.1 Descriptive statistics – average time per product

	All users		Advanced		Intermediate		Beginner	
	Mean	Std. dev	Mean	Std. dev	Mean	Std. dev	Mean	Std. dev
Short test	44.6s	19.57s	33.3s	17.50s	44.1s	16.02s	56.5s	18.58s
Medium test	33.0s	10.75s	26.7s	11.33s	32.0s	6.94s	40.2s	9.30s
Long test	32.9s	10.61s	26.5s	9.37s	30.5s	6.92s	41.8s	9.10s

Table 7.2 Scheffe comparison of between tests for all users – average time per product

Short (I), Medium (J)		Short (I), Long (J)		Medium (I), Long (J)	
Difference (I–J)	p value	Difference (I–J)	p value	Difference (I–J)	p value
11.6630	.000	12.0044	.000	.3415	.974

attributed to the week delay between the medium and the long tests, or fatigue associated with the longer product list.

As stated previously in this chapter, one of the key elements of usability is that a system is easy to learn (Mandel 1997; Preece 2000). This element is especially important for systems such as an online grocery system, because they are self-service and require a great deal of interaction from users. One method of assessing whether a system is easy to learn is to evaluate how long a task takes at different points in time. A benchmark for the analysis of time spent purchasing grocery products was in Polegato and Zaichkowsky (1994), which discussed the purchase of products at conventional self-service grocery stores. This study by Polegato and Zaichkowsky (1994) revealed that an average grocery shopping trip for females was about 60 minutes, while for males it was about 51 minutes. The average time travelling to and from the grocery store was approximately 30 minutes. In this study, the average time for the long test-ordering process was approximately 27 minutes, which is below the times stated in Polegato and Zaichkowsky's study.

7.6 Results – Post-Test Questionnaire Analysis

Although the time taken to add products to the online grocery system trolley suggests that using an online grocery system for grocery shopping is quicker than going to a grocery store, additional information was gathered on the users' perceptions of the system. Each user completed three post-test questionnaires, one after each of the tests. Analysis is based on the two constructs from the Technology Acceptance Model (Davis 1989): perceived usefulness and perceived ease of use. The Technology Acceptance Model (TAM) uses six questions with Likert scale responses (1 – strongly disagree, 7 – strongly agree). The results from these questions are averaged to give the overall rating on the perceived usefulness and perceived ease of use.

The results showed that beginner and intermediate users believed that the online grocery system was more useful than did advanced users during the short and medium tests. This outcome may be explained by Nielsen and Levy's (1994) statement that experienced users rate their satisfaction of systems lower than users with little or no experience. However, for the long test, which closely represents a typical visit to an online grocery system with over 50 items, the perceived ease of use was higher for intermediate and advanced users, who

Table 7.3 Means for perceived usability for the three tests

	Short test	Medium test	Long test
Advanced users	5.21	5.51	5.38
Intermediate users	5.25	5.54	5.15
Beginner users	5.68	5.57	5.62
Total	5.38	5.54	5.20

would have had more experience. Beginners appeared to struggle with the longer list of items based on their lower average ease of use score. Table 7.3 shows the means for the perceived usability of the three tests for each user group, with Table 7.4 showing the means for perceived ease of use.

Fifty-seven different studies were compared by Nielsen and Levy (1994). These 57 studies involved a comparison of two or more systems, with 40 of the studies measuring subjective performance. Nielsen and Levy's meta-analysis of these studies has allowed benchmarks to be created on subjective prefer-ences for systems. The results from Nielsen and Levy's study are comparable with the results from this study, as the methods that were used seem to be compatible. Nielsen and Levy's comparison normalised the studies with dif-ferences. The users Nielsen and Levy reported on were from a broad range of backgrounds (beginner through to advanced). The study reported that the subjective preference mean (at a 95% confidence interval) for a 7-point Likert scale was 4.82 ±0.19. However, Nielsen and Levy stated that this is not suitable as a benchmark for two reasons: it has been affected by both systems that the users liked and disliked; and the median of system satisfaction was higher than the numeric middle as users tend to be polite and give fairly high ratings unless they dislike a system greatly. Upon further study, Nielsen and Levy recommended a benchmark of 5.6 for the mean and median for a good quality system, based on the systems that were preferred by the users in the studies evaluated.

Overall, across the three tests in this research the mean for perceived usability was 5.37 ±0.17. This result is slightly lower than the benchmark for a good quality system. For the perceived ease of use, the mean was 5.63 ±0.14. This result shows that users considered the ease of use of the system to be high. Some of these results are also confirmed by the open-ended responses given by users.

Table 7.4 Means for perceived ease of use for the three tests

	Short test	Medium test	Long test
Advanced users	5.58	5.60	5.62
Intermediate users	5.58	5.88	5.73
Beginner users	5.70	5.80	5.30
Total	5.59	5.76	5.55

7.6.1 User Responses to the Open-Ended Question

The open-ended question asked users if they had any comments on the online shopping experience. Many users took this opportunity to state some of the issues that they had whilst shopping using the online grocery system. Some users also provided personal comments about their own shopping habits.

7.6.1.1 Short Test

There were numerous comments made by users in the open-ended section of the post-test questionnaire for the short test. The total number of participants that provided a response, number of comments of a positive nature and number of comments of a negative nature are shown below in Table 7.5 for each participant group.

The positive comments that were made by users after the short test referred to the way that users felt that this process was quicker than purchasing groceries via conventional self-service means. They also felt that searching was easy and that with products being categorised by product type, the lists were easy to navigate. The negative feedback that was given was mainly about the difficulties that users had when attempting to find items using the in-built search function or adding the item to the trolley.

In total, 29 responses (43.9%) of a positive nature and 37 responses (56.1%) of a negative nature were recorded for the short test. Users were impressed with the speed of locating products, and the convenience of the online grocery store overall. The most problematic issue with the online grocery store was adding an item to the trolley. Many of the negative comments from all types of users were due to users' misunderstanding of the online grocery store, indicating that the system should be simplified to address the needs of all users. While there were more negative comments than positive comments, overall the comments were neutral.

7.6.1.2 Medium Test

The total number of participants that provided a response in the medium test post-test questionnaire, number of comments of a positive nature and number of comments of a negative nature are shown below in Table 7.6 for each participant group.

Table 7.5 Participant responses to the short test

	Total responses	Positive comments	Negative comments
Advanced users	15	9	15
Intermediate users	15	12	10
Beginner users	14	8	12
Total	44	29	37

Table 7.6 Participant responses to the medium test

	Total responses	Positive comments	Negative comments
Advanced users	11	4	14
Intermediate users	14	7	10
Beginner users	13	6	10
Total	38	17	34

The positive comments that were made by users during the medium test referred to the way that users interacted with the online grocery store. A number of the comments referred to the fact that users felt it was quicker interacting with the online store the second time and now believed that it was definitely faster than visiting a conventional self-service grocery store. The negative feedback given was similar to that from the short test outlining difficulties using the search feature.

In total, there were 17 responses (33.3%) of a positive nature and 34 responses (66.7%) of a negative nature for the medium test. Users in all categories stated that using the online grocery store was faster and easier than conventional self-service grocery shopping, with some attributing this to their previous experience in the short test. Again, the majority of the negative comments were related to issues with adding products to the trolley. This was a major concern for users. The other issue repeatedly identified in the negative comments was the need for a spelling check facility or a facility to prompt likely product alternatives. The positive comments were widely supportive of the online grocery store, with the negative comments identifying small issues that could be rectified by the online grocery store owner.

7.6.1.3 Long Test

The total number of participants that provided a response in the long test post-test questionnaire, number of comments of a positive nature and number of comments of a negative nature are shown below in Table 7.7 for each participant group.

The positive comments that were made by users during the long test referred to the way that users interacted with the online grocery store compared to a conventional self-service grocery store. One user stated that 'I went shopping yesterday. It took over an hour. This is a lot quicker.' Others felt that the

Table 7.7 Participant responses to the long test

	Total responses	Positive comments	Negative comments
Advanced users	13	6	11
Intermediate users	13	5	14
Beginner users	11	5	8
Total	37	16	33

process became easier after using the system a number of times. The negative feedback given was similar to that from the short and medium tests outlining difficulties using the search feature. Users stated that a spell-checking facility was essential for a system such as this.

In total, 16 responses (32.7%) of a positive nature and 33 responses (67.3%) of a negative nature were recorded for the long test. Positive comments identified that using an online grocery store was faster than conventional self-service grocery shopping, required information (e.g. prices) could be easily identified, the system could be 'learnt', and the search box was easy to use. Negative comments for the long test repeated the comments in previous tests about issues associated with adding a product to the trolley, and the need for a spelling-check feature. Users also became more discerning about the naming and display of product information. As for the medium test, while there were more negative comments than positive comments, the negative comments identified issues that could be resolved by the online grocery store owners. The positive comments were of a more general nature, and included the following statement: 'The process became easy after some practice.'

7.6.1.4 Overall Feedback

Overall there were several comments that were made by a number of users in the different user groups across the three tests. These comments included

- The search facility has no error correction
- The users did not know if a product was not on the shelf or if they had searched using incorrect terms. Previous research (Raymond 2001) found that an inability to find products was one major reason customers do not return to an online store
- Problems with the shopping trolley, including no display of number of items added, total cost or a receipt
- Problems with truncations and plurals (This comment is referring to the system's inability to process truncated terms (e.g. 'bisc' does not return results for biscuit) and its inability to effectively deal with plurals (e.g. 'apples' does not find results containing the word 'apple'). These issues were compounded by the inconsistency of item names in the system.)

Some of the comments that were made by beginner users were actually incorrect. These comments included

- It would be difficult to use this system to find uncommon brands
  - The search facility provides users the ability to search for all products via the same mechanism. The linking is the same as conventional self-service aisles in a grocery store. Therefore, is should be no more difficult to find an uncommon brand compared to a common one
- Quantity has to be changed from zero before adding a product
  - When the check box is clicked, the quantity automatically changes to one

The overall negative comments presented above all identify serious concerns for the users. Addressing these concerns should be of high priority to online grocery systems because users in all user groups identified them, suggesting that experience using an online grocery system would not overcome these problems. The negative comments mainly identified specific problems, and were largely relating to issues associated with adding a product to the trolley. Many of these identified problems could be overcome with a relatively small investment from the online grocery system owner. The positive comments were of a more general nature, with users describing the system as 'quick' and 'easy to use'. On the basis of the content of the comments, it could be stated that the post-test questionnaire responses were of an overall neutral or slightly positive nature.

7.6.2 Stressors

Online grocery system usage styles and attitudes varied, with some testers preferring shopping for groceries online compared with conventional self-service means. This was shown with a number of users stating that online grocery shopping was faster and that they were going to recommend it to family and friends. However, there was no correlation to suggest that age, gender or experience impacted upon how users felt about using the systems. This result was different to previous studies, which stated that experience and age are the influencing factors when using such systems.

Table 7.8 shows the issues and stressors when a customer interacts with both conventional self-service and online grocery shopping environments. The results were obtained from users' feedback in the post-test questionnaire and from previous research (Ahuja et al. 2003; Geuens et al. 2003).

An online grocery store can potentially reduce the stress of grocery shopping as customers can purchase the products from anywhere which is convenient to them at any time. The products are delivered to an address the customer gives the grocery company during a specified time frame. A customer does not have to deal with crowds or trolleys that are difficult to manoeuvre as manual processes are handled by the supermarket staff in an online environment.

However, there are a number of new stressors that a customer could possibly be faced with when purchasing their groceries through an online grocery store. Privacy and security concerns with the website can be minimised by using a recognised company. Issues with the navigation of the system can be reduced through the development of thoughtfully designed websites by the store. While there is no conventional self-service customer service if the customer has an issue with using the site, help pages are generally available. A customer does not have the ability to touch or feel the product, which is traditionally important when selecting fruit and vegetables, requiring the customer to trust the store in providing good quality products. The customers

Table 7.8 Issues and stressors of grocery shopping

Conventional self-service grocery store issues only	Online grocery store issues only
Need to attend a busy store	Privacy/security concerns
The transport of a large quantity of items	Difficulty in finding products
Waiting in lines	Issues with the building search mechanism
Decayed products	Customer service
Melting products	Lack of interaction
Crowds of people	High prices including high shipping and handling costs
Elderly people	Inability to touch and feel the product
Annoying music	Loss of the trolley contents
No parking spaces	Issues with delivery
Badly manoeuvrable trolleys	Issues with the companies website
Bringing back trolleys on rainy days	Issues with the consumers Internet connection
Narrow aisles	
Unfriendly personnel	
Ignorant personnel	
Stress before closing hour	
Conventional self-service grocery store and online grocery store issues (shared)	
The possibility of out-of-stock products	

could also have issues with the website or with their Internet connection, which may cause frustration and stress.

One issue that is common to both conventional self-service and online grocery stores that can potentially cause stress to a customer is out-of-stock products.

7.7 Conclusion

The results from this study into users' interactions with online grocery systems have many benefits for designers of ISSTs. Users learnt how to use the online grocery system quickly, with a 26% decrease in average time per product between the short and the medium tests. The time difference per product between the medium and the long tests was negligible. This could have been due to the week delay between testing and/or fatigue associated with the longer product list. Results show that the interface of an online grocery system can be learned within a short period of time and all users can perform the majority of tasks for which the system is designed. Overall the experiences of users with this type of system were positive. Users described the system as 'quick', 'easy to use' and 'will recommend this to others'. These insights have shown that the use of online grocery systems can reduce some of the stressors associated with grocery shopping. Realistic solutions an online store can implement to reduce potential stressors for customers include: a smart search facility with in-built spell-checker; an intuitive shopping trolley system; clear presentation of product information and stock levels; and access to more detailed information on the current order. However, it is essential that online stores remember that the usability of the online interaction is only one element of a user's experience with online grocery shopping.

The statistics for adoption of online purchasing show increasing levels of use, and this growing demand is also being experienced in the grocery industry. Many studies have shown that one way to increase the number of households using such services is to offer a more usable and efficient service to the users. The results from the user testing phase of this research could be used by companies to set initial benchmarks for their online grocery systems, as the only benchmarks available to date relate to conventional self-service grocery stores. However, the benchmarks developed in this study are by no means comprehensive. Further analysis of other online grocery systems via usability testing with online grocery system users would be needed to provide a representative analysis for comprehensive online grocery system benchmarks.

An important area of further research is the impact of experience on issues such as usability for online grocery systems, and whether it is possible to make use of such systems intuitively. 'Bricks and mortar' grocery stores allow shoppers the ability to locate staff when help is required; however, no such support is available in an online environment with these systems. Such research would require greater rigour in the user selection process, with extensive knowledge of user experience gathered prior to tester selection. This study only asked users whether they had purchased any product or service online and if they had purchased any goods from an online grocery system.

Ensuring that online ordering systems follow usability guidelines will allow users to develop greater understanding and confidence in purchasing online, and provide benefits to both users and online sites. If websites adopt usability guidelines, shoppers are likely to be more willing to shop online, providing benefits to both users and website owners.

This chapter identified several issues that affected users in all experience categories. Addressing these concerns should be of high priority to online grocery systems because users in all user groups identified them, suggesting that experience using an online grocery system would not overcome these problems. These included numerous difficulties with the search facility and the shopping trolley, and a lack of information about product availability. Users believed these issues had an impact on their experience using the online grocery system, and thus had negative associations leading to stressful situations. In this self-service environment, where virtually no support from the online grocery store is available, these key elements of an online grocery store must function effectively for the store to be successful. Many of the identified problems could be overcome with a relatively small investment from the online grocery system owner.

This chapter has presented a case study of a self-service online grocery system. It has been shown that users of such systems experience some issues when interacting with the systems. Although most of the traditional stressors of self-service for groceries are removed when transferred online, new stressors are created that need to be managed.

References

ABS (2003–04) 6530.0 Household Expenditure Survey, Australia: Summary of results (Reissue), Australian Bureau of Statistics, Canberra

Ahuja M, Gupta B, Raman P (2003) An Empirical Investigation of Online Consumer Purchasing Behavior. Commun ACM 46(12):145–151

Aylott R, Mitchell VW (1998) An Exploratory Study of Grocery Shopping Stressors. Int J Retail Distrib Manag 26(9):362–373

Badre A (2002) Shaping Web Usability: Interaction Design in Context. Addison-Wesley, Boston, MA

Bannister P (2002) The Best Ten Practices of Online Retailing. http://ecommerce.internet. com/news/insights/trends/article/0,3371,10417_979861,00.html. Accesssed 12 December 2005

Bara J, Dorazio P, Trenner L (2001) The Usability Business Making the Web Work. Springer, London

Bellman S, Lohse GL, Johnson EJ (1999) Predictors of Online Buying Behavior. Commun ACM 42(12):32–38

Benbunan-Fich R (2001) Using Protocol Analysis to Evaluate the Usability of a Commercial Web Site. Inf Manag 39(2):151–163

Cochran WG, Cox GM (1957) Experimental Designs. Wiley, New York

Coles Myer Ltd (2005) Annual Report 2005: Maintaining Momentum. http://www. colesmyer.com/library/Investors/FinancialReports/2005/annual_report_2005.pdf. Accesssed 17 August 2006

Consumer Union of U.S. (2000) Food Fight. http://www.consumerreports.org/cro/index. htm. Accessed 2 May 2003

Davis FD (1989) Perceived Usefulness, Perceived Ease of Use, and User Acceptance of Information Technology. MISQ 13(3):318–340

Freeman M (2003) The Current State of Online Supermarket Usability in Australia. Paper presented at the 14th Australian Conference on Information Systems (ACIS), Perth, Australia, 26–28 November

Freeman M (2006) Perceptions of the ordering process of online grocery stores. Paper presented at the IR 7.0 Conference: Internet Convergences, Brisbane, Australia, 27–30 September

Freeman M, Hyland P, Soar J (2003) Usability of Supermarkets in Australia. Paper presented at the 4th Annual Conference of the ACM Special Interest Group on Computer-Human Interaction New Zealand Chapter, Otago, New Zealand, 3–4 July

Freeman M, Norris A, Hyland P (2006) Usability of online grocery systems: a focus on errors. Paper presented at the OZCHI 2006 Conference: design: activities, artefacts and environments, Sydney, Australia, 20–24 November

Geuens M, Brengman M, S'Jegers R (2003) Food Retailing, now and in the Future. A Consumer Perspective. J Retailing Consum Serv 10(4):241–251

Goldstein A (2002) Online Shopping Settles into Sensible Routine. E-Commerce Times

Hannen M (2002) Shopping That Clicks. Bus Rev Wkly 24(4):66–67

Harlam B, Lodish L (1995) Modeling Consumers' choices of Multiple Items. J Mark Res 32(4):404–419

Heikkila J, Kallio J, Saarinen T at al. (1998) Analysis of Expectations on Electronic Grocery Shopping for Potential Customer Segments. Aust J Inf Syst 6:56–69

Hicks M (2002) Plug in to Consumers - Usability Testing, Tools Help Prevent Site Flaws, Reveal Secrets to Web Success eWeek 19(4):45

Hölscher C, Strube G (2000) Web Search behavior of Internet experts and newbies. Paper presented at the WWW9 – Computer Networks Conference, Amsterdam, 15–19 May

Hong W, Thong J, Tam K (2004) Design product listing pages on e-commerce websites: an examination of presentation mode and information format. Int J Hum-Comput Stud 61:481–503

ISO 9241-11 (1998) Ergonomic Requirements for Office Work with Visual Display Terminals (VDTs) – Part II: Guidance on Usability, International Organization for Standardization

James M (2001) Site Usability Key to Converting Casual Users into e-Shoppers. New Media Age 17:7

Kempiak M, Fox MA (2002) Online Grocery Shopping: Consumer Motives, Concerns, and Business Models. First Monday 7(9). http://firstmonday.org/issues/issue7-9/fox/index.html. Accessed 2 September 2002

Lewison DM (1994) Retailing, 5th edn. Macmillan College Publishing Company, New York

Lohse GL, Spiller P (1998) Quantifying the Effect of User Interface Design Features on Cyperstore Traffic and Sales. Paper presented at the CHI'98 Conference on Human Factors in Computing Systems, Los Angeles, California, USA, 18–23 April

Mandel T (1997) The Elements of User Interface Design. John Wiley and Sons, New York

McGovern G (2001) Information Architecture Versus Graphic Design. http://www.clickz.com/design/site_design/article.php/945631. Accessed 2 December 2005

MyWebGrocer (2001) Online Grocery Shopping: Learnings From The Practitioners. www.fmi.org/e_business/webgrocer.html. Accessed 26 March 2004

Nielsen J (2000a), Designing Web Usability. New Riders, Indianapolis

Nielsen J (2000b) Test With 5 Users, Alertbox, March 19. http://www.useit.com/alertbox/20000319.html. Accessed 21 February 2005

Nielsen J (2001) Search: Visible and Simple (Alertbox). http://www.useit.com/alertbox/20010513.html. Accessed 31 May 2006

Nielsen J, Levy J (1994) Measuring Usability Preferences vs. Performance. Commun ACM 37(4):66–76

Oi WY (2004) The Supermarket: An Institutional Innovation. Aust Econ Rev 37(3):337–342

Phelps J, Nowak G, Ferrell E (2000) Privacy concerns and consumer willingness to provide personal information. J Public Policy and Mark 19(1):27–41

Polegato R, Zaichkowsky J (1994) Family Food Shopping: Strategies Used by Husbands and Wives. J Consum Aff 28(2):278–299

Preece J (2000) Online Communities: Designing Usability, Supporting Sociability. Wiley, Chichester

Pritchard WN (2000) Beyond the Modern Supermarket: Geographical Approaches to the Analysis of Contemporary Australian Retail Restructuring. Aust Geogr Stud 38(3):204–218

Raijas A (2002) The consumer benefits and problems in the electronic grocery store. J Consum Serv 9(2):107–113

Raymond J (2001) Databasics: No More Shoppus Interruptus. Am Demogr 23(5):39–40

Rubin J (1994) Handbook of Usability Testing: how to plan, design and conduct effective tests . Wiley, New York

Tilson R, Dong J, Martin S et al. (1998) A Comparison of Two Current E-Commerce Sites. Proceedings of the 16th Annual International Conference on Computer Documentation, Quebec, Canada, 24–26 September

Vrechopoulos AP, O'Keefe RM, Doukidis GI et al. (2004) Virtual Store Layout: As Experimental Comparison in the Context of Grocery Retail. J Retailing 80(1):13–22

Yen H, Gwinner K (2003) Internet retail customer loyalty: the mediating role of relational benifits. Int J Serv Ind Manag 14(5):483–500

Chapter 8
The Virtual Shopping Aisle: More or Less Work?

Dave Oliver and Celia Romm Livermore

Abstract This chapter explores Internet-based grocery shopping . A review of self-service and associated technologies is followed by a discussion of the three main styles of grocery shopping: over-the-counter, self-service and online. The chapter focuses on the distribution of work between the supplier and the customer in each of these modes. We observe some features of the self-service phenomenon which question prevailing assumptions about self-service activities, namely that they replace work done by employees with work done by customers.

8.1 Introduction

The widespread use of personal computers in the home, allied with the connection of many of these machines to the Internet, has extended the impact of information and communication technologies (ICTs) to the domestic environment. This has created a need for studies that explore the effects of ICTs on social behaviour in everyday life. One area of study involving e-commerce is the social implications of online shopping. This chapter explores grocery shopping , a mundane activity for many people, but nevertheless an important one involving most households on a regular basis, essentially for survival. This broad impact makes grocery shopping a significant and interesting field of study.

It is also complementary to a broader study we are engaged in across a range of industries on self-service on the Internet, which is reported in Chapter 13. This broader study is predicated on the belief that the intent of self-service is to transfer work from employees to customers, in order to achieve savings in processes. We focus on the transfer of work from organisations to consumers in the e-commerce arena. That study has identified a number of ways in which

D. Oliver (✉)
45 Mirrawena Avenue, Farnborough, QLD 4703, Australia
e-mail: dodave@gmail.com

D. Oliver et al. (eds.), *Self-Service in the Internet Age*,
DOI 10.1007/978-1-84800-207-4_8, © Springer-Verlag London Limited 2009

Internet-based self-service is achieved (Oliver et al. 2005; Romm et al. 2006; Romm Livermore et al. 2005). This chapter solely explores grocery shopping .

Initially, we introduce self-service and self-service technologies (SSTs), in particular those which are web-based. We explore the main operating styles of these websites, the reasons companies operate them, and the impact they have on the customer service experience. The context of this study, the grocery shopping industry is described. We derive observations from it with a particular focus on the allocation of work between customers and employees.

8.2 Self-Service and Self-Service Technologies

Self-service is associated with transferring work from the supplier of the service to the consumer of the service. That is, instead of having the fuel in the tank of your car filled by an employee of the service station, you, the driver, perform that task yourself. When self-service fuel was first introduced, there was a choice between those service stations that offered self-service and those that did not. In this transitional phase, customers of the self-service station may have perceived that they were saving time by filling their own tank, or saving money through lower fuel prices achieved through lower costs due to the reduced service level (Halbesleben & Buckley 2004). Re-fuelling one's own vehicle from a service station has now become the norm in western countries and full driveway service something of a rarity. Long-established practices like these have become so ingrained that we may fail to appreciate the roles we habitually fill in these "service encounters." Online grocery shopping is a comparatively new phenomenon, and one which is at different stages of development in different countries. We may be in a transitional phase that will see the eventual demise of the supermarket as we know it. Online grocery shopping appears to be growing in the UK. Fletcher (2006) reports "a record-breaking 1.3m shoppers ordered groceries and presents from Tesco.com in the run-up to Christmas, up from 1m last year."

Companies may believe that providing self-service can lead to competitive advantage through lower costs, increased satisfaction and loyalty of customers, and the ability to reach new consumer segments (Bitner et al. 2002). The motivation for businesses to reduce the cost of service is very strong. The main thrust of achieving process efficiencies through self-service is finding "ways to get the customer to do tasks previously done by a staff member" (Sayers 2003). Interest in this area by management specialists including Johnston (1989) goes back to the beginning of the twentieth century.

According to a study by Meuter et al. (2000), consumers elect to avail themselves of self-service technologies for a number of reasons; ease of use, avoidance of service personnel, saving time, availability of the service in terms of when and where the consumer requires it and saving money. Lee and Allaway

(2002, p. 553–4) reiterate these points but add that "SSTs can ... release service personnel from routine tasks so they can concentrate on more varied services" and decrease the heterogeneity of service quality.

Many SSTs are purpose built, for example automated teller machines (ATMs), airline checkin kiosks and supermarket self-scanning checkouts. On the other hand, web-based services are provided on SSTs (computers) that are purchased, maintained and housed by consumers themselves.

8.3 Web-Based Self-Service

Websites have only recently emerged as a place where a service encounter may take place. In many respects, websites have special advantages for companies providing services. A website may be constructed to function as a site for a service encounter relatively cheaply and easily. Much of the technology that enables the self-service process is owned and maintained by the customer. The customer provides the computer, pays for an Internet connection to the service site and trains him or herself in how to use the technology. Many of the technical problems that can occur in this type of service provision must be overcome by the customer. In this respect web-based self-service is different from ATMs or kiosks. The site for the service encounter may be extended to a large number of customers extremely easily in the case of websites. From the service provider's perspective, there is a comparatively low need for additional premises, technology and extra personnel. In management parlance, we may say that web-based self-service is highly scalable . All a service provider needs to do in order to open up a limitless number of web-based self-service outlets, is to set up and maintain a server site. These factors make websites a most attractive self-service technology.

Conneighton (2004) maintains that "web-based customer self-service is a vastly more cost effective way of managing customer interactions and inquiries than are channels that require any kind of human intervention." These reduced costs can be passed on to consumers in the form of lower prices. For example, the Australian domestic carrier VirginBlue website advises that fares booked by a service call attract a AU $15 loading compared to the Internet booking fee (VirginBlue 2006). The service that is being purchased, namely airline travel, is a physical provision which remains the same, whichever type of ticketing service the consumer elects. Depending on their circumstances, customers may choose between an Internet ticket purchase, a telephone ticket purchase or a face-to-face transaction at a travel agency.

Self-service websites are typically categorised into two main types: informational and transactional . Informational websites provide information about companies, services or products. Those which are transactional involve an Internet-mediated transaction such as placing an order, making a bank transfer or booking a flight (Conneighton 2004; Young & Benamati 2000). Young and Benamati (2000) report variations in the transactional capabilities of company websites in different industries. The grocery industry is a subset of the retail trade standard industry classification used in this North American study, which gave a 71.4% degree of transactional capacity compared to 34.7% overall. This figure is well below that for airlines, and savings institutions were both rated at 100%.

Providing information services on the Web also gives organisations the opportunity to reduce the cost of information provision. Such services also provide convenience to the customer rather than a cost saving, as in most cases seeking information from an organisation about goods and services does not incur a cost to the enquirer. Examples of such services are web-based shipment tracking systems and weather Services.

8.4 Evolutionary Changes in Grocery Shopping

8.4.1 Over-the-Counter Grocery Shopping

Prior to the self-service era, it was the norm in western countries for the shop worker to retrieve items for purchase in an over-the-counter style service. Writing about developments in grocery shopping in the UK, Curth et al. (2002) note that "only half a century ago, most food was acquired from staff who would pick, weigh and wrap it." In those days, a personal encounter took place between the purchaser and the shop worker in order for the shop worker to retrieve the required goods for purchase. The shop worker needed to be skilled in locating goods and also in weighing and packaging loose items. Also at that time when the use of motor vehicles was less common, shops might also arrange for the delivery of the items purchased.

We postulate a distribution of work in over-the-counter-service between the supplier and the customer in Table 8.1. We explain the reason for the low/high and high/low entries in the delivery row of Table 8.1 as follows. If the customer transports the purchases, the supplier work index is low and the customer work index for delivery is high. Conversely, if the supplier transports the purchases, the supplier work index is high and the customer work index is low.

Table 8.1 Counter service

Over-the-counter	Approximate work index	
	Supplier	Customer
Retrieval	High	Low
Payment	Low	Low
Delivery	Low/high	High/low

8.4.2 Self-Service Supermarkets

The retail grocery industry has adopted and extended self-service practices extensively over the last 100 years. They are believed to have originated in the USA at the beginning of the twentieth century and were motivated by a desire to save labour costs (Curth et al. 2002). The reduced labour costs meant that self-service stores could offer lower prices and hence attract more customers, increase sales volumes and expand profits.

In the UK, food shortages and the contingent need to conserve supplies, led to rationing both during and following World War II. This factor restrained the development of self-service supermarkets in that country. According to Curth et al. (2002), self-service supermarkets did not begin to burgeon in the UK until the mid 1950s when "it was estimated that some fifty new self-service shops were opening every month." Self-service has developed to the extent that in many industrialised countries the practice of doing anything other than self-selecting goods from shelves or cabinets for grocery items on a shopping expedition would seem unusual.

The transition from over-the-counter shopping to self-service shopping required shoppers to learn new roles. The shopper needed to learn to equip him or herself with a trolley or basket and to locate items for purchase him or herself. The shopper also needed to learn how to identify use-by-dates and other techniques applicable to making the most advantageous selection. The task of retrieving items is almost exclusively the responsibility of the shopper, although it is often the case that delicatessen items are weighed and packaged by shop workers. In line with the rise in standards of living, the range of items from which to select is also much greater than when the shop worker performed the retrieval, which adds to the complexity of the task. For many shoppers, locating desired items can be a challenging and time-consuming process. A moderate amount of shopping, say $100 or a week's supplies, could take half an hour of retrieval time. Then of course, there is queuing and payment processing time at the checkout as well as time spent going to and from the store, though this latter consideration applies also to the over-the-counter style. We postulate the estimated effort required by the supplier and customer for the self-service shopping mode in Table 8.2. Delivery by the supermarket appears to be less evident feature of this style of grocery shopping and the customer incurs a fairly high workload.

Table 8.2 Self-Service

Self-serve	Approximate work index	
	Supplier	Customer
Retrieval	Low	High
Payment	Low	Low
Delivery	Low	High

8.4.3 Online Grocery Shopping

Just as the transition from over-the-counter shopping to self-service shopping required shoppers to learn new roles, so too does the transition from self-service to online grocery shopping . Lee and Allaway (2002, p. 554) notes that the "replacement of human service by a technology usually requires both the development of new knowledge and behavior associated with the service and increased customer participation and responsibility in the production of the service." The ability to engage in online shopping is subject to the conditions that apply to Internet usage in general. A computer with an internet connection is necessary. The shopper must be able to link to the supermarket website. The shopper must be competent in navigating within the supermarket website to select items for purchase. As observed by Freeman (2006), online grocery shopping possesses complexities that do not arise in other common types of online shopping. The grocery shopper is rarely shopping for a single item as is usually the case when purchasing airline tickets or books. Fulfilling a weekly shop may require 50 or more separate individual items, some of which can be ordered in multiple quantities or varying weights. Finding everything you are looking to buy, just like in the real store, is not a simple exercise. Navigating the virtual aisle for multiple items requires much more effort than for one item.

In addition to the large number of items which need to be located down virtual aisles, the shopper also encounters a number of sophisticated interface techniques which need to be mastered. In addition to linking and keying operations, the online purchaser may encounter option buttons, spin buttons, check boxes and drop down lists. The interactive experience is complex as screens are often crammed with information and options. Online shopping requires considerable expertise in website use, and in its own way, is as demanding as negotiating conventional supermarket aisles. One convenience available to the online shopper is the facility to review the list of items placed in the trolley at any time. This ability to assess the financial outlay of a grocery shopping expedition prior to presenting at checkout is a facility not readily available to the physical shopper. The distribution of work tasks and the estimated effort required by the supplier and the customer is portrayed in Table 8.3.

Table 8.3 Virtual Self-Serve

Virtual-self-serve	Approximate work index	
	Supplier	Customer
Retrieval	High	High
Payment	Low	Low
Delivery	High	Low

8.5 Experiences of Online Grocery Shopping

Prospective online shoppers may teach themselves or be guided by more experienced friends and family. As the website interaction demands of online grocery shopping are relatively high, as Rowley points out, they are likely to impact fairly strongly on how the service is received: "both during the early stages of learning and later, the way that the customer experiences a service is significantly influenced by customer performance. This could have consequences for customer expectations and evaluation of service quality" (Rowley 2006, p. 343). This is closely related to one's opinion of oneself: "self-efficacy is defined as an individual's assessment of his or her ability to perform a behaviour (e.g. Bandura 1977, 1994). Some consumers may be more familiar with using technology-based products than others and may have higher self-efficacy" (Dabholkar & Bagozzi 2002, p. 187).

The online grocery shopping experience is not confined to online activities. Rowley (2006, p. 346) points out that "self-service or e-service is often part of a wider service delivery." Rowley p. 347 draws on Semejin in remarking "that offline fulfilment is at least as important as web site performance in impacting on customer satisfaction and loyalty." This is clearly true in the case of online grocery shopping as the transaction is incomplete until the goods are delivered and checked. Customer impressions of online grocery shopping will be tinged by this aspect of the service as well as the online encounter.

Attitudes and opinions of Danish and English people to online grocery shopping were surveyed by Ramus and Nielsen (2005). Participants in that study expressed both positive and negative views of online shopping. Participants appreciated the convenience of being able to place their order at any time, of not having to get dressed up to go shopping, avoiding hassles with finding a trolley, not having to carry heavy groceries, avoiding of checkout queues, avoiding challenges posed by parking, and general time saving. An interesting finding of this study was that experienced online shoppers in this survey detected a greater freshness of boxed meat and vegetable products compared to supermarket shopping. This they believed was due to a more direct supply line. Conversely, some online shoppers had either experienced damaged soft goods like fruit or thawed frozen products, and others were generally apprehensive about not being able to assess the quality of perishable goods like fruit, through touch and feel, prior to selecting them. The English groups of online shoppers felt that "the initial set up which includes this list of basic groceries was...a barrier to even begin shopping via the internet" (Ramus & Nielsen 2005). The time lag between ordering and delivery, and the need to be available for delivery were also considered drawbacks of online shopping. The most unwelcome feature mentioned by both Danish and English groups was the "the trouble the consumer had to go through if he or she for some reason had to complain about a product and/or return it" (Ramus & Nielsen 2005, p. 341).

8.6 Individual Preferences

Rowley (2006, p. 343), drawing from a number of sources, makes the point that perceptions of control is an online service encounter may vary from one person to another. Feeling in control of a situation increases individual acceptance and approval of a service. Dabholkar and Bagozzi (2002, p. 184), drawing on Meuter, Ostrom, Roundtree, and Bitner notes "some consumers may actually prefer using technology-based self-service over traditional service because they find it easier to use, or it helps them avoid interacting with employees." Clearly these are matters of individual preference. Ramus and Nielsen (2005, p. 349) makes the same point in their paper in noting that "a physically strong male shopper would probably not regard the advantage of escaping carrying heavy groceries home to be as important as a more fragile elderly person would." Salomann et al. (2006, p. 68) emphasise the importance of this issue, citing Bateson's study of self-service which also highlighted the importance of individual preferences as well as the time that the service takes and his/her control of the situation.

8.7 Failures

As other chapters in this book indicate, there are many successful Internet-based self-service businesses, including grocery shopping . Nevertheless, Ramus and Nielsen (2005, p. 336) report a number of unsuccessful attempts to establish online grocery businesses. Drawing on Tanskanen et al., they identify Webran, Streamline, Homegrocer, Homeruns and Shoplink as American internet-based supermarket failures and in their home country Denmark, the Internet-based grocery shops, ISQ, Favor/SuperBest and ISS. As these examples seem to indicate, the application of technological innovations such as Internet-based self-service do not automatically provide value to consumers or generate successful businesses. Consumer reaction to online grocery shopping is somewhat mixed. Online grocery shopping has its merits but it does not appeal to everybody, nor is it available to everybody. Some are outside delivery zones and others are digitally deprived. Others do not aspire to using it even if they are able to.

8.8 Work Implications – Who Does What?

Online grocery shopping as we have described it presents many of the aspects traditionally associated with self-service. Browsing a virtual shopping aisle on your own computer and filling your electronic shopping cart by clicking your mouse exhibit the characteristics associated with a self-service activity. The process of arranging payment is also fully automated via the supermarket website. We have an SST and interaction with it by a customer. The shopping activity has up to this point followed the self-service model. However, the grocery chain then selects and packs the items purchased and delivers them to the home address of the consumer.

In online grocery shopping, the tasks of selecting the physical items, packing them and delivering them to the home shopper involve work that is organised and carried out by the supermarket. We contrast this experience to the conventional self-service model for supermarkets where customers select groceries from supermarket shelves, place them in their cart, carry them to the cashier for payment, and typically transport the purchases to their home. These assessments are summarised in Tables 8.2 and 8.3. In Table 8.2, all the supplier work indices are low and two of the customer indices are high. In Table 8.3, for virtual self-service, the supplier has two high indices and the customer has one. Hence, comparing online grocery shopping to self-service shopping, the supplier workload has increased and the customer workload has decreased.

Online grocery shopping is unusual in that it requires a substantial element of service to be conducted by the supplier. In our attribution of the respective effort by customer and supplier shown in Table 8.3, both retrieval and delivery are rated as high effort for the supplier. The costs of undertaking these packing and delivery tasks are passed on to the online shopper in higher prices. In pure money terms, online shopping is therefore more expensive for the consumer. This retrieval, packing and transporting work undertaken by the grocery store characteristic of the virtual shopping experience did not exist under the conventional self-service model for supermarkets. We observe an instance of work being shifted back from the consumer to the supplier, which is unusual in the self-service paradigm. The home shopping service reverses the trend of increased customer effort and reduced employee effort towards one which requires less customer effort and more employee effort. This increased service results in a higher price of service and it seems this is what some people want. Consequently, we see technology as enabling service and also employment, instead, as is usually the case with SSTs, the other way round.

In our previous studies of self-service, we have assumed that SSTs are a vehicle for organisations to reduce costs by shifting work from the organisations supplying the good or service to the customer. Virtual grocery shopping on the other hand transfers work from the customer to the supplier. The delivery payment is an increased cost to the consumer but is one which is offset by eliminating the need for the consumer to visit the grocery store and transport the goods. The self-service aspect of online grocery shopping is confined to the selection of purchases.

Assuming all the options of over-the-counter, self-serve and virtual self-serve are available to the shopper, the relative convenience, preferences and cost to the shopper of each of the options need to be assessed by each individual shopper and a choice made between them. Stores may be assumed to engage in similar calculations of the relative costs involved in each of the presentation styles when pricing items for sale and determining delivery charges. Returning to the statement reported by Sayers earlier in the chapter, it seems that in the virtual store, re-engineering service is not solely pre-occupied with transferring work from employees to customers but in re-inventing new ways of conducting service interactions from which profitable business operations can be derived.

8.9 Conclusion

This chapter has explored the phenomenon of online grocery shopping . It has evolved from previous studies that explored the Internet as a vehicle for customers engaging in work during the service experience (Oliver et al. 2005; Romm et al. 2006; Romm Livermore et al. 2005). This paper notes that although websites are used by the grocery supermarkets in a similar fashion to those established in other industries, their use has some unexpected side effects. The conventional self-service phenomenon of increasing work done by customers and decreasing work performed by employees does not pertain in the case of online grocery shopping. The virtual process of selecting goods and paying for them while seated at home navigating a website, appears to result in a greater degree of work performed by the supplier, especially in the case of repeat shopping. The prospect of receiving groceries delivered to your doorstep instead of pushing a trolley and negotiating a car park, plus the driving to and from the store is closer to service than self-service. We also highlight how this form of web-based self-service produces a contrasting effect on employment to those of most other forms of self-service.

References

Bandura A (1977) Self-efficacy: Toward a unifying theory of behavioral change. Psychological Review 84:191–215.
Bandura A (1994) Self-Efficacy: The Experience of Control. Freeman, New York.
Bitner MJ, Ostrom AL, Meuter ML (2002) Implementing successful self-service strategies. Academy of Management Executive 16(4):96–108.
Conneighton C (2004) Self-Service Comes of Age – Part III. http ://www.crm2day.com. Accessed 4 March 2006.
Curth L, Shaw G, Alexander A (2002) Streamlining Shopping. History Today 52(11):34.
Dabholkar PA, Bagozzi RP (2002) An attitudinal model of technology-based self-service: Moderating effects of consumer traits and situational factors. Journal of Marketing Science 30(3):184–201.
Fletcher R (2006) Tesco online sales soar by 30pc. www.telegraph.co.uk/money/main.jhtml? xml = /money/2006/12/26/cntesco26.xml. Accessed 5 January 2007.
Freeman M (2006) Perceptions of the ordering process of online grocery stores. Paper presented at the Internet Research 7.0: Internet Convergences conference, Brisbane, Queensland, Australia.
Halbesleben JRB, Buckley RM (2004) Managing customers as employees of the firm - new challenges for human resources management. Personnel Review 33(3):351–372.

Johnston R (1989) The customer as employee. The International Journal of Operations and Production Management 9(5):15–23.

Lee J, Allaway A (2002) Effects of personal control on adoption of self-service technology innovations. The Journal of Services Marketing 16(6):553–572.

Meuter ML, Ostrom AL, Roundtree RI, Bitner MJ (2000) Self-service technologies: understanding customer satisfaction with Technology-based service encounters. Journal of Marketing 64(3):50–64.

Oliver D, Romm Livermore C, Farag NA (2005) Are You Being Served? - Exploring the Role of Customers as Employees in the Digital World. Paper presented at the CollECTeR Europe conference, Furtwangen, Germany.

Ramus K, Nielsen NA (2005) Online grocery retailing: what do consumers think? Internet Research 15(3):335–352.

Romm C, Farag-Awad N, Oliver D, Sultan A (2006) Turning Customers into Employees - Preliminary Results. Paper presented at the Sixth Annual Global Information Technology Management World (GITM) conference, Orlando, Florida, USA.

Romm Livermore C, Farag NA, Oliver D (2005) Turning Customers Into Employees - Research In Progress. Paper presented at the 6th Annual Global Information Technology Management (GITM) conference, Alaska, USA.

Rowley J (2006) An analysis of the e-service literature: towards a research agenda. Internet Research 16(3):339–359.

Salomann I, Kolbe L, Brenner W (2006) Self-services in customer relationships: Balancing high-tech and high-touch today and tomorrow. E-Service Journal 4(2):65–86.

Sayers J (2003) The JIT Service Labour Process and the Customer: New Possibilities for Resistance/Misbehaviour and Consumption in the Labour Process? Paper presented at the Critical Management Studies: 3rd International (CMS3) conference, Lancaster University.

VirginBlue (2006) Flight Bookings. bookings.virginblue.com.au/skylights/cgi-bin/skylights.cgi. Accessed 11 May 2006.

Young D, Benamati J (2000) Differences in public web sites: The current state of large U.S. firms. Journal of Electronic Commerce Research 1(3):94–05.

Chapter 9
The Customer Rules and Other e-Shopping Myths

Rachel McLean and Helen Richardson

Abstract This chapter discusses self-service and the Internet in the context of two studies, based in the UK, and undertaken during 1998–2005. They are united by a common framework of critically analysing discourses of e-shopping in the 'digital age'. Firstly, myths surrounding e-shopping are deconstructed with a view to analysing the 'sovereign consumer' and the e-shopping experience. The second study considers home e-shopping in the UK. In an atmosphere where we are urged to engage with ICTs (information communication technologies) in all spheres of our lives, the domestication of ICTs necessitates consideration of the gendered family in gendered households. In conclusion, we argue those self-service aspects of e-shopping are not signs of empowerment and self-determination . The notion of the sovereign consumer exercising power and control globally is an enduring myth.

9.1 Introduction

In this chapter, we discuss self-service and the Internet in the context of two pieces of research based in the UK, undertaken during 1998–2005 concerning the issues of e-shopping with regard to e-inclusion in e-society. One study (McLean) concerned deconstructing the myths of e-shopping, and this qualitative enquiry was conducted through in-depth interviews with 20 people who had experience of online shopping. The second study (Richardson) considered home-based e-shopping in the UK, and this involved qualitative and quantitative strategies, namely the use of focus groups, a longitudinal study of households and an online questionnaire survey. The two studies raise various issues of concern to the question of self-service and the Internet and are united by a common framework of critically analysing discourses of e-shopping in the 'digital age'.

R. McLean (✉)
The Business School, Manchester Metropolitan University,
Manchester M15 6BH, UK
e-mail: r.mclean@mmu.ac.uk

D. Oliver et al. (eds.), *Self-Service in the Internet Age*,
DOI 10.1007/978-1-84800-207-4_9, © Springer-Verlag London Limited 2009

In the late twentieth century, myths surrounding e-shopping proliferated generally regarding e-shopping self-service as an empowering and revolutionary experience. e-Shopping was to be a time-saving, convenient and leisurely encounter, and through customer sovereignty improve customer–company communication and individual access to information with a global reach. In this chapter, we deconstruct these aspects providing two contexts for our argument: that of gender and home e-shopping and also the individual e-shopping experience. We investigate the development of e-shopping from the perspective of its social, economic and political history, and discuss the realities encountered, which contrast strongly to the glorious utopian consumer dream world conjured up by e-shopping champions.

Our research follows a critical paradigm critiquing that which is taken-for-granted and to reveal the historical and ideological contradictions within social practices. As such we place our argument in the context of e-society and e-inclusion, where citizens are urged to engage with ICTs in all spheres of their lives in order to make a full contribution to the 'Internet Age'. In our 'Castellian' brave new world (Castells 1996), industrial society has apparently been left behind, knowledge has eclipsed manufacturing with human mind now cast as a productive force. It is supposedly a consumer-led society, and collective identities have ceased to exist (Campbell 1995). Instead individual patterns of consumption are deemed important and individual expressions – like that of shopping behaviour, sexuality and many other manifestations of class, gender, ethnicity and culture – are said to shape our atomised, particularised experience. Beck (1992) suggests that this 'ethics of individual self-fulfilment and achievement is the most powerful in modern society.' However, in considering self-service and the Internet we show a determination to reclaim collective identity from the individualistic 'human as sovereign consumer ' that pervades the dominant ideology of e-inclusion rhetoric.

Our field of study is 'cultures of consumption' and the political, historical, social, cultural and economic context that is implied. The ideology of cultures of consumption rests on dreams – keeping people going on dreams of consumer goods and consumer experiences in 'dream worlds' as Benjamin has called arenas of consumption like shopping malls, for example (Campbell 1995). Bocock (1993, p. 50) has described that

> Consumerism, that is, the active ideology that the meaning of life is to be found in buying things and pre-packaged experiences, pervades modern capitalism. The ideology of consumerism serves both to legitimate capitalism and motivates people to become consumers in fantasy as well as in reality

Consumption of mass-produced commodities constitutes a 'vital dimension of the modern capitalist economy' (Campbell 1995), despite being a neglected area of study (Miller 1987). Warde (2003), furthermore, suggests that consumer culture, a culture where what we consume and the way in which we consume goods and services provided in economic markets 'has come to represent our identities, mediate our interactions with others and even shape our politics'. In these terms Featherstone (1991) stresses how important it is to focus on 'cultures of consumption' rather than seeing consumption as arising in an unproblematic way from production. In the cultural market, the meaning of supply and demand is not simply production imposing itself on consumption or the effect of a conscious effort to serve the needs of the consumer, but the 'objective orchestration of two relatively independent logics – that of fields of production and fields of consumption' (Bourdieu 1994, p. 230).

9.2 Effective Engagement with Online Retail

We now consider issues of individual power and sovereignty in the context of e-commerce and self-service drawing on the concepts offered by the critical theorist Selwyn (2004). Selwyn (2004) reconsiders the relationship between 'access to ICT' and 'use of ICT', outlining four stages of access and engagement: as shown in Table 9.1. He reflects that consideration of the digital divide and the e-society should focus not only on access and use, but also on the impact and consequences of engagement. In reconstructing the digital divide as 'a hierarchy of access to various forms of technology in various contexts resulting in different levels of engagement and consequences', Selwyn notes that a 'single dichotomous' concept of the digital divide 'makes little sense' and is limiting in its potential to influence policymakers and bring about effective change. Whilst the digital divide is synonymous with the 'haves' and 'have nots'; the

Table 9.1 Stages in the digital divide (Selwyn 2004)

Formal/theoretical 'access' to ICTs and content	Formal provision of ICTs in the home, community and work settings that is available to the individual in theory
Effective 'access' to ICTs and content	Provision of ICTs in the home, community and work settings that the individual feels able to access. Contact with ICTs in any form. May or may not be 'meaningful' use. May or may not lead to medium/long-term consequences.
Engagement with ICTs and content	'Meaningful' use of ICTs. Use where the user exercises a degree of control and choice over technology and content. Use could be considered to be useful, fruitful and significant and has relevance to the individual.
Outcomes – actual and perceived Consequences – actual and perceived	Immediate/short-term consequences of ICT use and medium/long-term consequences of ICT use in terms of participating in society. Could be seen in terms of Production activity Political activity Social activity Consumption activity Savings activity

'connected' and the 'disconnected' little will be done to address the potential and problems of new channels of service delivery.

Further, the dichotomous construction of the 'informed', 'responsible' citizen as opposed to the 'uninformed', 'irresponsible' citizen, shifts responsibility rather than power onto the people, and provides a smoke screen to the real issues of training and skills and service provision. Significantly, through the perpetuation of the myth of the informed e-citizen, people could actually be experiencing poorer services. For example, an incomplete information search could result in information incompleteness and asymmetry placing the consumer in a *vulnerable* rather than powerful position. The vast amounts of information available today mean that the ability to structure a search and evaluate information retrieved is an essential skill in the avoidance of information overload and the execution of a productive search. Again, this (mis)construction of the 'informed', 'responsible' citizen as the norm is of benefit to service providers. Information seeking and retrieval incurs costs to the customer in terms of time, connection charges, print outs, subscriptions and so on. These are charges which have been passed to the customer by the company (Bakos 1991). The 'responsible citizen' is possibly doing the work of the organisation, cutting costs for them in terms of the need for informed staff, staff time and expensive manuals or brochures. However, not many individuals are able to effectively evaluate volumes of information. Harrison (2002) draws the distinction between information as passive 'relevant data' and advice which is 'information shaped to the needs of the individual'. It is not intended to imply that information *cannot* empower, but that a certain level of skill is required to retrieve and evaluate relevant information; providing access to the technology artefact alone does not automatically facilitate a skills revolution.

Bourdieu (1997) states that 'to appropriate and use' artefacts of technology, a person 'must have access to embodied cultural capital; either in person or in proxy.' We are increasingly reliant on 'knowledgeable' friends, to assist us in our interactions as 'e-citizens', again at a cost to individuals, and a benefit to the organisations providing the service. Selwyn (2004) builds on Bourdieu, showing how social capital can be collective: mobilised through social obligations between networks of individuals and organisations; or through expert sources (Kitchin 1998), which are increasingly remote and virtual (helplines and online help facilities). Research into technological exclusion has highlighted the benefit of 'localised face-to-face social capital' (Murdock et al. 1996). Such services are very under developed in the UK and further, new developments in mobile and broadband technologies open up the potential for digital service delivery on more familiar platforms such as mobile phones and television (Carey 2005). Both the familiarity of these devices and their long-established position within the domestic sphere make them fitting platforms for provision of effective access and engagement (see Table 9.1).

We proceed by discussing e-shopping, self-service and the Internet with two illustrations: firstly, that of the e-shopping experience based on interview data and secondly, that of home e-shopping in the UK based on focus groups, a longitudinal study of households and an online questionnaire survey.

9.3 The 'SovereignConsumer' and the e-Shopping Experience

This research involves deconstructing the myths of e-shopping and was conducted by McLean through in-depth interviews with 20 people who had experience of online shopping. Surrounded by mass media hype, online shopping promised a power shift to the consumer. This research set out to explore whether customers' experiences of online shopping were empowering. There are many forms of power: this study focused on the concepts of 'sovereign power' (people governed by an outside force by coercion), and power discursively embedded in forms of knowledge. It also explored the concepts of 'service' and 'non-service' (Ritzer 2006) in relation to the automation of retail activity. Through this, a number of myths surrounding online shopping were highlighted; namely, e-commerce offers greater choice and convenience, greater access to information and enables more effective communication with companies.

The following analysis of the interview data in relation to these myths will illustrate how e-shopping has brought about a redistribution of responsibilities. In terms of the concept of sovereign power, customers are 'coerced' into self-service. Using Selwyn's framework of effective engagement with ICTs (Selwyn 2004), this section will explore the issue of competencies and skills or how people learn to be 'self-servers'. Even though the participants of this research consider themselves to be technologically aware and IT literate, and have access to the Internet both at work and at home, they still experienced problems or frustration due to a lack of skills or knowledge of electronic engagement, or in some cases, due to the lack of engagement by the service providers.

9.3.1 Myths Deconstructed

The deconstruction (Derrida 1978) (taking apart of a narrative, hypothesis or theme to reveal the underlying vested ideology) of myths is a relatively well-established technique in both information systems and marketing research (Hirschheim & Newman 1991; Grover & Ramanlal 1999; Howcroft 2001). Myths promote a consensus view of solidarity and cohesion and often perpetuate a shared misconception of the phenomena they describe (Bolman & Deal 1984). For example, Howcroft (2001) explores the myths of the 'dot.com share bubble' questioning why investors were drawn into financially supporting Internet start-up companies with no attempt at a traditional evaluation. This chapter will now explore and deconstruct three myths that continue to perpetuate the justifications for the claim that e-shopping is empowering customers through self-service.

9.3.2 Myth 1: e-Commerce Offers Greater Choice and Convenience

The myth that through the Internet customers are offered more choice has a number of strands. Firstly, it is claimed that the Internet enables us to do business with any company wherever it is in the world. Through this 'global economy' we are offered a greater range of products and companies to select from. Secondly, there is the pervasive view that the Internet offers us convenience in the form of 24/7 shopping (shopping, 24 hours and 7 days a week), with no need to leave home.

In terms of the construct of the 'global economy', facilitated by technology, and implying a sense of the 'compression of time and space' and 'of the world as a whole' (Walsham 2001), a myth is formed that a 'level playing field' is created. All the companies of the world regardless of size or location are purported to be competing on equal terms. However, as Howcroft (2001) notes, the Internet yields similar advantages for both large firms and small niche players, and small firms remain at a disadvantage. This is because as larger firms have more resources to invest in establishing and running a web presence and infrastructure; in the e-commerce context they may effectively squeeze out or buy up smaller firms, continuing to dominate the market.

With this in mind, it is worth considering the importance of 'brand' in the electronic marketplace. Within the context of the myth of increased choice for consumers, an important contradiction can be identified. Whilst we are told that it is now as easy for us to do business with the small business on the other side of the country, if not the world, we are also advised that we should stay with 'well known and trusted brands'. The UK Department of Trade and Industry (1999) states that 'consumers can improve their security by shopping with reputable merchants whose products and policies they trust.'

A plethora of academic literature and consultancy reports support this view, theorising on brand power, brand and trust, and consumer confidence and brand (Brewer 2000). Deconstruction of the myth of a greater choice of products and companies points to an increasing homogenisation of the commercial Internet, mirroring that of our high streets and shopping centres. It is arguable that a new 'superbrand' dominating all channels across a number of sectors and locations has been facilitated by the Internet (McLean & Blackie 2002) effectively narrowing down, rather than opening up, choice. A number of participants commented that they tend to return to the same sites, or only use 'well known and well trusted' companies' websites (male, 24), implying limitation rather than increased choice.

The second strand to the myth of greater consumer choice is that the Internet offers us convenience and choice in the form of 24/7 shopping with no need to leave home. The 'reality' of e-commerce falls short of its promise of 'convenience'. Many of the interview participants recounted experiences of delays in purchases arriving, and the inconvenience of trying to contact the company to make enquiries. One in particular stated that her online shopping experience was 'anything but convenient'.

> I've done home shopping and that was a bit of a nightmare to say the least. Half the shopping was missing. Where online it had said things were out of stock were in stock and things that it had said were in stock were out of stock and some of the products were at the sell by date. It was more stressful than going to the shop I think. (female, 27)

In addition to ignoring the distance between the promise and the practice, this myth is rooted in the assumption that people actually want 24-hour access to shops from home. Exposure to capitalist consumerism is no longer limited in time (to shop opening hours) or space (the high street or shopping centre), but literally follows us into our homes, and arguably wherever we go through the development of m-commerce (commercial activity over a mobile device such as a phone or PDA). Information and communication technologies are the vehicles through which consumerism is being spread into the homes and private lives of individuals (Lyon 1993). Further, through online retail we are doing the work of the company assistant, almost subsumed into the company as boundaries begin to fade.

Deconstruction of the myth of greater convenience through the choice of when to shop, and the ability to shop from home, calls into question who this convenience actually serves. Whilst it does enable people to shop at any time of day or night from the comfort of their own homes should they wish to do so, it also allows the 'capitalistic enterprise' 24/7 access to the 'target consumer'. It could be argued that advertising per se has this level of access. However, traditional advertising does not actually facilitate an immediate response such as that encouraged by the discourse of advertising e-mails. Deconstruction of this myth suggests that in practice, choice is actually limited to a small number of well-known brands, and that the convenience of 24/7 access arguably serves the companies and more specifically the 'capitalist enterprise' more readily than the individual.

9.3.3 Myth 2: There Is Greater Access to Information

The myth of greater access to information via the Internet is one of the most instrumental in the perpetuation of the myth of consumer empowerment (Pitt et al. 2002; Economist 2004). The general belief is that access to such a volume of information on any subject at the click of a mouse must be empowering. However, access to information alone is not in itself empowering. The potential for empowerment lies in the ability to understand and evaluate the information (Harrison 2002).

The information gathering stage of a person's decision to purchase is well established in the traditional models of buyer behaviour (Howard & Sheth 1969; Blythe 1997). However, these models were generally developed before the 'information explosion'. An incomplete search could result in information incompleteness and asymmetry placing the consumer in a vulnerable rather than powerful position. The vast amounts of information available today mean that the ability to structure a search and evaluate information retrieved is an essential skill in the avoidance of information overload and the execution of a productive search. Many interview participants remarked that they experienced information overload, 'there's too much information' (female, 27), and 'you can spend so much time just trying to find the information that you want' (male, 38). A further participant likened the search for information on a website to being lost in a 'labyrinth':

> Some websites you get a list of topics and it could be in there, it could be in there, so you click on here and that gets you to somewhere else where it might be there or it might be there. It's a labyrinth and you get fed up with it. (male, 41)

It is not insignificant that the information available on the Internet comes from a range of voices or 'discourses' (expert, non expert, customer, professional). This access to multiple perspectives is regarded as contributing to the empowerment of customers through information accessibility. Some participants in this research referred to the range of perspectives of information or discourses available through the Internet, commenting on how this confused, baffled or was too 'technical'. A participant who was planning to buy a camcorder commented that he gathered information from a range of Internet sources before making a purchase:

> It was on company websites, and a lot of reviews were actual consumer reviews, bulletin boards as well. A lot of them were using these professionally for weddings, so they were very technical... There were some criticisms of the camera we were buying, but the group of people on the bulletin boards were all professional people who would actually notice that sort of difference. (male, 37)

Information from companies, fellow consumers and professional users was drawn upon here. However, the suggestion that the professional's reviews were 'very technical' and that the criticisms were of things that only experts 'would actually notice' implies a conflict of interests between the expert/non-expert culture (Snowden 1998) or 'speech communities' (Saussure 1965). This suggests that access to information from a range of perspectives or discourses is not necessarily empowering to the customer.

Pitt et al. (2002) hold up Edmunds.com (www.edmunds.com) as an example of information available to inform a buyer's decision and ultimately bring empowerment . They argue that the customer can now enter the car showroom in a much more powerful position. However, not all individuals are able to effectively evaluate such information. Harrison (2002) draws the distinction between information as passive 'relevant data' and advice which is 'information shaped to the needs of the individual'. Through the perpetuation of the myth of the informed consumer, customers could actually be experiencing a poorer service. Firstly, the responsibility for actively gathering information has been thrust on to the consumer. Terms such as the 'prosumer' (Toffler 1980) and the 'responsible consumer' (Gilliatt et al. 2000) have emerged and a UK government white paper explicitly defines the 'better consumer'. 'The better consumers are informed about what the market offers' (Department of Trade and Industry 1999) constructing the dualism (Derrida cited in Macey 2002) of the good consumer/bad consumer hierarchy, with the implication that an uninformed customer is irresponsible. Again, this construction of the 'informed consumer' as the norm is of benefit to companies. Information seeking and retrieval incur costs to the customer in terms of time, connection charges, printouts and so on. These are the charges which have been passed to the customer by the company (Bakos 1991). The 'better consumer' is doing the work of the company, cutting costs for them in terms of the need for informed staff, staff time and expensive manuals or brochures. Deconstruction of this myth is not intended to imply that information cannot empower, but that a certain level of skill is required to retrieve and evaluate relevant information. Finally, a challenge to the hierarchy of consumer types suggested in the government white paper Modern Markets, Confident Consumers (DTI 1999); perhaps it is the 'worse consumer' rather than the 'better consumer' who places greater demands upon a company and so assumes the position of power or sovereignty.

9.3.4 Myth 3: There Is More Effective Communication with Companies

It is as a communication channel that individuals have most readily adopted the Internet into normal routines and practices. Ironically, here the constructivist tradition or evolutionary user approach could actually be fuelling the determinist myth; people use the Internet to communicate, the technology is available for people and companies to communicate electronically; therefore, e-commerce must be enabling better communication between companies and their customers. Further, it is suggested that improved producer–customer communication removes distance between the two parties and is empowering to customers (Gilliatt et al. 2000). This claim again ignores the gulf between the promise and the practice. The dominant discourse is that the Internet is facilitating customer to company communication and knowledge exchange and so empowering customers. The challenge to this is, as Walsham notes, 'the communication capabilities of the Internet... (do) not eliminate the need to consider the human processes of communication' (Walsham 2001). Further, it does not eliminate the need to consider business processes and practices in relation to communication with customers. One interview participant noted that rather than bringing increased customer-to-company communication opportunities e-commerce is a 'one way thing' (male, 30) allowing companies to communicate to rather than with customers. In practice, the Internet appears to have opened up another channel for companies to disseminate a corporate line (Levine et al. 2000). The experiences of participants in this research suggest that companies often reply to e-mails with a stock message from a corporate script which fails to address the questions posed,

> If I get something personal saying 'so and so has received you order blah blah', you know, you can tell when it's not just an automatic reply (male, 38)

or simply do not reply at all. For example, one person commented how e-mail to one company:

> Just sits there for 5 days in an email box and nobody reads it and you're just 'Well what the hell's going on' (female, 27).

E-mail is generally used by companies as a marketing tool to send out promotional marketing messages which individuals experience as 'spam', often quoted as the most annoying aspect of the Internet:

> I hate it. It irritates the hell out of me. I hate being bombarded with junk email. I can't stand it. It's the scourge of the Internet. I really think that it needs controlling there's no control, you know with the Internet it's unstoppable isn't it? It's going to put people off (male, 38)
>   I don't like getting advertising material. I don't read it because if I want to find out about something then I will find out about it. So it just goes in the bin (female, 52)

Companies have not adopted the Internet as a means of personal B2C (business-to-consumer) communication. Few companies have adopted real-time chat with customers into their day-to-day practices. Many don't even respond to e-mails, or reply with a stock message that doesn't answer the particular individual query. Current business practice means that customer communication via the Internet amounts merely to marketing messages or SPAM (notably forcing consumers to purchase anti-SPAM software) and falling short of the promise.

Significantly, through companies neglecting to engage in conversations with customers via the Internet, this medium allows only lateral customer-to-customer communication. It does not facilitate vertical or business-to-consumer communication, reinforcing the boundaries or barriers and maintaining the company fortress. It could be argued therefore that two worlds are operating. The establishment of business-to-consumer communications from the corporate script which mirror offline interaction; and the pocket of dissenters, laterally connected through the Internet, muttering and complaining to each other, plotting a virtual revolution but in practice having limited transformative effect on the companies who choose not to listen. Interestingly, strategies suggested to companies who find that their services and products are the butt of 'unfavourable hate or spoof sites' include pre-empting and buying 'URLs for the firm's name preceded by 'I hate' or followed by 'sucks'' or 'offer to host the site' thereby gaining some control over the content, and ultimately 'sue the site owner' (Pitt et al. 2002). This illustrates how the economic power of the companies enables control of not only business-to-customer communication, but also customer-to-customer communication. Companies can effectively buy up the rights of customers to publicly discuss their products and services.

Deconstruction of the myth that e-commerce enables better C2B communication shows that although the Internet has the potential to empower customers, current business practices ensure that companies maintain a powerful fortress, controlling communication and limiting its effect.

In the next section, we introduce issues of home e-shopping that implies access to time, credit and technology in the home. This research questions the technologically determinist approach to home e-shopping as a leisure pursuit and uncovers the history and socio-cultural context of the domestication of ICTs. Rather than a time saving and leisure activity, home e-shopping particularly for women is another self-service chore that has to be dealt with.

9.4 Gender and Home e-Shopping

This research was initiated by Richardson in 1998 at the height of the dotcom boom. At the time the literature was divided. In the utopian-hyped fantasy world, the High Street by now would have ceased to exist (De Kare-Silver 1998). It was predicted that we would all be engaged in shopping through various media and shopping would have been transformed beyond recognition. On the other side of the spectrum, commentators suggested that e-shopping would have 'no impact' (Markham 1998) and be an irrelevance. Of course, the dotcom collapsed in 2000 dented the e-shopping hype, nevertheless the dotcom myths (Howcroft 2001) still reappear and re-invent themselves when the next 'revolutionary' media appears on the scene. This section continues by considering the history of 'consumption work' in the home, increasingly fulfilled by the 'housewife'. To understand home e-shopping also requires study of home-based shopping itself. Then introducing ICTs to this activity requires analysis of domestic technologies and the process of the domestication of ICTs. Here the relationships of gendered technologies in gendered households are apparent. So to begin with, the focus is on the household.

9.4.1 Focus on the Household

With the urge to home e-shop, the household becomes the focus of enhanced consumption and so the lens shifts to the family. In terms of discussing gender and home e-shopping, this cannot be divorced from considering the reality of everyday life in the UK households. Households involve relationships. They are the place to consume services – here you acquire clean clothes, eat food and consume media, for example. In other words, the 'reproduction of people happens in the household' (Weinbaum & Bridges 1976). Households can be places of love and hate where individuals can unwind or be wound up! As Engels (1972) discussed, the family is a 'haven and a hell' with the oppression of women rooted in the private domain of the family.

Green and Adam (1998) have noted how little is considered about the way in which ICTs impact on everyday life in the home, and in particular they observed the gendered social relation of domesticity which surrounds the use of ICTs. As Silverstone and Hirsch (1992) have pointed out, the household is a complex social, economic and political space that powerfully affects both the way technologies are used and their significance. We know little about the economic or social context of the use of technologies in the home and how ICTs are appropriated and consumed in households, including the gender dimensions of this and the negotiation involved (Green 2001). Generally, what findings there are, suggest that gender politics and sexual division of labour impact strongly on the use of domestic technologies and the appropriation of electronic leisure (Green & Adam 1998). Hynes (2002) adds another dimension in terms of how the routines and habits of everyday life are shaped by the use of technology, and how in turn the technology is shaped by everyday life. Often the gender dimension is ignored here. So the concept of domestication is seen as expressing a process of shaping a technology to an acceptable form within the family. We are being urged to engage with technologies including in the home. However, an absence of gender analysis – that technologies are gendered and the family is gendered – leaves gaping holes in understanding the future.

9.4.2 'Consumption Work in the Home'

Weinbaum and Bridges (1976) coined the phrase 'consumption work' involving not just buying 'things' but also buying 'services'. This has developed since the industrial revolution, when slowly 'the creative 'producing' tasks disappeared from the household replaced by the uncreative task of consuming' (Huws 2003, p. 25). In these terms, items like the radio, TV, washing machines, fridges, all 'come from' domestic labour and are commodities largely replacing women's activities in the home. Changes in the home are not gender neutral. Most consumption work is done by women and women are disproportionately affected by these changes (Huws 2003).

Various researchers have pondered why 'labour saving' devices don't save labour (for example, Huws 2003; Schwartz Cowan 1989; Wajcman 2000). Huws (2003) points out one factor. This is the way technology is introduced, with its drive for greater routinisation of work and increased productivity of service workers. In turn this has led to ever-increasing amount of 'consumption work' foisted onto the consumer. Consumers find stuff on the shelves themselves, pack and deliver goods home, for example. The time lost is the unpaid time of the consumer. Centralisation of services also transfers the expenditure of time and energy and transportation costs to the consumer (Huws 2003, p. 27). Further, Huws (2003) notes the ideological pressures related to changes in standards of cleanliness:

> from people who were stitched into winter underwear every autumn and unstitched in the spring to an expectation that we will wear clean knickers every day (2003, p. 28).

Moving to the modern day, Roz Petchesky asserts that

> It's the connection between the shit private production provided in the market and the miracles women are supposed to perform with it inside the family that's really the key. The cutting edge of consumption work isn't procuring but taking up the slack – trying to maintain goods designed for obsolescence; trying to prepare nourishing meals out of vitamin-depleted, over-processed food . . .trying to encourage and tutor kids that the schools doom to failure (cited in Weinbaum & Bridges 1976:97).

Consumption work involves a set of relations between 'housewives' as consumption workers on the one hand and wage labourers in stores and service centres on the other. 'Housewives' must work in relation to schedules developed elsewhere and these schedules are not coordinated with each other. 'Housewives' are expected to wait for weeks for installation and repairs, to wait in lines, to wait on the phone, for example (Huws 2003).

Wajcman (2000) discusses the early debates around domestic technologies, particularly the paradox that despite mechanisation of the house, this hasn't substantially decreased the amount of time women spent on household tasks. Clearly, domestic technologies and technologies in domestic settings are 'embodied with gendered meanings during their marketing, retailing and appropriation by users' and their symbolic meanings attached are continually being negotiated and reinvented (2000, p. 455). Although in the domestic sphere many technologies are used by women – from the microwave to the washing machine, yet the 'world of technology is made to feel remote and overwhelmingly powerful' (Faulkner 2000). The notion of 'hard' technology – use of industrial machinery, or solitary geeks programming computers – is commonly associated with a masculine world of work, whether or not women are engaged in these occupations. Hard technology implies a dualism of 'soft' technology – like domestic technology and ICTs used by women in clerical work, for example. In these terms, the 'hard-soft' dualisms factor out those other technologies which we all meet on a daily basis and can in some sense 'relate to' (Faulkner 2000). In conclusion, many changes between the household and economy 'passed almost unrecorded' (Huws 2003), yet without an understanding of these changes it is difficult to grasp the impact of ICTs on home and everyday life.

9.4.3 Domestication of ICTs

How does the domestication of ICTs fit in here? How are ICTs appropriated and consumed in households? In the literature there are a small but growing number of studies that consider ICTs in the home. These studies focus on 'smart homes' characterised as being 'intelligent, connected and wireless' (Patel & Pearson 2002, p. 106). When reviewing this literature, it is astounding how little the household itself is analysed in some of the studies and how gender and technology are not problematised or even considered worthy of any comment. Rather than a 'haven or hell' described above, some studies seem to view households as sterile places, neutral and bland.

Yet the PC has particular significance in the home, often housed in a communal area and taking up significant physical space. In addition, the PC has a symbolic link embedding a subtext of personal improvement through its reported educative role. Research – such as the Home Net project – has shown how home computers are used predominantly for communication by adults in households (Boneva et al. 2001), although PCs are often bought with children's education in mind. Home PC ownership has a strong association with the daily bombardment of digital divide rhetoric as well, demanding an individual commitment and responsibility to 'self-help'. In other words, the message is, embrace the ICT 'revolution' or be a victim of digital 'have-not-ness' brought about, it is implied, by personal inadequacy and culpable neglect.

9.4.4 Home e-Shopping

To understand cultures of consumption, we will now consider the recent trends which encourage e-shopping and the use of ICTs in the home. So what is the state of gender and home shopping and e-shopping and what can we learn about its relation to e-inclusion rhetoric and the ideology of individualism? On-line home shopping today has its origins in the traditional mail order business. Mail order shopping is strongly associated with the provision of credit to the customer by the mail order company. So in the 1850s 'Shilling' or 'Turn Clubs' brought credit to customers otherwise denied it (Baxter 1998). After the Second World War these 'clubs' became a major way to purchase. In effect, they offered interest-free loans. A significant feature of this traditional mode of home shopping is provision of credit, with women being community providers of credit as catalogue agents, and also consumers of credit as major catalogue users. Mail-order-catalogue home shopping is a localised market, centred on household-related goods. Its customers are mainly poorer women who are economically vulnerable. Women, as catalogue agents and therefore community credit providers, work part-time at this task and generally this fits in with their social and economic circumstances. There are social aspects involving meeting with relatives and neighbours whilst collecting weekly payments and hence is a club and community endeavour. This regulated form of credit and also unregulated forms like using loan sharks[1] or informal loans to friends and family, are crucial to low-income households as a mechanism to manage poverty.

Home e-shopping requires access to time in the home as well as credit and technology. Green's (2001) studies of women's leisure continue to show time synchronisation and time fragmentation dominating most women's lives leading them to find 'snatched' spaces for leisure and enjoyment rather than planned activities. A striking feature of everyday lives is how little leisure time people have or perceive themselves to have. Leisure time is often taken in snatched and fragmented moments and at times that precludes pre-planning. Leisure researchers also suggest that there is an objective decline in leisure time often referred to as 'time squeeze'. This is as a result of multiple role conflict and role overload (Peters & Raaijmakers 1999). The competing demands of labour market and domestic work are associated with a perception of a loss of control over time, often called 'time crunch', and research suggests that women with children feel more time crunched than men (Peters & Raaijmakers 1999). Leisure and employment patterns affect women's participation and currently e-shopping is likely to appeal to those affluent and time-pressed women who loathe shopping enough to persevere online.

Although 'there is nothing in shopping or going for health care or education *per se* that must be alienating and tiring' (Weinbaum and Bridges 1976), nevertheless the pattern of contested ownership of time does not stop at the factory gate (Huws 2003) and continues in the household and broader community. Disproportionate amounts of time spent on household and care tasks are regarded as 'clinching evidence' for the continuing social oppression of women (Huws 2003).

Being 'time squeezed' and 'time crunched', losing control over time, suffering from 'hurry sickness' (Pahl 1995), being 'time poor', all seem to suggest that home e-shopping would be a welcome relief. Indeed some make vast claims that 'the PC is the most significant appliance since the washing machine or microwave oven in terms of making a woman's life easier' (Weber 1999, p. 217). This sidesteps the issue that women bear a disproportionate burden of responsibilities in the home to the detriment of their leisure. Leisure is often viewed as a residual category by women but remains an unconditional entitlement for their male partners (Kay 1996).

---

[1] Loan sharks are people who offer loans to be repaid at excessive rates of interest. In the UK they often call 'door-to-door' offering loans to be repaid on a weekly basis.

9.4.5 Home e-Shopping and Self-Service Issues: Discussion of Empirical Work

This qualitative and quantitative enquiry involved focus groups of seven house-holds visited on a regular basis from 1999 to 2004. Experiences and attitudes to shopping and e-shopping and uses of ICTs in the home formed the basis of on-going discussions. These were related to topics of gender differences in relations to time, cost, after-sales service and other related household and money man-agement issues, trust, privacy and leisure. We discussed issues arising from Warde (1990) outlined below in Table 9.2, that formed the framework of understanding conditions of consumption and shaped the subsequent online questionnaire. This was sent between August and November 2004 and filled in by 216 respondents. A further six self-selected in-depth interviews of women known to use ICTs in the home were also conducted during 2004.

In terms of e-shopping from home this inquiry shows that whilst a lot of ICT use is going on in the home, with significant gendered experiences impacted by who owns and controls its use, e-shopping is not a major activity, particularly for women. Rather women prefer to search with a purpose, communicate and gather information. Going shopping is a pleasurable, social and sensorial activity, which is not fulfilled through electronic means. The chore of 'doing the shopping' whilst perhaps suggesting relief through using electronic chan-nels, rather is made more burdensome through the time it takes, the 'hidden' burden such as self-service and availability for delivery and returns and poor customer service (Richardson 2005). Despite attempts to capture the social and informational aspects of bricks and mortar shopping through, for example, avatar personal shoppers, personalisation of web sites and various 'virtual club' models, e-shopping fails to deliver and remains the domain of the time-poor, cash-rich, young men in the UK. Gender issues stand out in who has access to time and leisure and technology in the home and gendered attitudes to

Table 9.2 Conditions of consumption (Warde 1990) and how it shaped the inquiry

Elements of Warde's framework for understanding the conditions of consumption	How this shaped the inquiry
Process of production and provision	Non-store vs in-store; technology used; ordering; payment; delivery; after-sales; 24/7 aspects
Conditions of access	ICTs in the home; social context; access to technology, time and credit; motivation to e-shop
Manners of delivery	Nature of on-line shopping – social, solitary and sensorial aspects; virtual or physical interaction
Social environment of enjoyment	Gender issues in shopping; individual vs. communal elements

shopping – particularly the joy of 'going shopping' versus the purgatory of 'doing the shopping' act as barriers to e-shopping replacing bricks and mortar shops.

For many people 'doing the shopping' conjures up a picture of weekly purgatory – a stress-filled domestic chore to be endured. Yet 'going shopping', particularly for women is a pleasurable leisure pursuit involving browsing, meeting with friends and the anticipation of returning home clutching bulging carrier bags. It's not surprising therefore that shopping for pleasure is the most popular out-of-home leisure pursuit for women (MINTEL 1996).

A recent Which? report into e-supermarket shopping found that in 2004, £1 billion was spent with 6 million orders placed (Which? 2004). e-Shopping from supermarkets has a mixed reputation largely due to its unreliability. The unreliability of supermarket shopping can perhaps be explained by the logistics involved. E-supermarket shopping often entails an employee collecting the ordered goods off the shelves before the store opens – a disgruntled employee or one who has no knowledge of an item can therefore subvert the order. Substitutions are common – 70% of respondents to the Which? survey reported that they had goods substituted and although drivers are meant to highlight substitutions, often this doesn't happen due to tight deadlines (Which? 2004). Favourite substitutions from the questionnaire survey and the Which? report are red cigarette papers instead of red peppers; lemon toilet cleaner instead of lemon juice and condoms instead of organic carrots!

Internet shopping changes the relationship between the customer and company. Many respondents felt that the service provided was inferior and dealing with customer service issues was time-consuming. There were various bad experiences of online shopping, for example from this respondent: 'I dislike grocery shopping online, I have had experiences where items have been substituted when original item not in stock and have also found that sell-by dates are worse when shopping online.' There were problems with poor delivery: 'my main stress factors to do with online shopping is poor delivery service – if you work you cannot wait in between 8 and 6 for a delivery'; problems when goods failed to be delivered 'my flowers didn't arrive at all and I had the hassle of sorting out the non delivery problem'; subsequent long waits in responses to queries; hours of hanging on the phone to customer services; and difficulties in returning goods.

The Which? (2004) report also cited problems of sites frequently crashing and deliveries containing wrong items – all of which sent customers rushing back to their shopping trolleys. They report that in 2001, half the orders made with online supermarkets took more than an hour and a half to complete – longer than physically going to a local store to shop. Now, logging on and ordering is far less fraught and the average time spent online for regular users was 35 minutes. This is still 35 minutes that women in the home can't always spare and as Jane said: 'I can whiz round the supermarket in my lunch hour or nip in on my way to work – this takes much less time than going online and I can see what I'm buying'.

From the questionnaire survey many more women than men use mail order catalogues. They report that when you're stretched for time, catalogues can be picked up and put down with the order sorted out in snatched moments. They are less time consuming than online alternatives, and often there is a clearer path to customer services with better after-sales and credit arrangements.

There are gender differences in e-shopping with relation to household management. Ordering is just part of the e-shopping transaction, and after the order is placed e-shoppers have to deal with paying credit card bills, dealing with non-delivery or wrong delivery, returns and after-sales. The responses given to the questionnaire survey implies that women in the home deal more with post e-shopping transactions. Jane agrees that "Siggi said: 'there I've done it' [used the Internet to renew the car insurance] – 'that's all done' – he's got no idea that when the next credit card bill comes in I'll have to find the extra £700 to pay it off."

Women in this study in particular expressed how they liked the sensory aspect of shopping – touching, feeling and smelling goods – and this was a barrier to e-shopping. When asked why are you not a frequent online shopper women in particular said because of privacy concerns, security, leaving credit card details, the time it takes to order, delivery charges, lack of trust and concerns about keeping details private.

Men and women are under whelmed by multi-media-filled online shopping sites, for example one online respondent reported: the biggest drawbacks to online shopping I believe are the small range of goods available compared to the same shops on the high street, being unable to see and touch goods, and the bad planning of some websites that makes them difficult to use. Likewise problems over delivery were frequently raised, as one online respondent put it: 'private delivery companies are a pain in the bum!!!!!!!! I usually end up collecting the goods from their depot – usually on the second visit because I forgot the slip first time round.' Lastly, respondents were concerned about the environmental aspects of e-shopping, for example one online respondent said: I'm uneasy about the numbers of extra delivery vans, etc.

In this study taking a critical approach to home e-shopping has meant understanding the social, economic, political and historical context and the need to analyse the gendered household and gender and technology relations.

9.5 Conclusion

In this chapter, we have presented two separate studies as illustrations hoping to have provided alternative voices to that which is taken for granted in this age that urges us all to be engaged e-citizens. We critically analyse the domestication of ICTs and question the essentialist assumptions about technologies and those that consume them. A recurrent theme among advocates of technological deterministic perspectives that imbibe notions of a culture of consumption is that consumers and users are 'passive dupes' and 'impotent, malleable consumers, unthinking and unresisting in the face of media technology' (Heap et al. 1995). Aldred (2004), however, points out that 'people are not just prisoners of received ideas however strong they seem when the world is quiet: when we try and change the world we often start to see it differently' (2004, p. 121). She goes on to suggest that seduction by neo-liberalism's false promise of omnipotence – in the guise of the 'sovereign consumer' comes about through a sense of a fundamental *lack* of agency. We hope to understand the complex historical and cultural factors involved in the social relations of ICT use and highlight the contradictions between e-inclusion rhetoric in self-service e-shopping discourse and expose the reality for our everyday lives.

We have argued that self-service aspects of e-shopping are not signs of empowerment and self-determination. We have suggested that one of the myths surrounding e-shopping in the so-called 'Internet Age' is that the sovereign consumer can somehow reach powerfully over cyberspace exercising authority and control globally.

Ultimately, the meaningful use as defined by Selwyn (2004) 'where users exercise a degree of control and choice over technology and content' continues to reside in the hands of service providers and policy makers. We suggest that challenges to this hegemony or existing pattern of power and authority needs to be mounted to encourage collaborative design of technology and content and work towards citizen self- empowerment.

References

Aldred R (2004) In perspective: Judith Butler. International Socialism 103(Summer):15–135
Bakos JY (1991) A strategic analysis of electronic marketplaces. MIS Quarterly 15(3):295–310
Baxter J (ed) (1998) Home Shopping. Keynote Market Report. 6th edition
Beck U (1992) Risk Society: Towards a New Modernity. Sage, London
Blythe J (1997) The Essence of Consumer Behaviour. Prentice Hall, Harlow
Bocock R (1993) Consumption. Routledge
Bolman L, Deal T (1984) Modern Approaches to Understanding and Managing Organisations. Jossey-Bass, San Francisco. Cited In: Howcroft D (2001). After the Goldrush: deconstructing the myths of the dot.com market. Journal of Information Technology 16:195–204
Boneva B, Kraut R, Frohlich D (2001) Using E-Mail for Personal Relationships. The Difference Gender Makes American Behavioral Scientist 45(3):530–549
Bourdieu P (1997) The Forms of Capital. In: Halsey A, Lauder H, Brown P, Stuart-Wells A (eds) OUP, Oxford
Bourdieu P (1994) In other words. Polity Press, Cambridge UK
Brewer C (2000) Deepening brand loyalty. Computer User.com http://www.computeruser.com/articles/1910,2,3,1,1001,00.html. Accessed 2nd April 2002
Campbell C (1995) The Sociology of Consumption. In: Miller D (ed) Acknowledging Consumption. Routledge
Carey K (2005). Widening access to knowledge and choice. http://www.nesta.org.uk/ourawardees/profiles/4067/02_profile.html. Accessed 12 November 2005
Castells M (1996) The rise of the network society. Blackwell, Oxford

De Kare-Silver M (1998) E-shock. The electronic shopping revolution. Strategies for manu-
facturers and retailers. Macmillan

Derrida J (1978) Writing and Difference (A. Bass Translation) Routledge, London

DTI (1999) London: Modern Markets Confident Consumers. Department of Trade and
Industry. http://www.dti.gov.uk/consumer/whitepaper/wpmenu.htm. Accessed 26
January 2001

Economist (2004) E-Commerce takes off. The Economist 9(14 May)

Engels F (1972) The origin of the family, private property and the state in the light of the
researches of Lewis H Morgan. Lawrence and Wishart, London

Faulkner W (2000) The Technology Question in Feminism. A View from Feminist Technology Studies. Women's Studies International Forum June

Featherstone M (1991) Consumer Culture and Postmodernism. Sage, London

Gilliatt S, Fenwick J, Alford D (2000) Public services and the consumer: empowerment or
control? Social Policy and Administration 34(3):333–349

Green E (2001) Technology, leisure and everyday practices. In: Green E, Adam A (eds)
Virtual Gender. Technology, Consumption and Identity Matters. Routledge

Green E, Adam A (1998) On-line leisure. Gender and ICT's in the Home. Information,
Communication and Society 1(3):291–312

Grover V, Ramanlal P (1999) Six myths of information and markets: information technology,
networks, electronic commerce, and the battle for consumer surplus. MIS Quarterly
23(4):465–495

Harrison T (2002) Consumer empowerment in financial services: rhetoric or reality? Journal
of Financial Services Marketing 7(1):6–9

Heap N, Thomas R, Linon G, Mason R, Mackay H (eds) (1995) Information Technology and
Society. A Reader. Sage (published in association with The Open University), Milton
Keynes, UK

Hirschheim R, Newman M (1991) Symbolism and information systems development: myth,
metaphor and magic. Information Systems Research 2(1):29–62

Howard JA, Sheth JN (1969) The Theory of Buyer Behaviour. Wiley, London

Howcroft D (2001) After the Goldrush: Deconstructing the DotCom Market. Journal of
Information Technology 16:195–204

Huws U (2003) The making of a cybertariat: Virtual work in a real world. The Merlin Press,
London

Hynes D (2002) Digital multimedia consumption/use in the household setting. IAMCR
Conference, Barcelona 21–26 July

Kay T (1996) Women's work and Women's worth: The leisure implications of women's
changing employment patterns. Leisure Studies 15:49–64.

Kitchin R (1998) Cyberspace: The World in the Wires. JohnWiley, Chichester

Levine R, Locke C, Searls D, Weinberger D (2000) The Cluetrain manifesto: The end of
business as usual. In: Levine R, Locke C, Searls D, Weinberger D (eds) ft.com, London

Lyon D (1993) An electronic panopticon? A sociological critique of surveillance theory. The
Sociological Review 41:653–678.

Macey D (2002) The Penguin Dictionary of Critical Theory. Penguin, London

Markham JE (1998) The future of shopping – Traditional patterns @nd net effects.
Macmillan

McLean R, Blackie NM (2002) Virgin Lifestyle: the future of super brands in the new network
economy. In: Banwell L, Collier M (eds) Information Management Research Institute,
Northumbria University, Newcastle

Miller D (1987) Material Culture and Mass Consumption. Blackwell, UK

MINTEL (1996) Leisure Trends. MINTEL Leisure Intelligence, London

Murdock G, Hartmann P, Gray P (1996) Conceptualising Home Computing: Resources and
Practices. In: Heap N, Thomas R, Einon G, Mason R, Mackay H (eds) Information
Technology and Society. Sage, London

Patel D, Pearson ID (2002) Hype and reality in the future home. BT Technology Journal 20(2) 2 April

Pahl R (1995) Finding Time to live. Cited In: Aitchison, C, Jordan, F (eds) Gender Space and Identity. Leisure Studies Association 63 1998

Peters P, Raaijmakers S (1999) Time Crunch and the perception of control over time from a gendered perspective: the Dutch case. Society and Leisure 21(2):417–433

Pitt LF, Berthon PR, Watson RT, Zinkhan GM (2002) The Internet and the birth of real consumer power. Business Horizons July-August:7–14

Richardson H (2005) Consuming passions in the global knowledge economy. In: Howcroft D, Trauth E (eds) Handbook of Critical Information Systems Research: Theory and Application. Edward Elga, Cheltenham

Ritzer G (2006) The Globalization of Nothing. Sage, London

Saussure FD (1965) Course in General Linguistics. In: Wade Baskin (ed) McGraw-Hill, London

Schwartz CR (1989) More work for mother the ironies of household technologies from the open hearth to the microwave. Free Association Books, London

Selwyn N (2004) Reconsidering political and popular understandings of the digital divide. New Media and Society 6(3):41–362

Silverstone R, Hirsch E (1992) Consuming Technologies: Media and Information in Domestic Spaces. Routledge, UK

Snowden D (1998) A Framework for Creating a Sustainable Programme. Caspian Publishing/ Confederation of British Industry, London. Republished in Knowledge Management Year Book (1999) Butterworth

Toffler A (1980) The Third Wave. Bantam, New York

Wajcman J (2000) Reflections on gender and technology studies in what state is the art? Social Studies of Science 30(3):447–464

Walsham G (2001) Making a World of Difference: IT in a Global Context. Wiley, Chichester

Warde A (1990) Introduction to the sociology of consumption. Sociology 24(1):1–4

Warde A (2003) ESRC Cultures of Consumption Programme. Centre for Research in Innovation and Competition University of Manchester http://les1manacuk/cric/Alan_Warde/curreshtm Accessed 22 February 2005

Weber J (1999) Gender and computing. PC PRO September:212–217

Weinbaum B, Bridges A (1976) The other side of the pay check. Monthly Review July-August

Which? Report (2004) Its time to wave goodbye to wobbly trolleys crowded aisles and long checkout queues and do your weekly supermarket shop online. Which Magazine September

Chapter 10
Internet Banking: An Interaction Building Channel for Bank-Customer Relationships

Madhumita Banerjee

Abstract This chapter examines the weakening and strengthening of relationships in technology determined bank–customer interactions. It focuses on the use of Internet banking for long-term service maintenance in a multiple channel usage context. The research findings from a study conducted with retail banking customers in the UK, indicate how customers combine the concepts of 'convenience' and 'control' in performing banking activities through Internet banking. In addition, while the users demand enhanced functionalities, the non-users seek innovation in customer service to aid their understanding and initiate their use of Internet banking. Such a scenario creates situations that transfer work back from the customers to the bank employees with likely changes in the roles and responsibilities of the frontline staff. As a social consequence of Internet banking usage, issues about the dichotomy of convenience and stress are also discussed. The potential of a virtual and remote channel like Internet banking in creating enhanced bank–customer relationships becomes salient with implications for organisational strategies.

10.1 Introduction

'Technology has empowered customers to loosen ties with financial services providers, but it can also be harnessed to rebuild and strengthen relationships' states a recent research on the global financial services industry conducted jointly by the Economist Intelligence Unit and Deloitte Consulting (2006, p. 3). An examination of the technology determined bank–customer relationship weakening and strengthening tendencies is the central theme of this chapter. The focus in this chapter is on Internet banking , the fastest growing self-service technology (SST)-based channel.

M. Banerjee (✉)
Essex Business School, University of Essex, Southend-on-Sea SS1 1LW UK
e-mail: mbaner@essex.ac.uk

D. Oliver et al. (eds.), *Self-Service in the Internet Age*,
DOI 10.1007/978-1-84800-207-4_10, © Springer-Verlag London Limited 2009

The development and assimilation of electronic channels in the retail banking distribution channel strategy has, on one hand enabled banks to lower their costs of servicing customers. On the other hand, it has also facilitated the convenience for customers in banking at a choice of hour and location suitable to them. While the use of Internet banking in the retail banking business model has grown considerably, there is however, little by way of empirical research that goes beyond the adoption and diffusion issues and investigates the usage of Internet banking for long-term service maintenance activities.

This chapter presents findings from a research study conducted with retail banking customers in the UK investigating the use of Internet banking for long-term service maintenance in a multiple channel usage context. The research findings uncover issues that facilitate or inhibit the use of Internet banking and how the use of the Internet as an SST channel for everyday banking purposes can create conditions which actually enhance the bank–customer relationship. This chapter is organised as follows:

- The underlying issues that prompt organisations in the financial services sector, such as retail banks to provide SSTs are explored.
- The expectations of the organisation from its customers with regards to the use of the SSTs are examined.
- The research methodology adopted for the study is outlined.
- Customers' experience of using SSTs such as Internet banking is discussed.
- The social consequences that emerge from customer experiences of Internet banking are identified in the light of the research findings and discussed with the implications for organisational strategy and policies.
- The chapter concludes by drawing together the salient issues that emerge with regards to customer experiences and the social consequences of using an SST such as Internet banking.

10.2 Self-Service Technology and Internet Banking

SSTs are defined by Meuter et al. (2000, p. 50) as 'technological interfaces that enable customers to produce a service independent of direct service employee involvement.' In the financial services sector, technological advancements have led to the development of three principal electronic delivery channels, namely, automated teller machines (ATMs), phone banking and Internet banking . Additionally, new developments such as interactive television banking and mobile banking are being explored for their potential and these are in nascent stages. In retail banking, these technology driven channels join the primary channel of the branch network in reaching customers for service delivery.

The advancements in Internet-based technology led to the development of Internet banking , also known as online banking. The range of personal banking activities that customers can undertake includes viewing account statements, payment of bills such as credit cards, setting up direct debits and standing orders and the transfer of money across accounts. The online banking facility has manifested itself in two forms (Claessens et al. 2002):

- Banks with branch-based networks offering the customers the facility of undertaking banking activities through an Internet account developed as part of in-house online activities. This approach is often known as 'bricks and clicks'. In most developed economies of the world, banks now offer Internet banking facilities as a standard feature.
- Banks that have set up separate entities which offer only Internet-based banking, known as 'virtual banks', that is independent of branch-based banking. ING Direct, the Netherlands-based subsidiary of ING Bank with operations in Australia, Canada, France, Germany, Italy, Spain and the UK, is one of the best examples of this type of provision.

The growth and development of SST-based channels in retail banking is best understood by exploring the macro and micro environmental trends underpinning the developments in the broader financial services sector. The macro environmental trends driving the changes in the financial services sector include legislative reforms such as deregulation, economic integration within and across countries, and developments in information technology (Claessens et al. 2002; Harrison 2000). At the micro environmental level, increased competition and new product and service development have played a key role in the growth and diversity of the financial services sector and within that, in retail banking. However, indisputably, the biggest drivers of growth have been the technological advancements, manifest in the increasing role of technology in service delivery and the offering of multiple channels to customers for accessing bank services (Black et al. 2002; Harrison 2000; Ennew & McKechnie 1998).

The organisational motive for developing and offering SST channels to customers can be broadly categorised as facilitating *self-help* (information-seeking activity), *transactions* (making a purchase) and *customer service* (tracking a package, accessing bank account information) (Meuter et al. 2000, p. 52). In the context of retail banking, the growth of SST has been primarily driven by reducing the cost of servicing customers. When Internet banking was being introduced worldwide, research from the late 1990s calculated that the transaction cost on the Internet was $0.02. In contrast, the cost of providing the same service at a branch or telephone (both requiring a bank employee to service the transaction) was $1.00 (Hodes et al. 1999).

The first Internet banking provision was in 1997, developed jointly by First Direct and Fujitsu and offered to First Direct customers (Fujitsu n.d.). Since then, an interesting scenario has emerged. There is evidence of rapid growth in Internet banking, both in the customers' usage as well as the development of the channel by banks themselves. The success of Scandinavian banks such as MeritaNordbanken in introducing and encouraging customers to use Internet banking is a suitable example (Bughin 2001; Grief et al. 2000). Worldwide, there have been positive forecasts and actual growth in the adoption of Internet banking by retail banking customers. For example, in Europe, the number of online banking accounts was estimated to grow from 26 million in 2000 to 66.2 million in 2003 (West 2001). In the UK, the number of Internet banking users in 1999 was 2.0 million with an estimated growth to 14.5 million in 2004 (Key Note Report 2004). In China, from a 2.7 million user base in 2001, it was estimated to grow to 12.5 million users by the end of 2005 (Krebsbach 2003). As stated earlier, this increase in Internet banking has been made possible by technological advancements. The technology-based drivers and inhibitors for the development of Internet banking are summarised in Table 10.1.

Despite this growth, issues such as security of data and information have consistently discouraged more customers from using Internet banking (Key Note Report 2004; Bughin 2001). Worldwide, banks have been striving to build robust technology that would alleviate the security concerns and address the problems of network capacities and regulatory complexities to increase the attractiveness of Internet banking to their customers.

The above discussion has set the context regarding the key drivers underpinning the growth of Internet banking in business practice. Within the academic literature on services marketing though, certain research gaps can be detected. Extant research has essentially focussed on service encounters between service providers and customers and at an overall service level. Although customer experience with SST and its service outcome and satisfaction is mentioned as an important area of study (e.g. Dabholkar & Bagozzi 2002; Bitner et al. 2000), it has not been explored substantially (Jamal 2004; Meuter et al. 2003, 2000).

From a channel perspective, research has investigated issues of channel choice and adoption in banking (Black et al. 2002; Howcroft et al. 2002). However, the notion of technology-based channels has been researched from

Table 10.1 Technology-based drivers and inhibitors for the development of Internet Banking

Drivers	Inhibitors
• Possibility for services to be delivered using standardised modular software	• Customer security, although improved, remains an issue, not least in terms of customer perceptions
• Easy management of software	• Restrictions on the capacity of networks to cope with traffic remains for customers who do not own a broadband package
• A common browser front-end	• Complex regulations
• Possibility to be equipped with good security portals	
• Easy application of pre-packaged communications software, enabling customers to communicate directly with the bank	
• Instant access to the bank for all connected customers	

Source: Compiled from Key Note Report – Electronic Banking (2004:23)

the adoption–diffusion perspective as to when and whether customers choose to use technology-based self-service channels and for what banking purpose. While the long-term service maintenance role of channels and the fact that customers use a range of delivery channels for the long-term service maintenance activity is acknowledged in literature (e.g. Howcroft et al. 2002), it remains empirically under researched. The remainder of the chapter draws upon empirical evidence to examine customer experiences and the social consequences of Internet banking . Before doing so, the research procedures followed for investigating the phenomenon are briefly outlined.

10.3 Researching Customer Experience and Social Consequences of Internet Banking

This chapter presents insights from qualitative research conducted with customers of a UK retail bank regarding their experience of using human and SST-based channels for banking activities. The findings reported here are a part of a larger research programme to investigate multiple stakeholder perspectives on the role and contribution of multiple channel integration in building firm customer relationships conducted by the author in a case study of a UK retail bank (Banerjee 2006). This research study adopted a qualitative research methodology to facilitate an in-depth enquiry of the phenomenon by capturing people's experiences in their own words, study context specific influences and processes, isolate and define categories as precisely as possible and determine the relationships between them (Patton 2002; Cresswell 1998).

In order to ensure consistency, customers of the case study bank who were bounded by the common experience of the case study bank's retail products, services and channels were recruited for interviewing. The mass market customer segment of retail banking was chosen because of segment size and diversity in terms of age, income, products and channel used and life-stage needs. This customer segment was appropriate for 'maximum variation sampling' (Yin 2003; Miles & Huberman 1994). This sampling method enabled the selection of a wide range of cases that would help in identifying important common patterns cutting across variations (Patton 2002).

A screening questionnaire was used for recruitment using pre-determined criteria regarding the respondent's bank(s)/building society(s) association and its duration, types of products held and duration, channels used for banking activities, and demographic descriptors of age, education and occupation. All respondents were above 21 years of age. Out of a total 109 people contacted, 31 respondents were interviewed, divided equally across both gender and age groups. Data collection used in-depth face-to-face interviews with critical incident technique embedded in the interviews. Data management and analysis used QSR*NUDIST for data coding and memoing. The sorting and coding of critical incidents followed the suggestions of Bitner et al. (1990) and Van Dolen et al. (2001). Each interview was treated as a separate 'case' and within-case and cross-case analysis (Miles & Huberman 1994) was used for data analysis procedures. The key findings on customers' experiences and social consequences of Internet banking are presented next.

10.4 Customer Experiences of Internet Banking

A profile of the Internet banking users and non-users is presented in Table 10.2 that sets the context for the further presentation of the research findings.

As presented in Table 10.2, more than half of respondents were not using the SST channel of Internet banking . Among the non-users, the following sub-groups could be identified from the data. Those who are

- not computer literate
- not doing Internet banking but open to the idea
- using computers and Internet at work and for leisure but not inclined to use for banking activities
- using Internet banking with other banks but not the case study bank
- registered for Internet banking but are non-users

The respondent profile data was further analysed to determine whether there were any patterns with regards to demographic factors that could indicate reasons for non-usage. These details are summarised in Appendix A. No definitive pattern or connection between the demographic characteristics and the explanatory sub-groups for Internet non-usage could be detected.

While it would be easy to dismiss the non-user group and say they add no value to the findings, this is not the case. The use of qualitative in-depth interviews and the critical incident technique helped to draw out insights about barriers to the use of Internet banking and more importantly, ideas from the respondents themselves that would enable them to use Internet banking. The subsequent sections will address these issues as they become relevant. The research findings are organised along the following three key themes:

Table 10.2 Internet banking users and non-users profile (Banerjee 2006)

	Internet banking and usage groups	N	%
Non-users	Do not use Internet banking	18	15.1
Users	Use Internet banking only to check account balance and print monthly statements	5	16.1
	Use Internet banking to check account balance and pay bills but not confident of moving money between accounts	2	6.5
	Use Internet banking to check account balance, pay bills and move money across accounts	6	19.3
	Total	31	100

- Customers as service co-producers and/or employees
- Transfer of work from customers to employees
- Contradiction of convenience and stress

10.4.1 Customers as Service Co-Producers and/or Employees

Within the services marketing literature, customers and customer relationships are conceptualised as valuable resources of the firm because customers are perceived to be co-designers and co-producers of the service offered (Gauthier & Schmid 2003). In the era of SSTs, however, customers are increasingly turning into 'employees' of service firms (Oliver et al. 2007; Halbesleben & Buckley 2004; Keh & Teo 2001; Mills & Morris 1986). This notion of customers as employees is manifest in several service settings, such as online grocery shopping, online air ticket or holiday booking and purchase, online insurance quote generation and purchase, and online apparel purchase. These are a few examples of the ever increasing business situations where customers are increasingly taking on tasks through an SST channel such as the Internet, which would otherwise be performed by an organisational employee such as a grocery store staff member, travel agent, insurance provider or apparel retailing shop assistant.

Specific to Internet banking , customers who are using this SST channel are performing a range of banking activities that contribute to long-term service maintenance. These activities include checking account balances, printing account statements, paying bills, setting up direct debits and standing orders and transferring money across accounts. All of these activities were traditionally performed by a bank teller at the bank branch. In present times, banks that operate multiple channels such as branch, ATM, telephone and Internet, provide the option for customers to perform these activities through any of these channels. A recent and growing trend, though, is for pure Internet-based banks, as discussed earlier, where the bank has no physical entity and the Internet is the only medium through which a customer can perform these service activities.

Schneider and Bowen (1995) have argued that there are tangible benefits such as lower prices, and intangible benefits such as speedier service when customers turn into employees through the use of SSTs. In the context of retail banking, banks use a 'push' and 'pull' strategy to encourage customers to use SSTs. Specifically for Internet banking , as a 'pull' strategy, banks often use the incentive of higher interest rates on Internet-only-based savings accounts. The Dutch bank ING Direct has been successful in establishing a large customer base by employing this strategy of offering its savings accounts only through the Internet. Increasingly, high street retail banks in the UK are adopting a similar approach in migrating customers to Internet-based banking by offering increased interest rates on Internet-only savings accounts.

Where banks offer a human interface channel such as a branch, as well as an SST channel such as the Internet, both forms of employee engagement are evident, i.e. the bank's employees are performing the service activities as well as customers themselves. In the case of pure Internet-based banks, customers are operating as employees of the banks and carrying out the bank transactional activities through the Internet.

In the context of retail banking services, it is not enough to only understand whether customers are using Internet banking or not, but also to build an understanding of their level of comfort with the SST channel. In this study, some interesting findings were uncovered. Not only is there a wide spectrum of usage from limited to extended, but also a relationship between the activities performed and the degree of experience with Internet banking. The level of maturity with Internet banking did not correspond with the type of activities performed through Internet banking. It appeared to be more a consequence of the customer's comfort level with the Internet as a medium and hence its use for banking activities. For instance, a respondent had been using Internet banking for 2 years, but did so only to check account balances, as security concerns inhibited this person from paying bills and transferring money. On the other hand, another respondent had been using Internet banking only for 6 months but used it for a wide range of activities despite the security concerns. Also, there was no indication from the research data that younger people were using Internet banking to a greater extent than older people, in line with a general belief that the younger generation is more Internet savvy.

The above issue has implications for a retail bank's strategy of providing Internet banking . From a retail bank's perspective, the organisational motive of providing SST channels is to provide consumer choice and to lower transaction and operating costs. However, the insight that a customer's comfort level with the medium underpins the usage can be harnessed by the banks in providing support to customers who might be positively pre-disposed to the idea of Internet banking but are unable to do so, given their limited skills in understanding or using the medium.

10.4.2 Transfer of Work from Customers to Employees

The preceding discussion focused on how SST encourages customers to become 'employees' of the organisation by undertaking service tasks that would otherwise be performed by the organisation's employees. While SST creates the transfer of work from employees to customers, there is also research evidence suggesting that there are instances when Internet-based activities also transfer back work from the customer to the supplier organisation. Oliver and Romm (2006) in their research of grocery shopping on the Internet identify that while customers perform the task of virtually selecting their grocery items, they also create work for the supermarket staff to select, pack and deliver the items to the customer.

Similar evidence of transfer of work back from the customer to the supplier organisation can be found in the case of Internet-based retail banking. With reference to Table 10.2, the non-users (a) who had registered for Internet banking but did not use the service, and, (b) the ones who were not doing Internet banking but were open to the idea, expressed the need for a reference point that would guide them in the use of Internet banking. The branch as a channel was their preferred choice as a reference point because it physically represented the bank with the possibility of interacting with the branch staff for guidance in using Internet banking as opposed to receiving written instructions in the mail and trying to follow them on one's own.

A range of suggestions emerged during the data gathering process regarding educating people about Internet banking . These suggestions ranged from providing basic information on applying for Internet banking, ways of using the Internet banking facility for a variety of banking activities, educating people about malicious software and understanding the types of protection customers need to take to avoid compromising their personal financial information to hackers.

Further, there were suggestions of providing support and information at the branches through computer and Internet demonstrations by branch staff on Internet banking , providing kiosks within the bigger branches where people could learn more about Internet banking and how it can be useful for them. Another suggestion was that the bank could consider putting all the information on a user friendly CD-ROM that customers could either take home or go through at the branch and use as a learning tool. The following interview excerpts illustrate the point:

> Nobody educated me about that. One day if I go the bank [branch] and the bank [branch] has a section of Internet banking and they say ok if you want me to teach you how, just come over and I will show you, may be once a day or twice day – a morning or evening session.. In the beginning of course you have to educate people to do that otherwise they don't want to do that. [Male, 20s]
>
> They could at the branch set up the Internet kind of thing so that people could get used to setting up their account there. I wouldn't have held back if they had said that you visit the branch and set up the account there, probably I would have set it up faster. Some branches could offer you these facilities that you go there, they guide you, train you through the site. So if you don't have Internet at home, you can instead of waiting in the queue just sit there and do your transactions. [Male, 40s]

Banks, owing to competitive pressures, cost-cutting measures and the functionality offered through technology developments have attempted to migrate customers' everyday banking activities to SSTs such as the Internet. The provision of SST channels has allowed banks to reduce branch staff and even close branches. However, research findings such as the ones discussed above indicate that in order to increase the uptake of Internet banking , there is a need for employees located in branches to educate and encourage these potential Internet users. So, while customers and as these research findings indicate, specifically non-users of Internet banking, are open to the idea of using Internet banking, they see a need for the bank and its branch staff, to educate them about the use of Internet banking. If this were to occur, it would generate work for bank staff, and a change in the roles and responsibilities of the frontline staff interfacing with customers. In order to assist customers in learning to use SST channels, the role of the branch staff would change from a transaction-based activity such as branch teller to a more consultative and customer service support role.

10.4.3 Contradiction of Convenience and Stress

The contradiction of convenience and stress in the use of SST has been discussed in the extant literature (Richardson 2005). Undoubtedly, while banks have actively worked in migrating customers to SST channels such as the ATM, phone and Internet banking , customers too, have been attracted by the convenience of banking at a location and hour of their choice. However, this notion of convenience is also accompanied by stress, as discussed next.

In this study, several issues that lead to stress with Internet banking usage were identified. The most obvious concern is that of trust and risk of fraud, which is widely discussed in academia and business practice. Many users stated that they had migrated to Internet banking on their own initiative and learnt it themselves. Several of the non-users, who were open to the idea of Internet banking wanted more information, particularly about the perceived security risks. In fact, the security of information passed over the Internet was by far the biggest concern voiced by the respondents across genders and life stage groups. There was no difference between Internet banking users and non-users regarding their concern with the security of information. Differences, if any, were evident in the approach to security by respondents who used Internet banking extensively and were familiar with features such as firewalls and anti-spam software. This group of respondents took the security issue in their stride and tried to be cautious of spam mails soliciting account information. At the same time, they expected the bank to provide a very high level of security for online banking and educate them about security issues. Following from the security of information, the respondents raised their concern about the protection available to customers in case of information misuse by a third party. Respondents stated they were not aware of precautionary measures. During the interview, it was probed whether they had come across any information on the same in communications received from the bank. The respondents stated that either they could not recall getting any information or were not clear on it and felt the branch staff could help them understand these things better. The overarching need articulated by the respondents was to have clear and precise information from the bank regarding procedures to be followed and the extent of help to be provided by the bank in the event of any misuse.

The second issue leading to stress relates to mistakes committed by customers while performing their banking activities through Internet banking . The respondents stated that since they were still learning to do online transactions, they were apprehensive of making mistakes and resolving them. There was an expectation that the bank should help them in a difficult situation, for instance money getting credited to a wrong account during an online money transfer.

The third issue leading to stress related to technology malfunction and its consequences for customers. Several respondents said that they were apprehensive of doing more than just checking their account balance through Internet banking because of the fear of a technology malfunction and its unknown consequences. Specifically, they mentioned that if the onus of error was not on the customer, then there was no tangible proof to support their claim should anything go wrong. Additionally, the respondents were not comfortable with the option of communicating with channels such as phones and call centres where the customer has no record of the communication, and for a follow up, has to speak with different call centre service staff, and is required to repeat the query, request or complaint.

In all of the above situations, respondents voiced the need for integrating services between the two channels branch and the Internet because the branch offered the physical form of the bank where the customer could go for problem resolution in case of such eventualities of errors with Internet banking . The following interview excerpts provide salient examples:

> If there is a building like the branch – something solid and people you can actually contact then you are assured that you are dealing with someone. [Female, 20s]
>
> With doing transactions through Internet banking , to be able to go to the branch and tell them the date and the transaction and can you check if it is right or wrong. [Male, 30s]
>
> With doing things through the online banking, if things go wrong then I would want to speak to someone for peace of mind that it has been fixed, rather than me attempting to fix it and hoping that it is done. So no if I did something wrong, then I would like to be able to go to the bank [branch] and getting them to fix it. [Female, 30s]

What is revealing from these research findings is not just empirical evidence in the retail banking context of the apparent contradiction of convenience and issues leading to stress but a very clear expectation of the customers to receive support from a physical channel such as the branch, in the use of an SST channel like Internet banking . It is suggested by Meuter et al. (2003) that respondents with higher levels of technology anxiety use fewer SSTs. This research study did not set out to measure the levels of technology anxiety. Rather, this study finds different issues leading to stress, which can be alleviated with correctly managed service processes and procedures, as articulated by the respondents themselves.

10.5 Social Consequences of Internet Banking

Organisations such as retail banks provide SSTs with the motives of reducing service delivery costs and providing consumer choice for accessing their retail banking activities. The customer experience of using an SST such as Internet banking throws up a variety of issues, as discussed in the preceding section. Certain social consequences are borne out of this interaction between the organisational provision of Internet banking and the customers' experience of Internet banking.

In this study, firstly, the element of control emerged as a salient feature from the use of Internet banking . By no longer being restricted by branch opening times, the customers experienced a sense of control by conducting their banking activities at their convenience. This notion is in line with discussions in the extant consumer behaviour literature. In the digital environment, since the navigation can be structured by the consumer, there is a high level of perceived control over the experience (Dholakia & Bagozzi 2001). The sense of control appeared to be manifest in the customers being able to monitor the banking activity being performed, such as the movement of money across accounts by observing it happen on the computer screen. This is something they do not experience when a teller performs the activity at the branch or a call centre agent does it over the phone. This aspect of using an SST channel such as Internet banking as an instrument of control is consistent with the findings of Kapoulas et al. (2004). The following interview excerpts illustrate the point:

> Internet banking , I think is a really good service. I really enjoy that because I feel much more in control where things are going and it is in your time as well. [Female-30s]
>
> Earlier as I said I would use the telephone and do through that. But now I feel more in control because I am doing it myself then. I am transferring money, you see it is being transferred and confirmed that you want it transferred. Then you can go and look into the account that it has been. So I find that very good. [Female-50 +]

Secondly, is the aspiration of doing 'more' with this form of SST channel. As discussed in the previous sections, for some of the non-users, there is an aspiration of wanting to use Internet banking by suggesting ways in which their banks can enable them to do so. Among some of the users, as a manifestation of consumer expertise (Dholakia & Bagozzi 2001), there is an emerging desire to enhance their usage and thereby demand more functionality and features from Internet banking. The following quotations reflect this need for greater functionality to be made available for Internet banking.

> Do online applications for loans, overdrafts and go to the branch to collect the money. [Male-20s Male-30s, Male-30s]
>
> Excel spreadsheet facility on the website to analyse your spending patterns after seeing past monthly statements online – just to have the graphs and customers can calculate for themselves. [Male-30s]

Something like...a mortgage calculator and things like that so you can track the money. It is more about how I can use my money smarter by using my credit card doing things like that. If I paid an extra £50 every month, what difference would it make to my interest rate. Those kind of things just to help. [Female-30s]

... like a calculator if you are looking for loan or something you can add an extra amount and in how many months you want to pay it over and it will tell you..that type of thing is quite good I suppose to check how much interest to pay or the amount or the time. [Female-30s]

The overall social consequence relates to the interaction-building capability of Internet banking . It is evident that the branch (as a channel) by its nature facilitates personal interaction opportunities. Branch staff can build a relationship in the bank–customer interactions. Interestingly, the role of a technology-based channel, such as the Internet, as an interaction builder emerged from the study. Among the users of Internet banking, it was the main channel of interaction with the bank and not the branch. This was primarily for the convenience offered by the Internet in terms of not being restricted by branch opening times. So despite its impersonal nature, the virtual channel is the primary means through which a customer is connected to his/her bank. Internet banking customers use this channel of their own volition and are happy with it.

10.6 Conclusions

This chapter has discussed the potential of an SST like Internet banking to act as a relationship builder between a bank and its customers. The chapter outlined the organisational motives of banks in providing technology-based channels for everyday banking activities. The key drivers in this industry sector are the lowering of transaction and operating costs and offering customers the convenience of anytime banking. Drawing upon research evidence from a UK retail banking context, this chapter has then discussed the three key aspects of the customer experience of SST use: customers turning into employees, the transfer of work back from customers to employees and the contradiction of convenience and stress.

In the context of the research findings discussed in this chapter, for each of these three aspects, the potential of a virtual and remote channel like Internet banking to create better relationships between the bank and its customers became salient. The value of relationships is in improving the bank's ability to understand the needs of their customers and in making provisions to assist non-users in adopting Internet banking. This would open to more users the convenience offered by the medium, enhance usage and derive more benefits for both parties from this SST. From the point of view of the social consequences of SST use, this chapter demonstrates the potential for enhancing the interaction-building capabilities of Internet banking.

The chapter has discussed how banks have used a combination of 'push' and 'pull' strategy to increase the uptake of automated channels such as ATM, phone and Internet banking . Further, there is discussion in the literature of customers turning into employees and undertaking work on behalf of an organisation. The findings of the research study discussed here identify in certain cases, customer willingness and enthusiasm to increase the use of SST channels such as Internet banking. This group of Internet banking users have twinned the concepts of *convenience* and *control* and do not appear to view this as 'work' that they are undertaking in conducting the banking activities. The strategy of banks to influence their customers to use SSTs to perform banking activities that would normally be done by the bank staff is readily accepted by many customers. In turn, customers are pushing for innovations and new functionalities that would actually contribute to an increased use of Internet banking. So we find an emerging situation where both the banks and the customers are using 'push' and 'pull' strategies that can actually lead to an enhanced use of automated channels.

While the above discussion appears to indicate that the use of automated channels is growing and always positively received, this may not always be the case. As discussed earlier in this chapter, in times of technology malfunctions and service failures with automated channels, customers mention the need for a human interface for service recovery and problem solving. Where there is an element of convenience and control in using Internet banking , a system failure can turn that into frustration. Additionally, the use of an SST-based channel is not likely to be appropriate or meet the needs of every customer type. So, regardless of the convenience on offer, technology-based channels cannot completely eliminate the human channel.

Bitner (2001) and Bitner et al. (2000) argue that the technology in service encounters should be able to effectively customise service offerings, recover from service failure, and spontaneously delight customers. If the worldwide trends of innovation in technology-based banking are anything to go by, there appear to be efforts from the retail banks in that direction. The continuous developments in strengthening the technology to detect fraud and minimise the security risks of Internet banking are appropriate steps in the direction of allaying customer concerns that have hindered the adoption and usage of Internet banking. More recent developments include the offer of mobile banking services by Wells Fargo & Co. and ING Direct to their customers (Bills 2007a,b), and Power Financial Credit Union providing the facility to deposit checks through Internet banking (Wade 2007). These innovative service offerings not only attempt to address continuously evolving customer needs but also use the differentiation of services in an increasingly commoditised marketplace to attract and more importantly retain customers. Technological developments continue to play a key role in this service innovation process.

The research findings discussed in this study, contribute to our understanding of the customers' use of an SST like Internet banking , its current status and untapped potential. Further, this research was carried out within the context of a specific country. Just as banking regulations vary across countries, so do the motivations of banks to provide automated channels and encourage customers to use the same. There are situations of banking charges and fees to push customers towards the use of automated channels. An investigation of such a scenario can provide further insights into customers turning into employees, type of work transferred from the customer back to employees and the emergent social consequences of adopting automated channels such as Internet banking. Would customers be willing to enhance their use of Internet banking or would there be any negative implications, given the coercive nature of having to adopt it in the first instance? This can be an area of further investigation. Along with the diversity of banking regulations, business pressures to maintain competitiveness, evolving consumer behaviour trends and new technological developments on the horizon, the extent to which automated channels such as Internet banking can enhance bank-customer relationships and deliver on the promise, remains an area of further research.

Appendix: Demographic Profile of Respondents – Users and Non-users of Internet Banking

Non-users (n = 18)	Gender and age group	Salary band	Education	Occupation
Not computer literate (N = 2)	Males 50 +	Pensioner	School	Library Assistant
		< £20,000	School	
Not doing Internet banking but open to the idea (N = 3)	Male 40–49 years = 2	< £20,000	School	Self employed-business
		£20,000–30,000	School	Security Officer
	Female 40–49 years = 1	£20,000–30,000	University UG	Secretary
Use computers and Internet at work and for leisure but not inclined to use for banking purpose (N = 10)	Female 20–29 years = 2	< £20,000	University PG	Teacher
		< £20,000	University UG	Junior Nurse
	Males 20–29 years = 3	< £20,000	University PG	Student
		< £20,000	University UG	Temp Worker
		< £20,000	University UG	Marketing Executive
	Female 40–49 years = 1	< £20,000	School	Print unit staff
	Female 50 + = 3	< £20,000	School	Administrative Staff
		Pensioner	School	Voluntary Social Service
		< £20,000	School	Secretary
	Male 50 + = 1	£20,000–30,000	College Diploma	Car Salesperson

Appendix (*Continued*)

Non-users (n = 18)	Gender and age group	Salary band	Education	Occupation
Using Internet banking with other bank but not the case study bank (N = 2)	Male 20–29 years	< £20,000	University PG	Student
	Female 30–39 years	£20,000–30,000	University UG	IT Developer
Registered for Internet banking but non-users (N = 1)	Male 30–39 years	£30,000–40,000	University PG	Project Manager-Construction
Users (n = 13)				
Use Internet banking only to check account balance and print monthly statements (N = 5)	Male 30–39 years = 3	< £20,000	University PG	Student
		< £20,000	University PG	Student
		£30,000–40,000	University UG	Project Manager-IT
	Female 40–49	£20,000–30,000	University PG	Teacher
	years = 2	£30,000–40,000	University UG	Administration Manager
Use Internet banking to check account balance and pay bills but not confident of moving money between accounts (N = 2)	Female 20–29 years = 1	< £20,000	University PG	Student
	Female 30–39 years = 1	£20,000–30,000	University UG	Data analyst
Use Internet banking to check account balance, pay bills and move money across accounts (N = 6)	Female 20–29 years = 1	< £20,000	University PG	University research staff
	Female 30–39 years = 2	£30,000–40,000	University UG	Marketing Manager
		< £20,000	University UG	Secretary
	Male 40–49 years = 2	< £20,000	University PG	Mature student-career break
	Female 50+ = 1	£20,000–30,000	School	Secretary

Source: Banerjee (2006)

References

Banerjee M (2006) Multiple Channel Integration Process in CRM: Contribution to Firm-Customer Relationships, Case Study of a UK Retail Bank. PhD Thesis. University of Strathclyde, UK

Bills S (2007a) Wells starts a mobile service. American Banker 00027561, 172, (142), 7/25/2007

Bills S (2007b) ING Direct offers mobile banking. American Banker 00027561, 172, (131), 7/10/2007

Bitner M (2001) Self-service technologies: what do customers expect? Marketing Management 10(1):10–12

Bitner M, Brown S, Meuter M (2000) Technology infusion in service encounters. Journal of the Academy of Marketing Science 28(1):138–150

Bitner M, Booms B, Tetreault M (1990) The service encounter: diagnosing favourable and unfavourable incidents. Journal of Marketing 54(January):71–84

Black N, Lockett A, Ennew C, Winklhofer H, McKechnie S (2002) Modelling consumer choice of distribution channels: an illustration from financial services. The International Journal of Bank Marketing 20(4):161–173

Bughin J (2001) Giving Europeans an Online Push. McKinsey Quarterly. www.mckinsey.com. Accessed 28 July 2007

Claessens S, Glaessner T, Klingebiel D (2002) Electronic finance: Reshaping the financial landscape around the world. Journal of Financial Services Research 22(1/2):29–61

Cresswell JW (1998) Qualitative inquiry and research design: Choosing among five traditions. Sage, Thousand Oaks, CA

Dabholkar P, Bagozzi R (2002) An attitudinal model of technology-based self-service: moderating effects of consumer traits and situational factors. Journal of the Academy of Marketing Science 30(3):184–202

Deloitte Touche Tohmatsu (2006) Global Financial Services Industry Outlook: Shaping Your Strategy in a Changing World. www.deloitte.com. Accessed 12 December 2006

Dholakia U, Bagozzi R (2001) Consumer Behaviour in Digital Environments. In: Wind J, Mahajan V (eds) Digital Marketing: Global Strategies from the World's Leading Experts, Wiley, New York

Ennew C, McKechnie S (1998) The financial services consumer. In: Gabbott M, Hogg G (eds) Consumers and Services, Wiley, Chichester

Fujitsu (n.d.) First Direct. www.fujitsu.com/uk/casestudies/fs_firstdirect.html. Accessed 31 July 2007

Gauthier M, Schmid, S (2003) Customers and customer relationships in service firms: the perspective of the resource-based view. Marketing Theory 3(1):119–143

Grief S, Wetenhall P, Matre B (2000) Banking in Internet Time. Boston Consulting Group, www.bcg.com. Accessed 27 June 2007

Halbesleben JRB, Buckley RM (2004) Managing customers as employees of the firm – new challenges for human resources management. Personnel Review 33(3):351–372

Harrison T (2000) Financial services marketing. Heinemann, Oxford

Hodes M, Hall G, Roseberg L (1999) Issues and Outlook 2000: United States: E-Finance. Goldman Sachs and Co. Investment Research, New York

Howcroft B, Hamilton R, Hewer P (2002) Consumer attitude and the usage and adoption of home-based banking in the United Kingdom. The International Journal of Bank Marketing 20(3):111–121

Jamal A (2004) Retail banking and customer behaviour: A study of self-concept, satisfaction and technology use. International Review of Retail, Distribution and Consumer Research 14(3)July:357–379

Kapoulas A, Ellis N, Murphy W (2004) The voice of the customer in e-banking relationships. Journal of Customer Behaviour 3(1)Spring:27–52

Keh HT, Teo CW (2001) Retail customers as partial employees in service provision: a conceptual framework. International Journal of Retail and Distribution Management 29:370-378 Key Note Market Assessment Report (2004) Electronic Banking

Krebsbach K (2003) Taming the dragon. Bank Technology News September, 16(9):42–43

Meuter M, Ostrom A, Bitner M, Roundtree R (2003) The influence of technology anxiety on consumer use and experiences with self-service technologies. Journal of Business Research 56(11):899–906

Meuter M, Ostrom A, Roundtree R, Bitner M (2000) Self-service technologies: understanding customer satisfaction with technology-based service encounters. Journal of Marketing 64(July):50–64

Miles MB, Huberman AM (1994) Qualitative Data Analysis. Sage, Thousand Oaks, CA

Mills PK, Morris JH (1986) Clients as partial employees of service organisations: role development in client participation. Academy of Management Review 11:726–735

Oliver D, Livermore C, Farag N (2007) Self-service on the Internet: An explanatory model. Proceedings 20th Bled e-Conference on eMergence: Merging and emerging technologies, processes and institutions, Bled Slovenia, June

Oliver D, Romm C (2006) Grocery Shopping: Down the virtual aisle. Proceedings of Internet Research 7.0: Internet Convergences, Brisbane, Australia

Patton MQ (2002) Qualitative research and evaluation methods. Sage Thousand Oaks, CA

Richardson H (2005) Consuming passions in the global knowledge economy. In: Howcroft D, Trauth EM (eds) Handbook of Critical Information Systems Research: Theory and Application. Edward Elgar, Cheltenham

Schneider B, Bowen DE (1995) Winning the Service Game. Harvard Business School Press, Boston, MA

Van Dolen W, Lemmink J, Mattsson J, Rhoen I (2001) Affective consumer responses in service encounters: the emotional content in narratives of critical incidents. Journal of Economic Psychology 22:359–376

Wade W (2007) Credit union takes deposit data online. American Banker 00027561, 172, (131), 7/10/2007

West L (2001) Online banking becomes a commodity in Europe, Bank Technology News 14(5)May:64.

Yin R (2003) Case Study Research: Design and Methods. Sage, Thousand Oaks, CA

Chapter 11
Sense or Sensibility?: How Commitment Mediates the Role of Self-Service Technology on Loyalty

Sangeeta Singh and Line Lervik Olsen

Abstract It has been well documented that employing self-service technology (SST) results in considerable cost savings but few studies have examined its impact on consumers' behavior. We apply a well-recognized model from the field of services marketing in an SST context. We examine how the established relationships between satisfaction, affective and calculative commitments, and loyalty are affected when the service is provided through a technology interface as opposed to service personnel. We then present two alternative perspectives on the role of SST. The first is based on the predominant assumption that SST is a moderator of the relationship between customer loyalty and its drivers, while the other rests on the assumption that SST is just another context and that its role in affecting customer loyalty is mediated by drivers of loyalty. A cross-sectional study conducted in the banking industry shows that SST does not change everything. The classical model of how customers evaluate services and the predictors of loyalty are replicated in the SST setting. Interestingly, SST does not have a direct influence on loyalty by itself but its effects are mediated by commitment. However, it is the affective commitment that is more important in forming loyalty toward the service provider.

11.1 Introduction

One of the dilemmas facing firms in this age of technology is to what extent they should automate the services that have traditionally been provided by humans. While it has been documented that employing self-service technology (SST) results in considerable cost savings (Meuter et al. 2005), it has also been shown that firms that primarily adopt a revenue expansion emphasis perform better than those that emphasize cost savings (Rust et al. 2002). This indicates that one should focus on how SST may help expand revenues rather than save costs. The ability to compete in the business environment is dependent on how companies

S. Singh (✉)
BI Norwegian School of Management, Oslo, Norway
e-mail: sangeeta.singh@bi.no

D. Oliver et al. (eds.), *Self-Service in the Internet Age*,
DOI 10.1007/978-1-84800-207-4_11, © Springer-Verlag London Limited 2009

balance their short- and long-term cost cutting with revenue generating activities. According to Rust et al. (2004), one way of expanding revenues is to increase customers' lifetime value or customer equity, which is in part driven by retention equity (the other two being value and brand equity). Retention equity is defined as the gains from retention programs and relationship building (Rust et al. 2000). The literature on personal services suggests that to be able to build effective retention programs and lasting customer relationships requires a company to make customers loyal and committed by providing good and satisfactory service (e.g., Johnson et al. 2001). But in the literature on SST the predominant underlying assumption seems to be that technology is changing everything. According to Parasuraman and Grewal (2000) "technology is likely to be a (if not the) major force in shaping buyer–seller interactions in the future" (p. 170). Consequently, the question we examine in this chapter is if we can apply the insights from research on personal service to the SST context or does SST play such a dominating role that we have to start all over again, looking for new drivers of customer loyalty in this particular context? In order to answer these questions, we apply existing theories and a well-established model from the field of services marketing to an SST context. To investigate this research question, a cross-sectional study was conducted in the banking industry , an industry in which customers interact with their service provider in a variety of ways, including both personal interactions and those conducted remotely via SSTs.

11.2 Serving the Customer with Self-Service Technology

When reviewing the literature on SST within the marketing discipline, three main streams crystallize: research on adoption and implementation (Curran & Meuter 2005; Bitner et al. 2002; Meuter et al. 2003, 2005), attitudes toward SST (Simon & Usunier 2007; Dabholkar & Bagozzi 2002; Bobbit & Dabholkar 2001; Dabholkar 1996) and evaluations of SST vis-à-vis quality, satisfaction and loyalty (Froehle 2006; Fassnacht & Koese 2006; Meuter et al. 2000; Parasuraman et al. 2005; Beatson et al. 2006). In addition to these streams, some researchers also suggest a future research agenda for SST (Parasuraman & Zinkhan 2002; Parasuraman & Grewal 2000; Zeithaml et al. 2002; Zinkhan 2002).

11.2.1 Adoption of SST

Early research on the adoption of SST focuses on two aspects: consumers' readiness in adopting technology as a means of interface and the consumers' propensity for the initial trial. The predictors for both these behaviors are borrowed from the widely accepted adoption of innovation literature, where compatibility with existing behavior, the relative advantage of the new technology, complexity of the technology, the observability of the technology in use, its benefits and the ease of trial are the variables of interest. Some other predictors studied are the perceived risk of technology, the inertia of the customer to change to a new form of interface, anxiety related with the use of technology, the need for human interaction, previous experience with technology and demographic variables like age, sex, gender, education and income (for a review of this literature read Meuter et al. 2005). However, these studies merely establish the direct relationship between the predictor variables and the two dependent variables of interest: consumer's readiness to adopt technology and trial of technology rather than investigating more complex relationships.

Meuter et al. (2005) explore the key factors that influence the initial SST trial decision for situations in which the consumer has the option of using existing methods. The authors note that consumers' readiness as defined by their role clarity, motivation and ability mediates the trial and adoption of SST. Similarly, Zeithaml et al. (2002) expect the consumers' technology readiness, defined as their ability and competence to use technology, to affect their adoption of SST.

It is our belief that SST is no longer a new phenomenon and therefore our primary concern should not be that of adoption but rather acquiring an understanding of its impact on variables of traditional interest in services, namely, satisfaction, loyalty, and quality. Apparently, we are not alone in our thinking as more recent studies have examined how consumers evaluate services when offered through a technological interface.

11.2.2 Evaluation of Service Delivery

Studies examining consumers' evaluation of services have used two perspectives. One is the typical variables of interest in services marketing and the other uses attitudinal variables from the consumer behavior literature. In their synthesis, Zeithaml et al. (2002) conclude that consumers' evaluation of services offered through a technological interface is based on concerns for privacy/security, efficiency and ease of use of the technology. This evaluation or perception of service quality impacts consumers' satisfaction, intent to purchase and repurchase. A key factor, though little researched, affecting the consumers' evaluation of services is technology readiness.

Meuter et al. (2000) identify the sources for both consumers' satisfaction and dissatisfaction with SST. Consumers are more satisfied with SST when it helps them in an emergency situation, is better than the alternative and performs the expected job. However, dissatisfaction results when it fails, either because of poor technology or ineptitude on part of the consumer, or it is poorly designed. In a separate study in 2003, the same authors show technological anxiety (defined as the users' state of mind regarding their ability and willingness to use technology related tools) to not only influence satisfaction and future intentions to use SST but also the likelihood to participate in word-of-mouth.

Although well-known researchers who have contributed significantly to the field of services marketing and research on personal services apply cumulative insights from previous studies, they tend to consider SST as a phenomenon that is totally new, which has more impact than if it were yet another service context. They pose the following questions for future research: "Is customer retention/ loyalty harder or easier to achieve when customers interact with technology rather than with employees? What boundary conditions or moderating factors are likely to be relevant in this regard?" (Parasuraman & Grewal 2000, p. 172). We, however, believe that SST is something that customers are by now used to, especially in the banking industry , where ATMs, pay by phone, and Internet banking have been available for a long time. Therefore, we explore two alternative roles of SST in this study: one as having a direct impact on loyalty through established relationships between its (loyalty's) drivers and the other where this impact is mediated by one of the drivers of loyalty.

11.2.3 Goals of the Study

Parasuraman (1996) transformed the services marketing triangle of company–employees–customers suggested by Kotler in 1994, into a pyramid with the inclusion of a fourth dimension, technology. The addition of this dimension in the services triangle creates a need to study the three new linkages of technology–company, technology–employee, and technology–customer and how these may be incorporated in the quality-value-loyalty chain with the ultimate goal of building customer loyalty . Of these three linkages, the technology–customer one is the most critical in affecting every aspect of the quality-value-loyalty chain, as quality and value perceptions, as well as the resulting loyalty, represent customers' assessment of their interactions with the company.

As mentioned previously, one of the issues raised by Parasuraman and Grewal (2000) relating to this particular linkage, is whether it is easier or more difficult to maintain loyal customers when they interact with technology as opposed to when they are served by service personnel. They also question the need to examine boundaries and moderating factors that might be relevant to building loyalty and consequently retaining customers. The goals of this study are founded on these two issues. The ideas and discussions put forth in the previous paragraphs suggest that substituting people with technology may not be as straightforward and simple a decision as some academics and practitioners may lead one to believe. We need a better understanding of the repercussions of SST on consumers' behavior to make this decision. For this reason, we visit issues of interest in services marketing to understand the impact of SST on selected consumers' behaviors.

To the best of our knowledge, the models or relationships between constructs well established in service marketing have not been tested for when SST is employed for providing the service. Therefore, we first examine how the existing relationships between satisfaction, affective and calculative commitments, and loyalty are affected when the service is provided through a technology interface as opposed to service personnel. Researchers Parasuraman and Zinkhan (2002) have emphasized the importance of studying the drivers of loyalty when serving customers through SST. They conclude in their article that customer loyalty is difficult to maintain on the Internet. "With just one click", they state, "buyers can transport themselves to an entirely new shopping site" and "factors that initially draw a buyer to a Web site might not necessarily be the ones that motivate that same buyer to return" (p. 291). In this study, we do not make an attempt at identifying "new" drivers of loyalty. What this work attempts to achieve is to identify boundaries or conditions that affect the role of SST in building loyalty. In line with this thought, we present and test two alternative perspectives on the role of SST. The first is based on the predominant assumption that SST is a moderator of the relationship between customer loyalty and its drivers, while the other rests on the assumption that SST is just another context and that its role in affecting customer loyalty is mediated by drivers of loyalty. Our second goal, therefore, is to seek out under what circumstances SST is successful in increasing customer loyalty. We begin by outlining the constructs of interest and the relationships between them, followed by a description of the data collection procedures, the analyses and its results, and conclude with a discussion of these.

11.3 The Drivers of Loyalty

As previously mentioned, customer loyalty is a very important means of increasing customers' lifetime value (Rust et al. 2000). For many years customer loyalty has been considered a key factor in generating profits for companies, as demonstrated in the works of Heskett et al. (1997) on the service-profit chain and Reichheld's (1996) work on loyalty. This line of thinking is highly compatible with the quality-value-loyalty link identified among other places in some of his own previous work with colleagues (for a brief review of this research see Parasuraman and Grewal 2000). But, what is loyalty? The most widely used definition of customer loyalty in the marketing field is provided by Richard L. Oliver, according to whom "*customer loyalty* is a deeply held commitment to rebuy or repatronize a preferred product or service consistently in the future, *despite* situational influences and marketing efforts having the potential to cause switching behavior" (Oliver 1996, p. 392). Loyalty goes through different phases, starting out with a cognitive phase where "the information base available to the consumer compellingly points to one brand over another" (p. 392). This phase is followed by an affective one, where there is a "strong intervention of affect, both as attitude and as the affective component of satisfaction in this second loyalty phase" (p. 393). Then a conative (behavioral intention) phase follows where "conative loyalty is a loyalty state containing the deeply held commitment to buy" (p. 393). Finally, the consumer enters a phase where intentions are converted to action and the consumer decides to do an actual repurchase. There are some critical variables affecting customer loyalty across these different phases.

11.3.1 Customer Satisfaction

Customer satisfaction is the most well-established driver of customer loyalty (e.g., Johnson et al. 2001). Again, according to Oliver (1996), "*customer satisfaction* is the consumer's fulfillment response. It is a judgment that a product or service feature, or the product itself, provided (or is providing) a *pleasurable* level of consumption-related fulfillment, including levels of under- or over-fulfillment" (p13). It impacts repurchase intentions (Anderson & Sullivan 1993), retention (Bolton 1998), secures future revenues (Fornell 1992; Rust et al. 1995), and reduces the cost of future transactions (Reichheld & Sasser 1990). Satisfied members of loyalty programs discount or overlook negative evaluations of a firm vis-à-vis the competition (Bolton et al. 2000).

Satisfied customers affect the long-term profitability of a firm. They buy more of a particular product or service, transaction costs of serving such customers are reduced; they provide a ready base for add-on services, thus increasing cross-buying and faster market penetration. They also provide more recommendations and positive word-of-mouth, enabling a firm to charge higher prices and increase its bargaining power with suppliers, partners and channels. All these factors combined together help the firm not only to be competitive in the marketplace but also to increase the shareholders' value (Anderson et al. 2004). Although researchers so far have established that customer satisfaction is a key driver of customer loyalty (Johnson et al. 2001 summarize this research), they are also starting to recognize that satisfaction may be complemented by other drivers in predicting customer loyalty. Some research recognizes that customer commitment not only has an important role in predicting customer loyalty (Johnson et al. 2001, Hansen et al. 2003) and in service provider relationships (Morgan and Hunt 1994) but also is related with satisfaction (see Johnson et al. 2001).

11.3.2 The Nature of Commitment – Affective and Calculative

Commitment as a construct in the field of marketing has been typically used in understanding relationships in marketing channels, where it has been applied to explain the relational exchanges between buyers and sellers (Dwyer et al. 1987), shown to be a key variable in mediating successful relationships (Morgan & Hunt 1994), deemed an essential part of successful long-term relationships (Gundlach et al. 1995) and demonstrated to mediate future intentions of repurchase (Garbarino & Johnson 1999). This kind of commitment is considered to be mutual, coming from both partners involved in the relationship.

The concept of commitment has emerged from research in organizational behavior and a three component framework suggested by Meyer and Allen in 1990, where the employees' commitment to the employer is conceptualized to reflect a desire, a need and an obligation to maintain a relationship with the organization. The first dimension is the affective part that reflects the acceptance of the organization's values, a willingness to exert effort, and a desire to maintain the relationship. The second dimension reflects the calculative commitment based on the need to continue the relationship as a result of recognizing the costs associated with its termination. The less common third component of obligation exhibits the individuals' normative belief that they ought to remain with the organization. Meyer and Allen (1990) believe it more appropriate to consider these three dimensions as components of commitment rather than types as done by previous researchers.

These dimensions of commitment are also recognized by Geyskens et al. (1996), Verhoef et al. (2002), and Gustafsson et al. (2005). However, all of the mentioned studies employ only two of the dimensions – the affective and the calculative. These two dimensions of commitments are distinguished on the basis of the different motivations that underlie the behavior or intention (Geyskens et al. 1996). Affectively motivated commitment is described as a desire to continue the relationship because of attachment and positive feelings for the partner. Calculative commitment, on the other hand, is the need to maintain the relationship due to the perceived costs associated with its termination or switching costs associated with leaving combined with foregoing the benefits of investments already made. Thus, calculative commitment is a cold assessment of the relationship that results in a economic-based dependence on the partner (Gustafsson et al. 2005).

These two dimensions of commitment are especially important to service marketers where customers often form affective affiliations with service personnel and therefore, incur higher switching costs compared to the consumption of products. Research shows that consumers' commitment to the service employee has a carryover effect on the commitment to the firm and has a strong effect on loyalty (Hansen et al. 2003). SST eliminates the affiliations formed to the firm via the psychological affiliations with the service employees, therefore reducing the affective commitment to it.

Verhoef et al. (2002) consider calculative commitment to be associated with a negative motivation to continuing a relationship because switching costs associated with the termination of the relationship are high. SST users have invested time and effort to learn the technology that helps them obtain the service. The prospect of negating this investment by switching to an alternative provider may deter them from so doing. Often, SST users have done their "homework" to identify the least "costly" service provider and switching to another one requires them to do the groundwork all over again, which is a time-consuming process. Their choice has been based on rational evaluations of the alternatives. Thus, it would be expected that there is a relationship between commitment and the preferred type of interface. However, the role of SST in impacting loyalty is not clear.

11.3.3 Role of SST – Moderator or Mediated?

Research in services marketing perceives SST to be a moderator of loyalty but we consider SST to be merely yet another context in which the service can be provided. However, given the important mediating role of affective and calculative commitment in explaining loyalty, we propose that this construct will play a similar role when SST is incorporated in the relationship. Based on this, we propose two alternative models where SST plays different roles in the formation of customer loyalty . In the first instance, we test the established relationship between loyalty and its drivers, satisfaction, affective and calculative commitment (see Fig. 11.1), to see if SST moderates it.

Although we do not refute this relationship between loyalty and its drivers, we contend that the impact of SST on loyalty is mediated by one of the drivers of loyalty, commitment. This new configuration of relationship is presented in Fig. 11.2 below.

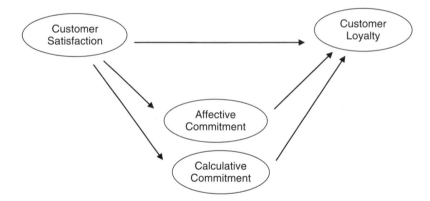

Fig. 11.1 SST as a moderator (adapted from Johnson et al. 2001) showing type of interface

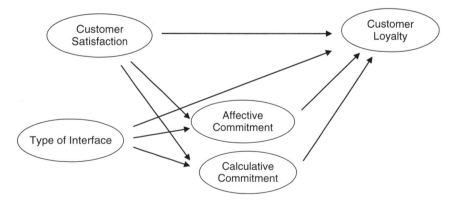

Fig. 11.2 SST mediated by commitment

11.4 Testing the Alternative Models

11.4.1 Data Collection

The banking industry is chosen as the context of investigation for this study for specific reasons. Financial institutions are progressively feeling the pressures of operating in an intensely competitive environment as a result of a greater than ever number of players in the marketplace vying with one another for a share from the same pie. Savvy and knowledgeable customers demand more from their banks than they used to. Better offers from competing institutions are able to wean them away from their current financial services provider and since there are few switching costs, this transition is relatively unhindered. The industry is thus characterized by a high number of "brands", furnishing very similar offerings in a market where there are few switching costs associated with moving from one brand to another. Building customer loyalty therefore, is critical. We believe this situation to be not typical for the financial services sector alone, but it provides a useful setting, as banking offers one of the most technologically advanced services available today. Customers can choose how to interact with the bank in various ways, including calling the bank, visiting it, ATMs, automated phone, or the Internet. The various methods of interface allow us to compare and contrast our proposed relationships under different circumstances and study the impact of SST on loyalty.

The data were collected in a cross-sectional study through the annual data collections of the leading customer satisfaction barometer in Norway. The data collection was conducted by a professional marketing research bureau, which interviewed the respondents by telephone. Prospective respondents who were not available on the first call were called back three times before a substitute was picked. Each interview lasted approximately 15 minutes. This subsample consists of the banking industry represented by the four largest banks in the country making up about 75 percent of the market share.

The sample consists of 743 respondents of which 358 prefer to visit the bank when using the bank's services, 151 prefer to use the automated phone bank, and 234 prefer to use Internet banking . Details of the sample are presented in Table 11.1.

11.4.2 Measures

Customer satisfaction, affective and calculative commitments and customer loyalty are all operationalized based on the works summarized in Johnson

Table 11.1 Sample description

Interface type	N	Men %	Women %	Average duration of relationship with bank
Visit	358	52	48	19 years
Phone	151	42	58	14 years
Internet	234	67	33	14 years

Table 11.2 Measures

Item	Variable
Likelihood of recommending service provider to others	Loyalty
Likelihood of speaking positively about service provider	Loyalty
Likelihood of continuing as customer	Loyalty
Overall satisfaction	Customer satisfaction
Performance versus the customer's ideal service provider in the category	Customer satisfaction
Expectancy disconfirmation (performance that falls short of or exceeds expectations)	Customer satisfaction
The pleasure taken in being a customer of the company	Affective commitment
Identification with what the company stands for	Affective commitment
Feeling of belongingness to the company	Affective commitment
The most profitable alternative	Calculative commitment
Location advantages versus other companies	Calculative commitment
Alternative service providers	Calculative commitment

et al. (2001). See Table 11.2 below for items. A 10-point Likert-type scale was applied when measuring the constructs, including exclusively positive values ranging from 1 to 10. The questionnaire consisted of two different scales anchored by "disagree" to "agree" and "dissatisfied" to "satisfied". Respondents were provided with a "don't know" and "cannot answer" option in case of indifference or lack of knowledge. The measures are presented in Table 11.2.

11.4.3 Data Analysis

Preliminary analysis of the data on the variables of interest (loyalty, satisfaction, affective, and calculative commitment) revealed that there were no significant differences between the groups of customers who preferred to use the automated phone bank and those who used Internet banking (means for these groups are presented in Table 11.3). Therefore, we combined these two groups using self-service technology as the interface with the bank to call them the SST group. The other group will now be referred to as the "Personal" group as shown in Table 11.4).

Alternative 1: Does SST moderate the relationship between satisfaction, commitment and loyalty or in other words, is loyalty of customers dependent on the interface method?

The objective of the first set of analyses was to confirm the already established relationship between satisfaction, affective and calculative commitment, and loyalty. This was done by exploring the following relationships:

1. Between satisfaction and affective and calculative commitment
2. Between satisfaction and loyalty
3. Between satisfaction, affective and calculative commitment, and loyalty

Table 11.3 Group means by interface type

Interface type	Loyalty	Satisfaction	Affective commitment	Calculative commitment
Visit	7.70	7.36	6.85	4.54
Phone	6.99	7.02	5.93	4.71
Internet	6.99	6.98	6.05	5.49

Table 11.4 Group means by interface type

Interface type	Loyalty[*]	Mediated loyalty	Satisfaction	Affective commitment[*]	Calculative commitment[*]
Personal	7.40	6.99	7.09	6.76	5.54
SST	6.82	7.14	6.87	5.93	4.73

[*]Significantly different at $p<.05$

These relationships were established by running four separate regressions as outlined in Table 11.5. In Regression 1, satisfaction was regressed on affective commitment, in Regression 2 on calculative commitment, and in Regression 3 on loyalty. Satisfaction, affective and calculative commitment were regressed simultaneously on loyalty in Regression 4. All of these regressions were significant at the 0.05 level. Moreover, the results show that the effect of satisfaction on loyalty is considerably reduced when affective and calculative commitment are included in the equation, which makes us conclude that the two commitments mediate the effect of satisfaction on loyalty. These results are in keeping with the findings of prior studies (Johnson et al. 2001).

The second objective of the first set of analyses was to see if the relationship was any different for the group that used SST and the one that used service personnel. For this purpose, the above analyses were run separately on the group that used SST and the group that visited the bank. The results from these analyses are presented in Tables 11.6 and 11.7 respectively. All of the relationships in Tables 11.6 and 11.7 were significant at the 0.05 level. Moreover, the patterns of the relationship are the same for the group that receives the service by visiting and the one that uses a technology interface, making us conclude that SST does not moderate this relationship.

Table 11.5 Relationship between satisfaction, commitment and loyalty – entire sample

Dependent variable	Regression1 affective	Regression2 calculative	Regression3 loyalty	Regression4 loyalty
R square	0.44	0.18	0.48	0.64
Adj. R square	0.44	0.18	0.48	0.63
Beta for satisfaction	0.86	0.54	0.92	0.34
Beta for affective				0.53
Beta for calculative				0.17

Table 11.6 Relationship between satisfaction, commitment and loyalty – personal interface

Dependent variable	Regression1 affective	Regression2 calculative	Regression3 loyalty	Regression4 loyalty
R square	0.45	0.21	0.47	0.63
Adj. R square	0.45	0.21	0.47	0.63
Beta for satisfaction	0.82	0.54	0.85	0.26
Beta for affective				0.55
Beta for calculative				0.15

Table 11.7 Relationship between satisfaction, commitment, and loyalty

SST interface

Dependent variable	Regression1 affective	Regression2 calculative	Regression3 loyalty	Regression4 loyalty
R square	0.42	0.14	0.48	0.63
Adj. R square	0.42	0.14	0.48	0.63
Beta for satisfaction	0.87	0.49	0.98	0.43
Beta for affective				0.51
Beta for calculative				0.20

Alternative II: Is the impact of SST on loyalty mediated by the two dimensions of commitment? That is, compared with service being provided by personnel, under which circumstances is SST more effective in producing higher loyalty?

The previous analyses demonstrate the importance of affective and calculative commitment in determining loyalty and how it might be misleading to conclude that increasing customer satisfaction by itself would result in higher loyalty. We showed that when affective and calculative commitment are included in the relationship, the impact of satisfaction in building on loyalty is considerably reduced, thus establishing the mediating role of the two dimensions of commitment. Satisfaction does build loyalty, but it does so through commitment. Keeping this in mind, we examined the impact of the interface method on loyalty vis-à-vis affective and calculative commitment. Again, this analysis also was run in several parts, as stated below, by examining the following set of relationships.

1. *Whether there were differences in affective and calculative commitment depending on the interface method used by customers.* Multiple analyses of variance using the interface method as the independent variable and affective and calculative commitment as dependent, was significant for both the dependent variables at the 0.05 level, with the F statistic for affective commitment being 22.27 and 19.90 for calculative commitment.
2. *Whether there were differences in loyalty based on the method of interface customers used for receiving the service.* Analysis of variance with method of interface as the independent variable and loyalty as the dependent, resulted in an F value of 20.1 which was significant at the 0.05 level with the average loyalty for customers who visited the bank being 7.70 and 6.99 for those who used SST.

3. *The relationship between the type of interface, affective and calculative commitment, and loyalty.* Analysis of covariance was the chosen method, with affective and calculative commitment being entered as covariates, type of interface as the independent variable and loyalty as the dependent. The model resulted in there being no significant effects for type of interface on loyalty. However, both affective and calculative commitments were significant at the 0.05 level respectively. The effects of contact type on loyalty disappear when the two types of commitments are included in the regression along with satisfaction, thus confirming the mediating affect of commitment. This would make us conclude that it is not the type of contact with the service provider but the commitment that is responsible for the effects on loyalty.

11.5 Discussion

The first analysis replicates the expected relationship between loyalty, satisfaction, affective and calculative commitment. Evidence from our study shows that this relationship remains unchanged when the sample is divided into two groups based on their method of interaction with the bank, thus showing that the interface method might not be a moderator as assumed by previous researchers.

The second analysis reinforces the findings in the first part by demonstrating that it is the two dimensions of commitment that mediate the impact of type of interface on loyalty. When only the effects of the type of interface on loyalty are observed, subjects who have personal contact with the service provider are shown to be significantly more loyal than those who use technology to receive the service, as demonstrated by the significant differences in the means for loyalty in Table 11.4. However, when the effects of the two dimensions of commitment are accounted for, it is customers that interact via a technology interface who are more loyal than those who do so through a personal interface as shown by Table 11.4, means for mediated loyalty.

Affective and calculative commitment have been used in marketing to understand relational exchanges between the buyer and supplier and have been shown to mediate successful long-term relationships and future intentions of repurchase. Our findings support these previous findings: it is the commitment to the service provider rather than the method of interface that is responsible for the degree of loyalty the customer feels toward the service provider.

The results from our study indicate that SST does not change everything. The classical model of how customers evaluate services and the predictors of loyalty are replicated in the SST setting. We find that customer satisfaction has a direct effect on customer loyalty , as well as an indirect effect, through affective and calculative commitment when the analyses are performed on the sample as a whole, and also when they are performed on the two groups separated by method of interface. In other words, consumers' evaluation

processes are the same when using SST as when being served by service personnel. Interestingly, SST does not have a direct influence on loyalty by itself but its
effects are mediated by commitment. Furthermore, in the SST sample we find
that affective commitment (Beta coefficient = 0.51) is the stronger driver of
loyalty followed by satisfaction (Beta coefficient = 0.43). Calculative commitment is important but a weaker driver of loyalty (Table 11.6, Regression 4,
B = 0.20). One of the reasons why we find this result may be that customers tend
to have very long relationship with their banks. On average the length of the
customer relationship is 19 years in the sample of customers visiting the bank,
and 14 years in the SST sample.

11.6 Further Research

Loyalty has been difficult to explain so it might be more fruitful to examine two
of the variables that it has been proven to depend on: satisfaction and commitment. Instead of trying to understand loyalty under different interface methods,
future research could focus on the drivers of satisfaction and commitment when
the interface method is technology and compare them with those for when the
service is provided by people. An insight into the drivers of these two variables
under different interface methods would provide marketers with an effective
tool that could leverage their customers' loyalty.

It has been proposed in the literature that consumers who receive the service
through a technology interface are going to be more calculative in their relationships with the service provider as the costs of switching are apparently lower.
This could very well be true in an industry other than the banking industry,
which is marked by long running relationships. Banking is classified as a continuous delivery service with a formal membership (Lovelock 1983) that is "sub-
scribed" by the consumer. In a service that is nonsubscription based and one in
which each transaction is discrete, we might observe a different behavior, e.g., in
the airlines industry.

11.7 Conclusion

Several streams of research have emerged within the SST field and common to
many of these is the underlying assumption that SST changes everything and
that SST is a means of cutting costs. Our findings contest this by demonstrating that SST is not necessarily changing everything but is yet another way for
customers to make use of services and for service companies to enable innovations
and growth through improved efficiency in service delivery. IBM recognized this
in making the shift from a product-oriented company to a service-oriented one
because it foresaw its clients "seeking to integrate advanced technology with their
business processes and operations, not primarily to reduce costs, but to enable

innovation and growth" (www.ibm.com/annualreport/2006/higher_value.shtml). Managers should first and foremost focus on building relationships with their customers the old fashioned way, by making the customers happy and committed. The SST should therefore be designed for the purpose of improving service quality and thus satisfaction rather than to cut costs.

Despite the new and interesting findings, our study is not the last word in research on the role of SST in building loyalty. However, we can conclude that though both consumers' sense (calculative commitment) and sensibility (affective commitment) mediate the role of self-service technology in forming loyalty, the sensibility is noticeably more important.

Acknowledgment The authors would like to acknowledge the Norwegian Customer Satisfaction Barometer at the Norwegian School of Management-BI for its help in providing the data that made this study possible.

References

Anderson EW, Sullivan MW (1993) The Antecedents and Consequences of Satisfaction for Firms, Marketing Science 12(2):125–153

Anderson EW, Fornael C, Mazvancheryl SK (2004) Customer Satisfaction and Shareholder Value. Journal of Marketing 68(4):172–185

Beatson A, Coote LV, Rudd JM (2006) Determining Consumer Satisfaction and Commitment through Self-Service-Technology and Personal Service Usage. Journal of Marketing Management 22:853–882

Bitner MJ, Ostrom AL, Meuter ML (2002) Implementing Successful Self Service Technology. Academy of Management Executive 16(4):96–108

Bobbit ML, Dabholkar PA (2001) Integrating Attitudinal Theories to Understand and Predict use of Technology-Based Self Service. International Journal of Service Industry Management 12(5):423–450

Bolton RN (1998) A Dynamic Model of the Customer's Relationship with a Continuous Service Provider: The Role of Satisfaction. Marketing Science 17(1):45–65

Bolton RN, Kannan RK, Bramlett MD (2000) Implications of Loyalty Program Membership and Service Experience for Customer Retention and Value. Journal of the Academy of Marketing Science 28(1):95–108

Curran JM, Meuter ML (2005) Self-Service Technology Adoption: Comparing Three Technologies. Journal of Services Marketing 19(2):103–113

Dabholkar PA (1996) Consumer Evaluations of New Technology-Based Self-Service Options: An Investigation of Alternative Models of Service Quality. International Journal of Service Research 13:29–51

Dabholkar PA, Bagozzi RP (2002) An Attitudinal Model of Technology-Based Self-Service: Moderating Effects of Consumer Traits and Situational Factors. Journal of the Academy of Marketing Science 30(3):184–201

Dwyer RF, Schurr PH, Oh S (1987) Developing Buyer-Seller Relationships. Journal of Marketing 51(April):11–27

Fassnacht M, Koese I (2006) Quality of Electronic Services: Conceptualizing and Testing Hierarchial Model. Journal of Service Research 9(1):19–37

Froehle CM (2006) Service Personnel, Technology, and their Interaction in Influencing Customer Satisfaction. Decision Sciences 37(19):5–38

Fornell C (1992) A National Customer Satisfaction Barometer: The Swedish Experience. Journal of Marketing 56:6–21

Garbarino E, Johnson MS (1999) The Different Roles of Satisfaction, Trust and Commitment in Customer Relationships. Journal of Marketing 63(April):70–87

Geyskens I, Steenkamp JBEM, Scheer LK, Kumar N (1996) The Effects of Trust and Interdependence on Relationship Commitment: A Trans-Atlantic Study. International Journal of Research in Marketing 13(4):303–317

Gundlach GT, Achrol RS, Mentzer JT (1995) The Structure of Commitment in Exchange. Journal of Marketing 59(January):78–92

Gustafsson A, Johnson MD, Roos I (2005) The Effects of Customer Satisfaction, Relationship Commitment Dimensions, and Triggers on Customer Retention. Journal of Marketing 69(October):210–218

Hansen H, Sandvik K, Selnes F (2003) Direct and Indirect Effects of Commitment to a Service Employee on the Intention to Stay. Journal of Service Research 5(4):356–368

Heskett JL, Sasser Jr WE, Schlesinger LA (1997) The service profit chain: how leading companies link profit and growth to loyalty, satisfaction, and value. Free Press, New York www.ibm.com/annualreport/2006/higher_value.shtml. Accessed 26 October 2007

Johnson MD, Gustafsson A, Andreassen TW, Lervik L, Cha J (2001) The Evolution and Future of National Customer Satisfaction Indices. Journal of Economic Psychology 22(2):217–245

Kotler P (1994) Marketing Management: Analysis, Planning, Implementation and Control. Prentice-Hall, Englewood Cliffs, NJ

Lovelock CH (1983) Classifying Services to Gain Strategic Marketing Insights. Journal of Marketing 47(39):9–20

Meuter ML, Ostrom AL, Roundtree RI, Bitner MJ (2000) Self-Service Technologies: Understanding Customer Satisfaction with Technology-Based Service Encounters. Journal of Marketing 64(3):50–64

Meuter ML, Ostrom AL, Bitner MJ, Roundtree R (2003) The Influence of Technology Anxiety on Consumer Use and Experiences with Self-Service Technologies. Journal of Business Research 56:899–906

Meuter ML, Bitner MJ, Ostrom AL, Brown SW (2005) Choosing Among Alternative Service Modes: An Investigation of Customer Trial of Self-Service Technologies. Journal of Marketing 69(2):61–83

Meyer JP, Allen N (1990) A Three-Component Conceptualization of Organizational Commitment. Human Resource Management Review 1(1):61–89

Morgan RM, Hunt SD (1994) The Commitment-Trust Theory of Relationship Marketing. Journal of Marketing 58(July):20–38

Oliver RL (1996) Satisfaction: A Behavioral Perspective on the Consumer. McGraw-Hill, New York

Parasuraman, A (1996) Understanding and Leveraging the Role of Customer Service in External, Interactive and Internal Marketing. Paper presented at the 1996 Frontiers in Service Conference, Nashville, TN

Parasuraman A, Grewal D (2000) The Impact of Technology on the Quality-Value-Loyalty Chain: A Research Agenda. Journal of the Academy of Marketing Science 28(1):168–174

Parasuraman A, Zinkhan GM (2002) Marketing to and Serving Customers Through the Internet: An Overview and Research Agenda. Journal of the Academy of Marketing Science 30(4):286–295

Parasuraman A, Zeithaml VA, Malhotra A (2005) E-S-QUAL: A Multiple-Item Scale for Assessing Electronic Service Quality. Journal of Service Research 7(3):213–233

Reichheld FF, Sasser Jr WE (1990) Zero Defects: Quality Comes to Services. Harvard Business Review 68(5):105–111

Reichheld FF (1996) The Satisfaction Trap. Harvard Business Review 74(2):58–59

Rust RT, Zahorik AJ, Keiningham TL (1995) Return on quality (ROQ): Making Service Quality Financially Accountable. Journal of Marketing 59(2):58–70

Rust RT, Zeithaml VA, Lemon K (2000) Driving Customer Equity: How Customer Lifetime Value Is Reshaping Corporate Strategy. The Free Press, New York

Rust RT, Moorman C, Dickson PR (2002) Getting Return on Quality: Revenue Expansion, Cost Reduction, or Both? Journal of Marketing 66(4):7–24

Rust RT, Lemon K, Zeithaml VA (2004) Return on Marketing: Using Customer Equity to Focus Marketing Strategy. Journal of Marketing 68(1):109–127

Simon F, Usunier JC (2007) Cognitive, Demographic, and Situational Determinants of Service Customer Preference for Personnel-in-Contact over Self-Service Technology. International Journal of Research in Marketing 24(2):163–173

Verhoef PC, Franses PH, Hoekstra JC (2002) The Effect of Relational Constructs on Customer Referrals and Number of Services Purchased From a Multiservice Provider: Does Age of Relationship Matter? Journal of the Academy of Marketing Sciences 30(3):202–216

Zeithaml VA, Parasuraman A, Malhotra A (2002) Service Quality Delivery Through Web Sites: A Critical Review of Extant Knowledge. Journal of the Academy of Marketing Science 30(4):362–375

Zinkhan GM (2002) Promoting Services via the Internet: New Opportunity and Challenges. Journal of Services Marketing 16(5):412–423

Chapter 12
Web-Based Self-Service Systems for Managed IT Support: Service Provider Perspectives of Stakeholder-Based Issues

Vanessa A. Cooper, Sharman Lichtenstein, and Ross Smith

Abstract This chapter explores the provision of after-sales information technology (IT) support services using Web-based self-service systems (WSSs) in a business-to-business (B2B) context. A recent study conducted at six large multinational IT support organisations revealed a number of critical success factors (CSFs) and stakeholder-based issues. To better identify and understand these important enablers and barriers, we explain how WSSs should be considered within a complex network of service providers, business partners and customer firms. The CSFs and stakeholder-based issues are discussed. The chapter highlights that for more successful service provision using WSSs, IT service providers should collaborate more effectively with enterprise customers and business partners and should better integrate their WSSs.

12.1 Introduction

The effectiveness of after-sales services has a significant impact on customer satisfaction and, ultimately, the profitability of the service provider (van Riel et al. 2004). Utilising the World Wide Web ("the Web") to provide after-sales support services is a recent and growing trend. A Web-based information system that facilitates support service provision is called a Web-based self-service system (WSS). WSSs are an important type of network-based customer service system (NCSS) which has been defined as "a network-based computerised information system that delivers service to a customer either directly (e.g. via a browser, PDA or cell phone) or indirectly (via a service representative or agent accessing the system)" (Piccoli et al. 2004, p. 424).

In a business-to-business (B2B) setting, there are specific concerns for WSS use that are relevant to different stakeholders at the service provider firm, business partners working with the service providers and customer firms. We argue that service providers would benefit from understanding and addressing

V.A. Cooper (✉)
RMIT University, Melbourne, VIC 3001, Australia
e-mail: vanessa.cooper@rmit.edu.au

D. Oliver et al. (eds.), *Self Service in the Internet Age*,
DOI 10.1007/978-1-84800-207-4_12, © Springer-Verlag London Limited 2009

the complex stakeholder-based issues involved in WSS support provision. In this chapter we consider the topic in the context of B2B information technology (IT) after-sales support provision. The contracting of IT support to an IT service provider is an increasing trend for non-IT organisations and WSSs are increasingly used in this context.

Stakeholders in customer service settings are concerned with a broad range of issues surrounding marketing and information systems, customer service and security and privacy risks. Relationship marketing emphasises the role of marketing in establishing, maintaining and enhancing service provider relationships with stakeholders, so that the objectives of all stakeholders are met (Grönroos 1994). Services marketing also addresses stakeholder-based issues such as service quality (Parasuraman & Grewal 2000) which can influence customer satisfaction and profitability. Previous studies have highlighted the importance of *after-sales* service to customer loyalty and retention (van Riel et al. 2004). When providing technology-mediated customer service, stakeholders may also be concerned with security and privacy risks (Zeithaml et al. 2000). We will explore these and other issues in the managed after-sales IT support context in this chapter.

The chapter commences with a brief background. Some of the main findings from a research project conducted at six large multi-national IT support organisations (Cooper et al. 2005, 2006a,b, 2007) are reported to illustrate the issues central to the chapter. We review categories of critical success factors (CSFs) that an IT service provider should address to provide effective after-sales IT support to enterprise customers, when using a WSS. The chapter also discusses a set of stakeholder-based challenges and suggests several solutions. It concludes with a summary of key insights developed in the chapter.

12.2 Background

12.2.1 WSSs and After-Sales IT Support Provision

The World Wide Web offers important opportunities to develop and manage customer relationships. Customer relationship management (CRM) assists an organisation in retaining its customers, managing the customer experience and facilitating cross-selling and up-selling. CRM can leverage customer interactions to provide information and knowledge that might be helpful in future dealings with the customer (Fjermestad & Romano 2003). WSSs are an important type of operational electronic CRM (eCRM) application (Geib et al. 2006; Khalifa & Shen 2005).

Three significant innovations provide the value in WSSs. Firstly, Web-based services provide a common platform for communication and information within and between organisations using Web-based interfaces (Kalakota & Robinson 2003). Business processes can be improved when enabled by Web-based services,

leading to greater internal efficiencies, increased profitability from a more effi
cient supply chain and greater customer reach.

Secondly, effective management of customer, solution, contact and supplier
knowledge and information can add value to customer support (Davenport &
Klahr 1998). The transfer of knowledge such as best practices, cases and problem resolutions, internally as well as to external customers, can assist a service
provider by improving employee productivity, reducing future support costs and
improving support service quality and customer satisfaction (Ciccolini & Sorkin
2003; Szulanski 2000). Information management and knowledge management in
Web-based after-sales support provision can also improve a service provider's
financial performance (Barua et al. 2004).

For internal knowledge transfer, IT service (help) desks are typically organised into three support tiers. Help desks aim to distribute as many support
issues as possible to the least-expensive resources – Level 1 "Support Agents".
Senior (and usually more expensive) technology experts can then concentrate
on the more challenging support issues. To realise the productivity and cost-
saving benefits of this type of structure, IT support personnel should share
knowledge to reduce the re-solving of prior support issues: a problem should be
solved once, but the solution should be re-used many times. This type of
structure enables a service provider to provide efficient and consistent service
to external customers. The Web and knowledge repositories accessed by a Web
interface provide a convenient way for support agents to access and reuse
solutions developed by senior technology experts. During this process knowledge of a solution is transferred to Level 1 support agents. However, some
support personnel can find this method of knowledge transfer personally
unsatisfying compared with the creativity, excitement and challenges of personally solving a customer's support problem. Thus providing more interesting
work is important for support agent recruitment and retention. Support agents
may also be reluctant to share their expertise if they know they will go unre-
warded and unrecognised for doing so. They may also anticipate loss of power
within the current hierarchy of the organisation if their specialised knowledge is
commonly known. IT support agents on help desk duty have notoriously high
turnover levels and are increasingly difficult to source in an era where fewer and
fewer students choose IT for higher education study. Thus, there can be challenges for knowledge sharing and reuse within a tiered IT help desk structure.

Thirdly, self-service in an after-sales enterprise, customer support context is a
convenient approach to service delivery for customer firms. Support is available
24/7, support costs are lowered for the provider and customer firms, the volume
of customer interaction is reduced, and customer service is often improved
(Pujari 2004). Yet while providers highlight the convenience of self-service
support, they focus less on the resulting reallocation of support work from
their own support staff to the customer firm. Support organisations should
further consider the potentially negative impact of this reallocation of work on
customer satisfaction and CRM.

Despite the potential benefits of WSSs for after-sales support reviewed above, a recent survey revealed that only 14 percent of the UK companies offer good customer self-service via the Web (CRM2day 2007). Another survey found that consumers significantly use electronic mail and telephone channels far more than a Web-based self-service channel for after-sales support (McGeary et al. 2007). Consumers complained mainly about static site content (lack of content currency) and inadequate keyword search (lack of findability) in the Web-based self-service channel. Clearly there is scope for improved WSSs.

12.2.2 Managed IT Support Services and Knowledge-Centred Support (KCS)

This section reviews the use of WSSs for after-sales support in managed IT support services. In this environment, customer firms ("enterprise customers") are supported in their post-sales IT support needs by IT service providers. The use of a "Best Practices" customer support methodology is also discussed.

In the emerging services economy, corporate IT management in non-IT organisations is evolving towards service and relationship-oriented business approaches. Such approaches strive to offer continuous evaluation and improvement of application, communication, delivery and support services to internal and external customers (Dahlberg & Nyrhinen 2006; Peppard 2003). In managing IT infrastructure, the focus is increasingly on the value of the *services provided by the technology* rather than the value of the hardware and software per se. IT services outsourcing exploits existing software, hardware, processes, methodologies and expertise to provide improved service, economic advantages and other benefits (Peppard 2003). According to Dahlberg and Nyrhinen (2006), IT services outsourcing has become more complex due to the emergence of large IT service providers, more complex and substantial services, transfer of responsibility to IT service providers, new partnership roles with customer firms, the involvement of multiple service providers, and the maturation and professionalism of customer firms and IT service providers.

To address the complexities of managed after-sales IT support, a knowledge-based approach is used to leverage customer, solution, contact and supplier knowledge and information (Davenport & Klahr 1998). *Knowledge-Centred Support (KCS)* is a recently developed managed IT support "Best Practices" methodology (CSI 2002) that uses knowledge management principles to address many reported user concerns in managed IT support. Examples of key issues addressed by KCS are findability and information currency (McGeary et al. 2007). KCS was developed in 2002 by the Consortium of Service Innovation (CSI 2002), a not-for-profit industry consortium of leading IT service organisations including Dell, Intel, Microsoft, Nortel, Primus and Serviceware. The methodology leverages knowledge management principles and focuses on effectively managing IT solution-oriented knowledge for better supporting customers (CSI 2002). KCS is based on the knowledge processes of knowledge capture, re-use and publication. It defines a set of principles and practices that enable IT support organisations to improve the quality of service for customers, gain operational efficiencies, and increase the value of IT support services (CSI 2002).

The potential benefits of KCS stem from applying the principles of knowledge management to solve a particular IT support problem once, and re-using and extending the resulting IT solution. KCS aims to create and manage IT solutions that are findable and usable by a range of users. In a B2B context such users can include IT support agents working at IT service providers, relevant support employees in business partner firms, and employees acting as IT users in customer firms. KCS also leverages the valuable knowledge developed from the experiences and interactions of IT service providers with business partners and enterprise customers. The service department is often the hub of critical product information at enterprise customers and business partners and this information can be captured by the use of KCS.

Knowledge transfer is regarded as central to KCS, as "all support strategies and services are dependent on the effective transfer of knowledge" (CSI 2002, p. 7), regardless of "whether the knowledge is driven outward over the internet into the customer's environment, inward through product engineering, and throughout the organisation over to service partners in other organisations, or used explicitly to create new value to sell for a separate fee" (CSI 2002, p. 21).

While it is quite well used in practice, KCS has several important limitations. For example, KCS does not specify which factors are critical to the successful implementation of enterprise customer IT support when WSSs are used. It also does not specify which challenges are thorny to resolve, particularly those challenges relating to the interactions and conflicts between the different stakeholders involved in managed IT support. Finally, KCS does not identify the CSFs that are relevant to specific stakeholder types. Therefore in this chapter we discuss the key concepts and processes involved in knowledge transfer of IT support-oriented knowledge to customer firms when WSSs are used, rather than focusing on the KCS methodology.

12.2.3 Stakeholder-Oriented Relational Web-Based Enterprise Customer Service

A consideration of stakeholder relationships, and related knowledge flows, is important to the successful implementation of WSSs. Issues for different stakeholders should be considered together (Zeithaml et al. 2000) as stakeholder requirements often conflict. Adopting a relational approach best explains system success or failure in Web-based enterprise customer service (Mollstedt & Fredriksson 2004). In B2B service provision, stakeholders interact with each

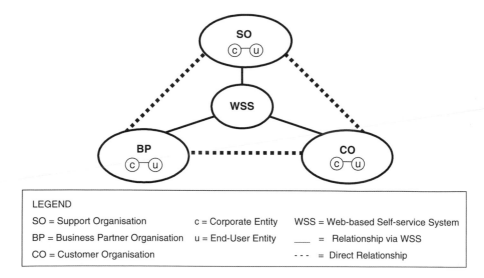

Fig. 12.1 Stakeholder-oriented relational framework for Web-based enterprise customer service (Cooper et al. 2005, 2006b)

other directly and indirectly via a WSS. Web-mediated knowledge flows can be exploited for relationship marketing purposes as the knowledge is captured by technology (Geib et al. 2006).

The framework in Fig. 12.1 (Cooper et al. 2005, 2006b) depicts relationships between key stakeholders and a WSS during Web-based enterprise customer service. The three key types of stakeholder organisation are service provider ("support organisation"), business partner and customer organisation. At each organisation there are corporate entity representatives (e.g. managers) who interact with end-users. The framework highlights the importance of knowledge flows between key stakeholders and a WSS in a managed IT support environment.

12.2.4 Knowledge Transfer in Managed After-Sales IT Support Using WSSs

Figure 12.2 depicts a typical WSS encounter in after-sales enterprise IT support. IT support organisations respond to enterprise customers' after-sales enquiries, incidents and problems regarding core IT products and services by providing support-oriented knowledge (Negash et al. 2003). Enterprise customers comprise small, medium or large organisations in various profit and not-for-profit industries. WSS encounters can provide informational, transactional and proactive types of support. Informational support includes "break-fix" support which provides customers experiencing technical problems with resolutions to

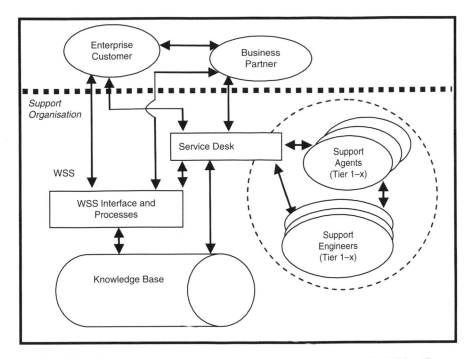

Fig. 12.2 Knowledge transfer in enterprise after-sales IT support with WSSs (Cooper et al. 2006b)

their problems. This type of support includes unassisted support, such as answers to frequently asked questions (FAQs) and downloading of software patches, and assisted support such as peer-to-peer online fora, e-mail and online chat. Other informational support includes the provision of information and knowledge to assist with enquiries and enable customers to access best practice, by the publication of white papers, for example. Transactional support includes case tracking, whereby the customer initially documents the IT problem scenario, requests assistance from the support organisation, and subsequently monitors the support organisation's progress in resolving this problem. Proactive support includes the embedding of problem detection support software on customer end-user computers, and personalised messages directing the customer to potential product or service purchases.

When a customer firm experiences IT incidents or problems, IT professionals employed at the customer firm may telephone the support organisation's service desk or directly access the support organisation's Web site seeking a solution. If the customer professional does not find a solution in the form of explicit knowledge, first tier support agents at the support organisation identify potentially successful solutions from their tacit knowledge of the subject matter or from searching the solutions knowledge base. Complex problems are escalated to experienced second and third tier support agents. Downstream are tiers of support engineers – technology specialists who ultimately resolve the most difficult problems. New and evolving solutions are captured in the knowledge base as explicit knowledge and re-organised for re-use. Sometimes IT support is provided by a business partner, in which case an enterprise customer's IT professionals may interact directly with the partner firm's IT professionals. Business partners may also contribute to the WSS knowledge base via the WSS interface (e.g. via user fora). Partners may also locate solutions via the service desk or from the WSS knowledge base in order to assist customers.

Next we review key results arising from a recent research project. We discuss a number of stakeholder-based issues that enable or constrain the success of WSSs. The project, based in Australia, involved an initial case study of a large multi-national IT services firm that used WSSs successfully to provide IT support to enterprise customers. This study was followed by a focus group comprised of representatives from five multi-national IT services firms. At these firms, support services offered included informational, transactional and proactive types of support. Support was delivered by multiple integrated channels including the Web, and was based on a multi-vendor solutions knowledge base. An adapted CSF research approach helped to identify the CSFs, categories of CSFs and key issues including the stakeholder-based issues discussed next (Cooper et al. 2007).

12.3 Stakeholder-Based Issues in Managed After-Sales IT Support Using WSSs

12.3.1 Stakeholders and Categories of CSFs

Low-level CSFs for B2B IT support provision via WSSs can be grouped into six categories as shown in Table 12.1, relevant to the three types of stakeholder organisations (support organisation, business partner organisation and customer organisation). A comprehensive set of CSFs is provided in Appendix 1.

Organisational commitment and readiness. Various supporting strategies demonstrating commitment and readiness are critical to ensure that organisations are able to work successfully with WSSs. Firstly, the marketing of

Table 12.1 CSF Categories for B2B IT support provision via WSSs

Categories of CSFs
Organisational commitment and readiness
Manage for strategic and operational benefits
Knowledge management capability and process
IT infrastructure capability
Experience management
Content

Web-based support to customers is important, particularly during the initiation stage. Secondly, support processes should be aligned with WSSs which should in turn be integrated with other support channels, applications and processes. Possessing knowledge management capability is also important to support WSS use in customer support.

Providing adequate customer education and training to assist customers in applying an IT resolution shows commitment but may only be available with a relevant support contract. An organisation's culture will support knowledge sharing and WSS-based support when it is customer-oriented, open and trusting. Finally, the ability to measure support performance in terms of service levels demonstrates true commitment to service improvement.

Manage for strategic and operational benefits. Each stakeholder organisation should manage for the delivery of anticipated benefits. For example, for the support organisation, such benefits might include customer loyalty, reduced costs and increased efficiency. There is also a need to manage the development and offers of new opportunities to customer firms. Managing relationship development between the different firms is critical with respect to enabling open communication and developing trust between a support organisation, its business partners and customer firms to facilitate knowledge flows.

Knowledge management capabilities and processes. Knowledge management capability and competence help enable WSS success. The advantages of a knowledge management strategy include the ability to identify gaps, bottlenecks, barriers and deficiencies in current business processes, and enable a support organisation to gain a better understanding of how support-oriented knowledge flows within the company and to its customers. Such a strategy can provide an improved understanding of customer expectations and so improve support.

Explicit support-oriented knowledge includes the captured knowledge of support agents and customers during support, such as resolutions, case histories and customer feedback. Tacit support-oriented knowledge exists in the minds of key stakeholders including support agents, business partner employees and customer contact personnel. Tacit knowledge is notoriously difficult to transfer. Key knowledge processes at a support organisation required for successful WSS include the capture, transfer and re-use of support-oriented knowledge.

There are several knowledge processes that are considered key enablers of successful knowledge transfer in the provision of after-sales IT support services to enterprise customers using WSSs. Firstly, the transfer of knowledge between the support organisation, its business partners and customer firms is critical to WSS success. Secondly, knowledge capture is an important process, particularly the capture of support-oriented knowledge, such as new resolutions, developed following problem escalation. Such knowledge must be validated before it is codified and stored. Service provider representatives in the study by Cooper et al. (2007) stressed that it is critical to educate support agents on how knowledge capture can benefit them individually, to help overcome their reluctance to share hard-won knowledge.

Thirdly, capturing an understanding of how effectively resolutions are applied by customers is considered essential, and can be done with the help of customer feedback.

IT infrastructure capability. Each organisation must have an adequate IT infrastructure to support Web-based self-service. The technical infrastructure must be able to support internal knowledge workers and large numbers of support transactions over the long term. It must also meet challenging security and privacy requirements. Technical infrastructure readiness in terms of sufficient and reliable high speed Internet access is particularly important. For example, a support organisation could have a fast and reliable Internet service supporting its WSS. However, if a customer firm only has slow dial-up Internet access provided by an unreliable Internet Service Provider (ISP), use of the WSS for certain support tasks may not be successful.

Experience management. The WSS should manage the experience of all stakeholder organisations, both at the corporate and end-user level because this will affect satisfaction levels and potentially ongoing use of the WSS. At the corporate level, it is important to encourage the economic decision maker within the enterprise to migrate to WSSs. This might involve offering favourable cost structures for organisations which use Web-based self-service over more expensive support channels such as a service desk. For end-users, providing education and training on how to use a WSS will be important.

Content. The WSS should contain useful, accurate and up-to-date content in order to resolve the end-user's support issue or knowledge requirement. Ultimately, the ability of the WSS to resolve an end-user's requirements will determine the usefulness of the WSS to the support organisation, business partner and customer organisations. End-users will also require the content to be presented in a way which maximises their understanding and ability to apply the knowledge quickly.

12.3.2 Critical Success Factors for Stakeholder Types

In this section we describe a stakeholder-oriented taxonomy of the CSFs. If a support organisation is able to understand the relevance of CSFs to particular stakeholders, it should be better able to manage its WSS. For example, it is important for a support organisation to distinguish between a corporate entity and end-users at a customer business. This is because, while the end-users at the customer organisation may be well satisfied with the WSS, the corporate entity may be dissatisfied and vice versa. If these issues are mismanaged a service contract may not be renewed.

With these issues in mind, participants representing a multi-national IT support organisation (Cooper et al. 2007) discussed the relevance of each CSF to the six stakeholder types, end-users and the corporate level, at each of the support organisation, business partner and customer organisations. Four groupings of

CSFs were identified as shown in Table 12.2. Almost half of the CSFs were considered critical to ensuring a successful WSS to all six types of stakeholders. This highlights the interdependencies of stakeholders in a B2B WSS context and the importance of a relationship-based approach. To illustrate, *CSF-2 provision of additional value and cross-selling* was seen as important from a corporate perspective at all three stakeholder organisations. This is because customer organisations increasingly expect maximum value in all dealings with the support organisation and its business partners. Consequently, the support organisation and its business partners seek a WSS strategy which is able to meet these customer demands. Offering additional services such as free white papers and information on best practice were commonly cited as a means of providing additional value. From an end-user perspective, end-users at the customer organisation desire products and services which enable them to perform their jobs more effectively. When rewards

Table 12.2 Stakeholder-oriented CSFs for knowledge transfer in enterprise customer IT support using WSSs (Cooper et al. 2007)

CSFs perceived as relevant to the corporate and end-user entities at all stakeholder organisations	CSFs perceived as relevant to end-users at all stakeholder organisations
CSF-2 Provision of additional value and cross-selling	CSF-3 Critical mass: knowledge content, knowledge contributors
CSF-4 Usefulness: provision of knowledge which meets end-user requirements	CSF-7 Effective information architecture (and search engine)
CSF-5 Efficiency	CSF-9 Ease of use
CSF-8 Security, privacy and assurance	CSF-12 Confidence in solution
CSF-11 Ongoing positive experience	CSF-15 Provision of additional support
CSF-13 Customer focus: understand needs of customer	CSF-22 Presentation of knowledge
CSF-14 Positive relationship between all parties using the WSS	CSF-25 Web-based customer self-service recovery/over-ride
CSF-16 Employee focus	CSF-26 Ease of re-initiation
CSF-20 Knowledge validation	
CSF-23 Measurement and feedback of Web-based self-service	
CSF-24 Aligned with IT/business processes	
CSF-27 Top management support	
CSFs perceived as relevant to the corporate entity at all stakeholder organisations	CSFs perceived as relevant to end-users at all stakeholder organisations and to the corporate entity at the support organisation
CSF-1 Cost effectiveness	CSF-6 Access, connectivity and performance
CSF-18 Awareness and marketing of Web-based self-service	CSF-10 Early positive experience
	CSF-17 Culture
	CSF-19 Knowledge creation, capture and re-use
	CSF-21 Knowledge storage and retrieval

and recognition at the support organisation and business partner organisations are tied to an employee's ability to provide a customer with additional value, or cross-selling products and services, they too are interested in this CSF.

Eight CSFs were relevant only to end-users at each stakeholder organisation. The factors were primarily associated with two main issues surrounding ease-of-use and usefulness. The first is the end-user's perception of the availability, relevance and accessibility of the knowledge. For example, *CSF-3 critical mass: knowledge content, knowledge contributors, CSF-12 confidence in solution* and *CSF-22 presentation of knowledge*. The second issue surrounds the design of the WSS and surrounding processes, as represented by factors such as *CSF-9 ease of use* and *CSF-26 ease of re-initiation*.

Five factors were considered a concern for end-users at all stakeholder organisations and were also perceived to have important implications for the corporate entity at the support organisation. These factors further illustrate the importance of end-user requirements to WSS success and ultimately to support organisation profitability and success. For example, end-users are concerned with having a positive experience when participating in Web-based self-service and in particular, an early positive experience because "first impressions count". If an end-user is not satisfied with early experiences, they are unlikely to adopt this method of gaining IT support. Therefore, it is important to the support organisation to ensure a favourable outcome when an end-user first uses the WSS. Indeed, the support organisation may decide to forgo early cost effectiveness benefits and "over-service" the end-user initially, to ensure long-term adoption.

Finally, two CSFs, *CSF-1 cost effectiveness* and *CSF-18 awareness and marketing of Web-based Self-service,* were considered a corporate concern only at all three types of stakeholder organisation. The rationale is that these CSFs address issues of profitability, and in a B2B context, end-users are more concerned with job effectiveness and efficiency than financial matters. Of course in a business-to-consumer (B2C) context, where the end-user is effectively the "financial controller", these issues will be more important to these end-user stakeholders.

12.3.3 Critical Success Factors Specific to WSS Strategies

It was noted that many of the CSFs were applicable to IT projects in general and were not specific to the provision of after-sales B2B IT support services via WSSs. Given that management is likely to have an awareness and understanding of the generic factors, it was considered useful to highlight those factors which are unique or which have a specific relevance in a Web-based self-service context. The eleven CSFs which were identified by representatives of the IT support organisations as specific to WSS projects are listed in Table 12.3. However, this is not to imply that the CSFs which are generic to IT projects

Table 12.3 CSFs specific to WSS projects

CSFs specific to WSS projects
CSF-2 Additional value and cross-selling
CSF-3 Critical mass: knowledge content and knowledge contributors
CSF-4B* Provision of knowledge which meets user requirements
CSF-6 Access, connectivity and performance
CSF-7 Effective information architecture and search engine
CSF-19 Knowledge creation capture and re-use
CSF-20 Knowledge validation
CSF-21 Knowledge storage and retrieval
CSF-22 Presentation of knowledge
CSF-25 Web-based service recovery and over-ride
CSF-26 Ease of re-initiation

in general are less important in a WSS context, but rather that they are commonly reported in other contexts. For example, *CSF-1 cost effectiveness* is frequently identified in an IT project context but was still one of the most commonly cited CSFs in this study. Service provider representatives saw this factor as a specific driver of WSSs strategies for support organisations.

Participants in the cross-organisational focus group argued that highlighting the eleven factors shown in Table 12.3, which may have a specific interpretation in a WSS context, can potentially provide valuable insights for support organisations and thus they are assembled as a distinct set.

12.3.4 Stakeholder-Based Issues for Enabling Successful WSSs in Enterprise IT Support

Eight stakeholder-based issues (Cooper et al. 2007) were identified (Table 12.4) and are discussed below.

Table 12.4 Key Stakeholder-based issues in B2B WSS IT support

Stakeholder-based issue
1. Consideration of all stakeholder views
2. Specific stakeholder interpretations of CSFs
3. Stakeholder interdependencies and performance management and measurement in a B2B WSS context
4. Impact of WSS on stakeholder relationships
5. B2B stakeholder relationship complexity
6. Customer co-contribution to service
7. Intellectual property, security and privacy
8. Complexities within strategic alliances

12.3.4.1 Consideration of All Stakeholder Views

All WSS stakeholder viewpoints should be considered together. However, different stakeholder types may have different perceptions of the CSFs, making it difficult to satisfy all stakeholder requirements. For example, while a support organisation may find the transfer of IT solutions via the WSS highly desirable, in order to limit repeated support calls to the service desk for the same concern, end-users at a customer firm may not mind repeatedly requesting support for a particular concern whenever it arises. Customer end-users may simply want their problem solved with as little effort as possible. This presents an interesting dilemma because if an end-user at a customer firm is not interested in learning from an IT solution provided by a support firm, strategies will be needed to stimulate that interest. For example, perhaps the contract can specify that repeat questions to the service desk on the same concern will be charged at higher rates, to encourage customers to seek solutions from the WSS.

Support organisations should also consider the differing requirements that individuals within the stakeholder types may have. To illustrate, some end-users at the customer organisation may simply desire only to resume IT operations using a supplied solution. In contrast, others have specialised role-based needs, such as database administrators, and may be highly interested in learning about a solution and gaining more general knowledge which could be useful in performing their jobs in the future. On the other hand, if an end-user at a customer firm builds full knowledge of a product or service, this may reduce the customer organisation's dependence on the support organisation, thus reducing revenue for the support organisation. To avoid this scenario, there may be knowledge which a support organisation chooses not to transfer to customer firms.

12.3.4.2 Specific Stakeholder Interpretations of CSFs

Service provider representatives questioned whether different stakeholder types might interpret the requirements for CSFs differently. For example, in describing *CSF-9 ease of use* it was mentioned that regular end-users of the WSS interface would prefer an efficient interface, whilst novice users would prefer easy-to-use interfaces. As a second example, individual customers will have different IT infrastructure capabilities that are subsequently used to access the WSS. Consequently, customers will have varying perceptions as to whether the requirements for *CSF-6 access, connectivity and speed* have been satisfactorily achieved. It may be that an organisation who has invested in a high-speed broadband connection will expect the WSS to exploit the benefits of this connection by catering to the transfer of knowledge in the form of high-speed multi-media resources (see also *CSF-22 presentation of knowledge*). In contrast, an organisation using a dial-up connection may prefer that knowledge is presented in a text-based format which will enable the knowledge to be received within an acceptable time frame. Thus, the support organisation must consider how different stakeholders might interpret the requirements of each individual CSF.

12.3.4.3 Stakeholder Interdependencies and Performance Management and Measurement in a B2B WSS Context

In a B2B WSS context, stakeholders are interdependent and will influence the performance and ultimate success of the WSS strategy. While the previous discussion of individual stakeholders highlighted that the six stakeholder types will have different emphases and requirements on each individual CSF, the six high level CSF categories shown in Table 12.1 will be a concern for all stakeholder organisations. The performance of each stakeholder organisation on each category and relevant factors will impact on the success of the providing organisation's WSS strategy. For example, the success of the WSS will be affected by whether or not the customer organisation has an adequate *IT infrastructure capability*. If corporate customers or business partners in a managed IT support situation do not address their CSFs and the six categories, the support organisation's WSS may be less successful. In practice, however, a support organisation will have very little control over whether a customer organisation and business partner organisation address these factors, making performance measurement and management of WSS strategies in a B2B context challenging. It may be necessary for the support organisation to educate business partners and customers about the CSFs, or even specify standards in service level agreements (SLAs).

12.3.4.4 Impact of WSS on Stakeholder Relationships

Some interesting issues were raised regarding the feasibility of relationship development when a WSS is used, and when relationships are therefore mediated by technology. A two-way relationship may be possible because if an end-user trusts the WSS and the organisation providing the system, this trust forms part of the relationship. Here, the WSS was seen to provide the underpinning communication method between the parties to the relationship. Others, however, saw Web-based relationships as one way only. When end-users access a WSS anonymously, is there a relationship between the end-user and the providing organisation, as the support organisation does not know the identity of the end-user? Under these circumstances, the support organisation would be unable to contact this end-user directly, as part of its CRM strategy.

12.3.4.5 B2B Stakeholder Relationship Complexity

While Fig. 12.1 depicts typical stakeholder relationships in a B2B WSS context, in some instances the relationships can vary. For example, in some instances, a business partner is not required in supporting the customer firm and will not play a role. In other circumstances, the relationship between stakeholder organisations is conducted primarily online, with no direct or "face-to-face" contact involved.

As the size of stakeholder organisations increases, the relationships become more complex. There may be multiple relationships developed at individual, departmental and corporate levels. This finding is significant, as while it has been acknowledged in a large body of literature that developing relationships with partners is important there is little attention paid to partner-unit-based relationships and companies would be interested to find out more.

12.3.4.6 Customer Co-contribution to Service

In managed IT support, customers contribute to services provided in various ways. The study revealed that when customers used online fora, they sometimes contributed solutions which were not formally captured by the IT service providers. Nor was there formal capture of the feedback provided by end-users following the application of the solutions. The feedback from such applications was lost forever. This represents a lost opportunity for not only updating the support organisation's more formal knowledge base but also from a CRM perspective. In another example, while there was some monitoring of the content of fora, the primary support organisation in this study did not invest significant resources in this task. Rather, it relied on a "merit" based system implemented in the online fora, whereby users were allocated a number of points based on the number and usefulness of their postings. These points built up to various ratings to assist a user to assess the merit of a solution and to encourage users to share valuable knowledge. As a third example, online fora are accessible to a variety of end-users, some of whom may post inaccurate solutions which may cause problems for other end-users if applied in their organisations. While support organisations may rely on the terms and conditions of using the WSS and invest significant resources in their legal teams, there is still the potential for a negative impact on the support organisation's reputation in the marketplace. Indeed, customers negatively affected by inaccurate solutions may expect some form of support (or compensation) from the support organisation to address any problems caused, despite the presence and visibility of official disclaimers. This may in part arise because where customers are aware that the support organisation employs people to act as forum monitors, they expect the monitors to assess the accuracy of *all* posted content.

12.3.4.7 Intellectual Property, Security and Privacy

Intellectual property (IP), security and privacy issues are important concerns. There are complexities inherent in working with organisations which frequently operate across international borders. Participants in the study argued that support organisations must consider issues of security, privacy and IP within the context of an off-shore environment. National legal systems are unable to deal with some of the complex issues raised. For example, customer end-users may be unaware of the location where their personal information is stored and retrieved. Unless customers are confident with the management of intellectual property, security and privacy, they may be reluctant to participate in B2B IT support using WSS.

12.3.4.8 Complexities within Strategic Alliances

Service provider representatives identified that in a B2B IT support context there is a blurring of relationships. In some projects an organisation may be considered a business partner, while in others it would be considered a competitor. Consequently, the organisations will be concerned with sharing knowledge in a joint project, which might be used in another project where the companies are competitors. Lei (1997) argues that with respect to strategic alliances, regardless of the various types of legal structures which may be put in place, over time companies will absorb and internalise skills, regardless of the amount of formal, legal ownership that is demarcated by the alliance structure. Service provider representatives in the study expressed a need for greater understanding of this complex area and suggested that associated concerns are likely to continue into the foreseeable future.

12.4 Conclusion

This chapter has shown that in the managed enterprise after-sales IT support context, a stakeholder-based perspective is important to understanding successful use of WSSs.

Key insights were that the interdependencies between stakeholders in a WSS context, and consequently the performance of all stakeholders, may impact on WSS success. The chapter highlighted that not all stakeholders are necessarily interested in adopting self-service because they perceive that such methods of gaining support will increase their own workload. Thus there is a need for the service provider to motivate WSS adoption. Relationship-based issues, such as trust, were also identified as important for WSS success.

The chapter highlights that *all* stakeholder viewpoints and issues should be considered by an IT support organisation when planning, implementing and managing WSSs in a managed enterprise IT support context. Yet it has clearly shown that there can be difficulties satisfying some conflicting requirements, such as in the areas of security, privacy and IP. Several of the challenges have highlighted the evolving complexities of working with business partners in the provision of electronic services. The chapter also points to a need for IT service providers to engage with customers and business partners in collaborative and integrative development of WSSs. Industry level support for regulation change, and collaborative infrastructure development, would also be beneficial.

Appendix 1: CSFs for Knowledge Transfer from Support Organisation to Customer Organisation Using WSSs

CSF		Description
1	Cost effectiveness	The cost equation for providing/using Web-based self-service must be better, or at least not worse, than providing/using non-Web-based self-service.
2	Additional value and cross-selling	Current WSS transactions are used proactively as an opportunity to offer the customer organisation additional advice and services.
3	Critical mass: knowledge content and knowledge contributors	A sufficient number of end-users must proactively contribute sufficient knowledge content to the WSS knowledge base, to encourage all stakeholders to use, and continue to use, the WSS as a means of resolving the customer's support issues or information requirements.
4	Usefulness: provision of knowledge which meets user requirements	The WSS must provide the functionality and knowledge required to meet the objectives of all stakeholders.
5	Ability to provide efficiency	Use of the WSS to resolve a support issue or provide other knowledge resources must be perceived as efficient by all stakeholders. This is inclusive of not only the performance of the WSS tool but also surrounding processes for using the WSS.
6	Access, connectivity and performance	The support organisation, relevant business partners and the customer organisation must have sufficient technology infrastructure in place, to enable all stakeholders to participate in Web-based self-service.
7	Effective information architecture and search engine	The WSS must have an effective information architecture and search engine such that the information system that organises and retrieves knowledge in the knowledge base is perceived as effective by end-users.
8	Security, privacy and assurance	All stakeholders must feel secure, private and confident in all aspects of WSS transactions including the stored data components of transactions. Issues surrounding information security and information privacy and the need to keep confidential related company secrets (intellectual property) must be addressed.
9	Ease of use/usability	The end-user must perceive that use of the WSS does not demand excessive cognitive and ergonomic effort.
10	Early positive experience	The first few end-user experiences using the WSS must result in a positive outcome, where the end-user's needs are met and they

(continued)

CSF		Description
		feel valued, in order for the end-user to adopt Web-based self-service long term.
11	Ongoing positive experience	Using the WSS on an ongoing basis must result in a positive outcome, where corporate stakeholders' needs and all types of end-users' needs are met and they feel valued.
12	Confidence in solution	The end-user must have confidence that the solution provided by the WSS will resolve the customer's issue and will not result in any additional issues. The end-user must also have confidence in their own ability to apply the offered solution.
13	Customer Focus: understand the customer and their requirements	The support organisation (and relevant business partners) must understand the individual business and technical needs of individual customer organisations and their end-users. With this understanding, Web-based self-service is tailored to meet those individual needs.
14	Positive relationship	The relationship between the support organisation, business partners and the customer organisation must be one which supports open communication and trust. This positive relationship should exist at both the corporate and end-user levels.
15	Provision of additional support: education and training	Additional assistance, or education and training as to how to use the WSS must be provided by the support organisation when requested by end-users.
16	Employee focus	Management within the support organisation, business partner and customer organisations must have an understanding of the work processes and conditions which will affect the ability and willingness of employees to adopt the WSS and associated strategies. With this understanding, management must focus on meeting the needs of their employees where possible, in order to maximise employee productivity and the benefits received from the WSS strategy.
17	Culture	The support organisation should foster an environment that recognises that Web-based self-service is part of the way it wants to conduct business. In addition, an open, sharing culture is needed. The culture should extend externally to customers and business partners.
18	Marketing and awareness of Web-based self-service	Marketing programs which raise awareness of and support for the adoption of Web-based self-service, must be in place.

(continued)

CSF		Description
19	Positive relationship	The relationship between the support organisation, business partners and the customer organisation must be one which supports open communication and trust. This positive relationship should exist at both the corporate and end-user levels.
20	Provision of additional support: education and training	Additional assistance, or education and training as to how to use the WSS must be provided by the support organisation when requested by end-users.
21	Employee focus	Management within the support organisation, business partner and customer organisations must have an understanding of the work processes and conditions which will affect the ability and willingness of employees to adopt the WSS and associated strategies. With this understanding, management must focus on meeting the needs of their employees where possible, in order to maximise employee productivity and the benefits received from the WSS strategy.
22	Culture	The support organisation should foster an environment that recognises that Web-based self-service is part of the way it wants to conduct business. In addition, an open, sharing culture is needed. The culture should extend externally to customers and business partners.
23	Marketing and awareness of Web-based self-service	Marketing programs which raise awareness of and support for the adoption of Web-based self-service, must be in place.
24	Knowledge creation, capture and re-use	Processes to ensure that useful knowledge is created and captured into the WSS knowledge base by end-users, must be in place. Processes to ensure that this knowledge is subsequently accessed and re-used by end-users, must also be in place.
25	Knowledge validation	Processes to ensure the accuracy of the knowledge which is captured into the knowledge base and ensuring that once it is captured, that it is frequently reviewed and updated to ensure its currency, must be in place.
26	Knowledge storage and retrieval	Processes to ensure that the structure and format of captured knowledge facilitates finadability, must be in place.
27	Presentation of knowledge	The knowledge must be presented in a form which maximises the understanding acquired by end-users.

(continued)

CSF		Description
28	Measurement and feedback of the WSS strategy	Sufficient methods to assess the effectiveness of the WSS strategy must be in place.
29	Alignment and integration	There must be alignment and integration between the WSS and other channels' support processes, as well as with related business processes in the context of the business/industry environment.
30	Web-based self-service over-ride and recovery	A strategy for the end-user and/or system to over-ride the WSS transaction must be in place, whereby if an end-user is not finding a satisfactory resolution via the WSS, the transaction is launched into an alternative mode of service delivery in order to find a satisfactory resolution (e.g. a chat session or telephone call).
31	Ease of re-initiation	A process must be in place whereby an end-user can easily re-initiate a support transaction to re-locate a previously retrieved resolution or other knowledge resource.
32	Top management support	Top management must provide ongoing support and commitment to the WSS and associated strategies.

Appendix 2: Glossary of Technical Terms

Term	Description
After-sales support services	Services offered to the customer after the initial sale of the core product or service.
Break-fix support	Support that provides customers experiencing technical problems with resolutions to those problems.
Business partner organisation	An organisation, distinct from the support organisation, that works with the support organisation to provide support services to the customer organisation.
Business-to-business (B2B)	The transaction of goods or services between businesses, as opposed to that between businesses and other groups (e.g. consumers).
Content	A category of CSFs that identifies that the WSS must contain useful, accurate and up-to-date content in order to resolve the end-user's support issue or knowledge requirement.
Critical success factor (CSF)	The limited number of areas that, if an organisation performs satisfactorily, will ensure its successful competitive performance.

(continued)

Term	Description
Customer organisation	A small, medium or large organisation, in a range of profit and not-for-profit industries, which receives support services.
Customer relationship management (CRM)	An organisational strategy that assists an organisation in retaining customers, managing the customer experience and facilitating cross-selling and up-selling.
Enterprise customer	See *Customer Organisation*.
Experience management	A category of CSFs that identifies that the WSS should manage the stakeholder's experience, both at the corporate and end-user level. The stakeholder experience will directly affect satisfaction levels and therefore ongoing use of the WSS.
Explicit knowledge	Knowledge that is articulated, codified and communicated in symbolic form and/or natural language (e.g. documents released to the WSS incorporating the trouble-shooting steps a customer should follow to resolve a support problem).
IT infrastructure capability	A category of CSFs that identifies that an organisation must have an adequate IT infrastructure in place, to enable it to participate in Web-based self-service.
IT outsourcing	The contracting out of IT operations (by the customer organisation) to an external entity (the support organisation) that specialises in the management of IT infrastructure and associated services.
IT support organisation	Organisations offering hardware, software and IT consulting services.
IT solution-oriented knowledge	The content developed and shared between the support organisation and the customer that describes all facets of the (IT) problem situation and how it can be resolved.
Knowledge management	A strategy that aims to support the creation, storage, transfer and application of organisational knowledge in order to improve organisational efficiency, effectiveness and competitiveness.
Knowledge management capabilities and processes	A category of CSFs that identifies that an organisation must practice the principles of knowledge management and implement associated knowledge management processes, to maximise the benefits received from the WSS strategy.
Knowledge-centred support (KCS)	A methodology built upon knowledge management concepts and the management of IT solution-oriented knowledge to resolve industry-wide IT support problems.
Manage for strategic and operational benefits	A category of CSFs that identifies that a WSS strategy must assist the organisation in attaining its strategic and operational objectives.
Managed IT services	See *IT Outsourcing*.
Net-based customer service system	A network-based computerised information system that delivers service to a customer either directly (e.g. via a

(continued)

Term	Description
	browser, PDA or cell phone) or indirectly (via a service representative or agent accessing the system).
Organisational commitment and readiness	A category of CSFs that identifies that an organisation must manage the policies, processes and cultural issues that will affect its ability and willingness to embrace Web-based self-service.
Relationship marketing	A marketing strategy that considers the importance of establishing, maintaining and enhancing relationships with stakeholders, so that the objectives of all stakeholders are met.
Service level agreements (SLAs).	Contracts between the IT support organisation and its customers, that detail the services and quality of those services required of the IT support organisation by the customer.
Services marketing	Marketing designed to market services (as opposed to products), that are typically intangible, heterogeneous, inseparable and perishable.
Support agent	IT support personnel whose primary role is to assist customers resolve their IT support problems.
Support engineer	Technology specialists who resolve the most difficult IT problems.
Tacit knowledge	Knowledge that is observed in individual action, experience and involvement in a specific context and consists of technical and cognitive components (e.g. A support engineer will have experience of how to efficiently trouble-shoot specific technologies).
Web-based self-service system (WSS)	A type of Net-based customer service system that is accessed via a Web-browser.
WSS stakeholders	A party who affects, or can be affected by, the IT support organisation's WSS. These include the corporate entity (e.g. managers) and end-users (e.g. Support Agents) at the support organisation, business partner and customer organisations.

References

Barua A, Konana P, Whinston AB (2004) An empirical investigation of business value. MIS Quarterly 28(4):585–620

Ciccolini C, Sorkin B (2003) The key to cost-effective support for specialised applications. DM Direct Newsletter. http://www.dmreview.com/article_sub.cfm?articleId = 6872. Accessed 14 November 2007

Cooper VA, Lichtenstein S, Smith R (2005) Emerging issues in after-sales enterprise information technology support using web-based self-service systems. Proceedings of the 16th Australasian Conference on Information Systems (ACIS 2005), 29 November-2 December, Sydney

Cooper VA, Lichtenstein S, Smith R (2006a) Knowledge transfer in enterprise information technology support using web-based self-service systems, International Journal Technology Marketing 1(2):145–170

Cooper VA, Lichtenstein S, Smith R (2006b) Enabling the transfer of information technology support knowledge to enterprise customers using web-based self-service systems: critical success factors from the support organisation perspective. Proceedings of the 17th Australasian Conference on Information Systems (ACIS 2006), 6–8 December, Adelaide, Australia

Cooper VA, Lichtenstein S, Smith R (2007) Enabling successful web-based information technology support for enterprise customers: a service provider perspective of stakeholder-based issues. Proceedings of the 20th Bled Conference eMergence: Merging and Emerging Technologies, Processes, and Institutions, 4–6 June 2007, Bled, Slovenia

CRM2day (2007) UK companies failing in web-based customer self-service. crm2day.com. http://www.crm2day.com/news/crm/121775.php. Accessed 14 November 2007

[CSI] Consortium Service Innovation (2002) Getting started with KCS. Official Consortium Service Innovation Site. http://www.thinkhdi.com/files/pdfs/GettingStartedKCS.pdf Accessed 19 July 2007

Dahlberg T, Nyrhinen M (2006) A new instrument to measure the success of IT outsourcing. Proceedings of the 39th Hawaii International Conference on System Sciences http://csdl2.computer.org/comp/proceedings/hicss/2006/2507/08/250780200a.pdf. Accessed 14 November 2007

Davenport TH, Klahr P (1998) Managing customer support knowledge. California Management Review 40(3):195–208

Fjermestad J, Romano NC (2003) Electronic customer relationship management, advancements in management information systems. London

Geib M, Kolb L, Brenner W (2006) Collaborative customer management in financial services alliances. In: Fjermestad J and Romano NC (eds), Electronic Customer Relationship Management. Armonk, New York

Grönroos C (1994) From marketing mix to relationship marketing, towards a paradigm shift in marketing. Management Decision 32(2):4–20

Kalakota R, Robinson M (2003) From e-business to e-services: why and why now? Addison-Wesley, New York

Khalifa M, Shen N (2005) Effects of electronic customer relationship management on customer satisfaction: a temporal model. Proceedings of the 38th Annual Hawaii International Conference on System Sciences (HICSS'05), IEEE Society Press

Lei DT (1997) Competence-building, technology fusion and competitive advantage: the key roles of organisational learning and strategic alliances. International Journal of Technology Management 14(2/3/4):208–237

McGeary Z, Daniels D, Matiesanu C, Mitskaviets, I, Sehgal, V (2007) Online Self-Service Effectiveness: Tactics for Measurement, Vision Report, April 12, Jupiter Research

Mollstedt U, Fredriksson O (2004) Information systems failure and adoption of internet-based after-sales service in a business-to-business context. Proceedings of the International Colloquium in Relationship Marketing (ICRM). IEEE Society Press

Negash S, Ryan T, Igbaria M (2003) Quality and effectiveness in web-based customer support systems. Information and Management. 40(8):757–768

Parasuraman A, Grewal D (2000) The impact of technology on the quality-value-loyalty chain: a research agenda. Journal of the Academy of Marketing Services 28(1): 168–174

Peppard J (2003) Managing IT as a portfolio of services. European Management Journal 21(4):467–483

Piccoli G, Brohman MK, Watson RT, Parasuraman A (2004) Net-based customer service systems: evolution and revolution in web-site functionalities. Decision Sciences 35(3):423–455

Pujari D (2004) Self-service with a smile? self-service technology (SST) encounters among canadian business-to-business. International Journal of Service Industry Management 5(2):200–219

Szulanski G (2000) The process of knowledge transfer: a diachronic analysis of stickiness. Organisational Behavior and Human Decision Processes 82(1):9–27.

van Riel ACR, Streukens S, Lemmink J, Liljander V (2004) Boost customer loyalty with online support: the case of mobile telecoms providers. International Journal of Internet Marketing and Advertising 1(1):4–23.

Zeithaml VA, Parasuraman A, Malhotra A (2000) A conceptual framework for understanding e-service quality: implications for future research and managerial practice. Marketing Science Institute, Cambridge, Massachusetts

Chapter 13
An Explanatory Model of Self-Service on the Internet

Dave Oliver, Celia Romm Livermore, and Neveen Awad Farag

Abstract This chapter describes research that identifies and classifies the dimensions of self-service activity enabled through the Internet. Self-service is effected by organizations providing ways and means whereby customers perform tasks related to the procurement of goods and services. We describe how an instrument used to measure Internet-based self-service was developed, validated and applied. The results from applying the instrument to a large number of Web sites, covering a range of industries, countries and cultures, are analyzed and discussed. The study presents a model in which type of industry, level of technological development, income and cultural factors are proposed as explanatory variables for Web-based self-service. We conclude with an assessment of this program of research's achievements so far.

13.1 Introduction

This chapter presents an explanatory model of self-service on the Internet. The initial proposition taken to explore this phenomenon is the notion that self-service involves customers performing tasks that would otherwise be undertaken by employees of the organization providing the service. The Internet provides a mechanism whereby self-service activities may be conducted from almost anywhere in the world. Self-service on the Internet brings together two major dimensions of modern life: the independence afforded by helping oneself and the freedom from time/space constraints provided by the Internet. The provision of self-service on the Internet affects how people go about achieving their goals in life. Moreover, the continual expansion of the Internet suggests that any impacts that may be discerned from the current level of Web-based self-service activity are likely to increase in the future. Self-service on the Internet is changing lives all over the world.

D. Oliver (✉)
45 Mirrawena Avenue, Farnborough QLD 4703, Australia
e-mail: dodave@gmail.com

D. Oliver et al. (eds.), *Self-Service in the Internet Age,*
DOI 10.1007/978-1-84800-207-4_13, © Springer-Verlag London Limited 2009

There is much to explore in the role that Web sites play in transforming aspects of the service experience that used to be performed by employees, into ones that are now performed by customers. In previous works (Oliver et al. 2005; Romm Livermore et al. 2005), we focused on the development of an instrument for measuring the potential of customer service Web sites for shifting work from employees to customers. In this chapter we revisit our approach to defining, documenting, categorizing, measuring, and theorizing about the phenomenon. Our data collection has been on a global front and our theorizing from the broad perspectives of industry, country and culture , levels of income, and technological development. The explanatory model we present in this chapter extends that of Oliver et al. (2007) by including per capita income as an additional explanatory variable. In addition there are some differences in the statistical analysis.

The structure of the chapter is as follows. We begin by introducing the concept of self-service and self-service technologies (SSTs) and in particular how the Internet facilitates forms of Web-based self-service. We then describe how we develop an instrument to measure the extent of Web-based self-service. The results achieved from applying the instrument to a large number of Web sites and industries are then presented, analyzed, and discussed. Finally, we conclude with an assessment of this program of research's achievements so far.

13.2 Self-Service

People in the developed world are thoroughly accustomed to the notion of self-service. Self-service has completely colonized many service areas. For example, it used to be the case, when grocery shopping in Western countries, for shop workers to retrieve the items a customer wished to buy. Today, in the self-service era, customers select their own purchases from the shelves and storage cabinets, place them in a trolley or basket provided by the store, which they then present to the cashier. In more extreme versions of self-service, customers may also scan these purchases and tender payment unaided by an employee. Refueling a car at a service station is another activity where self-service rather than customer service is the norm. In both of these examples, it is clear that to receive the service, the customer engages in activities that would otherwise constitute paid work for an employee.

Sayers (2003), drawing on Fitzsimmons et al., highlights how consumers are perceived as service providers within the supply chain:

> re-engineering service to take full advantage of self-service is now a full-blown science. 'Process Design' specialists map out service interactions, timing and measuring each component of a service chain so that ways to gain efficiencies in the system can be achieved, including ways to get the customer to do tasks previously done by a staff member.

Following this perspective on the role consumers play, we define the process in which "aspects of the customer service experience that used to be provided by the company's employees are now provided through the interaction of customers with the company's website" as "turning customers into employees" (TCIE) (Romm Livermore et al. 2005).

It should be noted that this is an *interpretive definition* that may or may not fit the subjective perception of either the company or its customers. Thus, customers may perceive self-service as an opportunity to achieve increased customization of a product, convenience, faster speed of service, or lower prices (Halbesleben & Buckley 2004; Meuter et al. 2000; Schneider & Bowen 1995), while companies may believe that self-service will lead to competitive advantage through lower costs, increased satisfaction, loyalty of customers, and the ability to reach new consumer segments (Bitner et al. 2002). The suggestion that the interaction between the customers and the company reflects TCIE is thus an interpretation of reality that may or may not be shared by either the companies whose Web sites we intend to study, or the customers of these companies.

We accept Lengnick-Hall's (1996) definition of the relationship with customers and employees as "co-production" and we view customers as "partial employees" (Mills et al. (1983), Mills and Morris (1986), Keh and Teo (2001), and Harris et al. (1999)). Note also that we use the term "employee" to identify those instances that reflect the role of the customer as a provider of labor in the service experience. Customers may receive a "benefit" in the form of lower prices, greater satisfaction, greater speed of service, and greater customization (Schneider & Bowen 1995).

13.3 Self-Service Technologies

The phenomenon of customers performing tasks that used to be provided by employees of companies is now facilitated through electronic networks, including the Internet. Automatic teller machines (ATMs) enable bank customers to make deposits and withdrawals from their accounts without any assistance from bank employees. Internet Banking, which does not require ATM technology at all, enables customers to obtain balances of accounts and view transactions, as well as paying bills using the bank's Web site.

Online self-service Web sites are typically categorized into two main types: informational and transactional . Informational Web sites provide information about companies, services, or products. Those which are transactional involve an Internet-mediated transaction such as placing an order, making a bank transfer, or booking a flight (Conneighton 2004), (Young & Benamati 2000). This distinction may simply reflect different evolutionary stages in the development of a particular Web site. Other, more detailed analyses of the stages of Web site development have been made such as that developed, and those cited in, Krawczyk (2007). Conneighton (2004) maintains that "Web based customer self-service is a vastly more cost effective way of managing customer interactions and inquiries than are channels that require any kind of human intervention." He adds the proviso "so long as customer service quality is maintained." Companies can reduce operating costs by providing the opportunity for customers to self-serve using the Internet. These reduced costs can be passed on to consumers. For example, the Virgin Blue Web site (an Australian domestic carrier) advises that fares booked by a service call attract a $15 loading compared to the Internet booking fee (VirginBlue 2006). The service that is being purchased, namely airline travel, is a physical provision which remains the same whichever type of ticketing service the consumer chooses (Internet ticket purchase, a telephone ticket purchase, or a face-to-face transaction at a travel agency).

Information services that organizations provide do not usually command a fee for service; however, there is clearly a cost to providing them. Providing information services on the Web gives organizations the opportunity to reduce the cost of information provision. Customers may prefer Web-based information provision for reasons of convenience, even though there is no clear cost benefit to them. Examples of Web-based information provision are shipment tracking enquiry systems and weather reporting services.

Consumers interact with many SSTs without needing to acquire their own technology infrastructure. ATMs are provided by financial institutions, airline checkin kiosks are provided by airlines and self-scanning checkouts are provided by supermarkets. On the other hand, Web-based services are only available to those who have access to computers with Internet connections; so consequently, only those people who customarily use the Internet are likely to avail themselves of these services. This technology effect suggests that there may be a relationship between the level of Internet connections within a country and the level of Web-based self-service.

13.4 Development of the Self-Service Model

We assume that the process of turning customers into employees is not uniform across countries and cultures, companies, or industries. It is reasonable to assume that in countries where the cost of labor is relatively high, there is a greater incentive for organizations to focus upon strategies to lower their requirements for employees, compared to countries where labor costs are low. One strategy is to turn customers into employees by adopting self-service. The other is to replace labor with technology. We would expect, since per capita income is a suitable measure of labor costs, that the level of self-service would be higher in countries that have a higher per capita income than those with a lower per capita income. In other words, per capita income should be positively correlated with self-service levels.

Similarly, a higher level of technology in a country suggests there would be a greater capacity for self-service. Since we are focusing specifically on self-service on the Internet, we have chosen the number of personal computers (PCs) and the number of Internet users as variables to measure technology. A positive correlation between our measure of Web-based self-service and these measures of technology is anticipated.

Given that in some industries there is an apparently high tendency toward Web-based self service, for example the airline travel and banking, it appears that type of industry should be included in the model . Also, we considered it possible that cultural traits might create a disposition toward self-service. Consequently, we used the cultural classifications developed by Hofstede (1980a,b, 1984a,b, 1994a,b) to assess this characteristic. We present an outline model reflecting the contributory factors of income, technology, industry and culture in Fig. 13.1.

The process used to develop the measurement instrument from our interpretive definition of TCIE is shown in Fig. 13.2. An initial set of criteria to measure the TCIE phenomenon was developed from an exploratory examination of Web sites made by teams of MBA students (the majority of whom are employed full time and doing their MBA part time). These students were organized into groups of about nine students. The student groups were directed to select three Web sites from the US, three from either the UK or from Australia, and three from a culture "very different" from either the US, the UK, or Australia (such as Japan or India). This was in order to explore different cultural settings as defined by Hofstede (1980a,b, 1984a,b, 1994a,b). In determining which cultures are "very

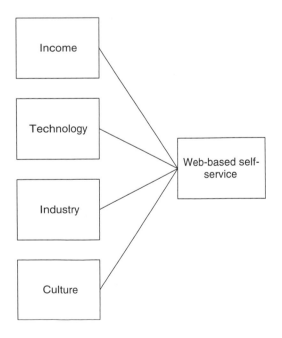

Fig. 13.1 Outline model of Web-based self-service

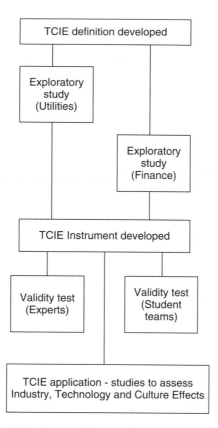

Fig. 13.2 TCIE Instrument development framework

different" from the US, Australia, and the UK a culture was deemed to be at least ten points different from the US, UK, or Australia on at least two dimensions of the Hofstede model .

Each team was asked to share with the other teams and with the instructor the organization, industry, and country they intended to focus on, to make sure that there was no overlap between the teams in terms of the Web sites studied. These teams were instructed to study each Web site and to identify between four and ten distinct tasks that reflected TCIE in their sample. Teams were instructed to reach consensus on the tasks they identified. Finally, once identified, the student teams were asked to describe the TCIE tasks in detail and to accompany their description with examples that reflected the various tasks.

A large number of Web sites, around 100, were reported on by the student groups over two successive offerings of this class. These responses were analyzed by one of the authors, who consolidated these findings into a single list of identifying criteria as shown in the Appendix using a form of grounded theory analysis (Glaser & Strauss 1967; Strauss & Corbin 1990, 1997). The measurement instrument is based on this list.

13.4.1 Assessing the Validity of the Instrument

This list of identifying criteria was tested for validity by asking two reference groups to check the items in the list against the definition of TCIE that was presented earlier in this chapter. One group comprised six experts. The experts included, two professors of IT with expertise in issues related to e-commerce and Web design, two professors of organizational behavior and human resource management, and two executives with special expertise in establishing and managing a Web-based business. Their task was to check each item in the list of criteria against the definition of TCIE and to assess the extent to which the item is an example of an aspect of the service experience that can be undertaken by a customer instead of an employee. From these responses a Kappa statistic of 0.79 was generated (Landis & Koch 1977). Landis and Koch suggest the following coefficient benchmarks: poor (<0), slight (0–0.19), fair (0.20–0.39), moderate (0.40–0.59), substantial (0.60–0.79), and near perfect (0.80–1.00). The other reference group was formed from a subsequent class of MBA students who performed the same task. The Kappa statistic from the student group was 0.66. Both groups were therefore in the "substantial" range.

The same class of MBA students who assessed the validity of the instrument, also applied the instrument to a further sample of Web sites from the retail sector. This application of the instrument constitutes some of the data that informs the studies that are described in the next section. From this study we computed the Kappa statistic on the use of the instrument by the student groups. A calculation was made for each group separately because each team was studying a different set of Web sites. We ended up with six scores for reliability representing each of the six teams. The Kappa statistics from this process were unusually high, with the lowest being 0.88. This has caused us to reflect that in this initial application of the instrument, group members were possibly not acting independently as directed. Since these results were averaged later in the process to form a consolidated measurement of a Web site, this apparent collaboration in coding is not perceived to be of detriment to the accuracy of the study.

13.5 Application of the TCIE Research Instrument

In the course of a number of classes we applied the instrument to a number of different industries as shown in Table 13.1, which include, manufacturing (automobile, construction materials), retail (book, clothing, cosmetics, food) and utilities (electricity, gas, telephone). These were selected from a range of countries that reflected different cultural profiles as described earlier. The classes were organized into groups comprising six students, although some groups comprised only four or five. Each student rated each Web site against the instrument and a consolidated rating for each Web site was obtained by

Table 13.1 Industry/country groups studied

Industry	Country				
Automobile	Australia	Japan	Russia	UK	USA
Book	Australia	Norway	Singapore	UK	USA
Clothing	Australia	India	Japan	UK	USA
Construction materials	Australia	Denmark	Malaysia	UK	USA
Cosmetics	Australia	Bangladesh	Japan	UK	USA
Electricity			Japan	UK	USA
Food	Australia	France	Italy	UK	USA
Gas	Australia	Italy			USA
Telephone	Australia	Spain	Taiwan	UK	USA

averaging these individual ratings. The rating was a number between 1 and 30. Although it may be possible in theory to obtain a 0 rating, none occurred in these rounds of data collection. The primary data collected by the students consisted of 756 observations across the 41 industry/country groups shown in Table 13.1, which were consolidated into a data set of 141 Web sites in the manner just described, to yield a value between 0 and 30 for each Web site.

From this data we endeavor to substantiate the four explanatory variables in the model outlined in Fig. 13.1. One major difficulty we face is that Table 13.2 has a large number of vacant cells, which reduces our capacity to draw firm conclusions.

13.6 Industry

The results we present from the application of the TCIE instrument are in the form of a single value obtained from applying the instrument as described earlier. The TCIE instrument may therefore be seen as a strength indicator, where a high measurement from the TCIE instrument indicates an industry with a high degree of TCIE activity and vice versa.

Table 13.2 shows the industry/country measures for TCIE activity obtained from the study so far. The last row of this table shows considerable variation in the TCIE metric across industries. This average is not computed from the values in the column but is directly calculated from the Web site values obtained from the application of the instrument. As the number of Web sites studied for each country/industry combination can differ considerably, a simple column average will not yield the same figure as that shown in the last row of Table 13.2. This means that some of the values in Table 13.2 are more representative than others.

Table 13.2 shows that different industries have substantially different levels of Web-based self-service activity and therefore supports the inclusion of Industry as an explanatory variable in the model of Fig. 13.1. These results also confirm those of Young and Benamati (2000) who report variations in the transactional capabilities of company Web sites in different industries. This is a

Table 13.2 TCIE measures for industry/country combinations

	Automobile	Book	Clothing	Construction materials	Cosmetics	Electricity	Food	Gas	Telephone
Australia	10.7	15.7	16.3	10.5	18.0		17.3	9.3	19.7
Bangladesh					5.3				
Denmark									
France			9.7	5.7			9.3		
India								10.7	
Italy	11.0		11.0		14.3	10.0	17.3		
Japan				8.0					
Malaysia									
Norway		20.7							
Russia	5.0	17.0							
Singapore									
Spain									13.0
Taiwan									12.0
UK	13.0	17.3	17.3	8.0	14.7	14.0	6.7		20.0
USA	15.4	21.2	16.5	8.4	19.3	16.7	13.7	12.7	20.7
Average	11.5	18.8	14.6	8.0	15.2	13.6	13.0	10.9	17.7

strong pointer to the incidence of TCIE in an industry. Engaging in transactional activity will almost certainly involve the customer in doing some work that would otherwise have been performed by an employee.

The automobile industry, the gas industry and the construction materials industries exhibit the lowest TCIE measures. This suggests the capacity for customers to engage in Web-based self-service over the Internet is low in these industries. That the gas industry records a low value is puzzling since the perception of the authors was that utilities would record a high level of TCIE, as they require meter values to be input periodically, a function users could perform online.

The findings reported here do not necessarily confound these assumptions. It may be that the TCIE instrument at this stage of its development is too blunt as it does not distinguish between potentially high customer workload activities and low ones. The instrument simply takes an indicator of TCIE at face value and ranks each attribution equally without any assignment of strength or importance. So an industry with few TCIE indicators used intensively would register a low rating, whereas another industry with many little-used TCIE indicators would register a high rating. A consumer survey may be needed to develop a deeper understanding of what the TCIE activities mean to those consumers who undertake them and their relative workloads.

The electricity and telephone utilities show high TCIE values compared to gas. This result also poses some questions, for whereas gas and electricity consumption is measured by meters located at the consumer end, which can therefore be easily read by consumers, that is not the case for the telephone industry where the metering is done centrally and therefore does not present the same capacity for consumer work. Nevertheless the instrument records a substantially higher level of TCIE activity for the telephone industry compared to gas and electricity. This is clearly due to other TCIE factors.

The book and telephone industry yielded the highest levels of TCIE involvement at 18.8 and 17.7 respectively. The book industry is known to have a high profile in terms of e-commerce activity, so this result serves to confirm the effectiveness of the instrument . However, both these levels are still less than 66% of the maximum value possible. This again points to the issue of the broad scope of the measurement instrument, distilled as it was from a study of many Web sites in many industries, which perhaps inhibits the possibility of achieving a very high score in a single industry.

13.6.1 Income

To test the assumption that the provision of self-service on the Internet is determined by wage levels, we correlated per capita income with the TCIE measure shown in Table 13.2. The values for income per capita were taken from the World Bank Web site (World Bank n.d.) shown in Table 13.3.

Table 13.3 Income, internet users and personal computers, 2004 (World Bank n.d.)

Country	Income per capita	Internet users per 1000 people	PCs per 1000 people
Australia	20,640	497	616
Bangladesh	350	2	4
Denmark	33,040	556	648
France	24,210	399	414
India	440	23	11
Italy	20,090	321	232
Japan	32,350	606	425
Malaysia	3,670	392	170
Norway	34,310	546	567
Russia	2,260	91	113
Singapore	30,170	559	565
Spain	14,100	317	199
UK	21,410	533	496

Figure 13.3 shows the scatter plot of this data, which yielded a Spearman rank correlation coefficient value r of 0.42. It should be noted that the distribution of Web sites studied is not uniform across all countries. As is evident from the sparseness of Table 13.2, there are many industry/country combinations that do not provide any data. This is the reason for the vertical clustering evident in Fig. 13.3. Also the global nature of the Internet introduces some difficulties with respect to this variable. A Web site in one country may well target customers in other countries and this will tend to weak the impact of local national income. Despite these reservations, there is some evidence to suggest that higher income levels generate higher levels of Web-based self-service.

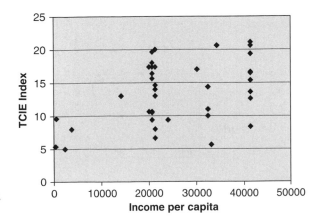

Fig. 13.3 Scatter plot of income per capita and TCIE index

13.6.2 Technological Development

To answer this question, we correlate the results from applying the TCIE instrument across industries and countries as shown in Table 13.2 with suitable measures for technological development. The measures of technological development we selected were the number of Internet users and the number of PCs per 1000 of the population in 2004 obtained from the World Bank Web site (World Bank no date) as shown in Table 13.3. These measures seemed appropriate for technological development, as we are investigating an SST that requires Internet connectivity and a PC. The scatter plots for these are shown in Figs. 13.4 and 13.5. The vertical clustering reflecting the uneven spread of

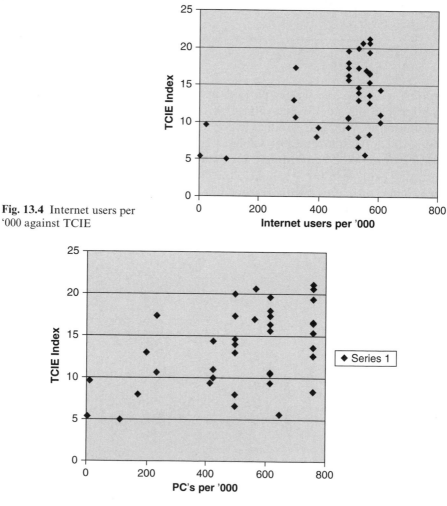

Fig. 13.4 Internet users per '000 against TCIE

Fig. 13.5 PCs per '000 against TCIE

countries is also evident here. We expect a positive correlation between these measures and the TCIE metric if the level of technological development is associated with TCIE activity.

The coefficient of correlation between the number of Internet users and the TCIE index was 0.42 and that between the number of PCs and the TCIE index was 0.48. This moderate degree of correlation supports the inclusion of technology as a factor influencing TCIE in the model in Fig. 13.1. The same caution needs to be applied to this determination as that for income in the previous section. As Web sites were not selected evenly across countries, there is a bias toward those who were sampled more frequently. Perusal of Table 13.2 shows that Australia, the UK, and the USA provide the most data. Not only do they occupy more columns, but also the number of Web sites studied in these countries tends to be higher, especially those from the USA.

13.6.3 Culture

It will be recalled from earlier in this chapter, that the student teams that collected data for this project were instructed to select three Web sites from the US, three from either the UK or from Australia, and three from a culture "very different" from either the US, the UK, or Australia. To discern the effect of culture, we correlated each of the four measures power distance index (PDI), individualism (IDV), masculinity (MAS), and the uncertainty avoidance index (UAI) of the Hofstede model with the measure of TCIE obtained from each Web site. The values for the Hofstede measures for the countries visited in this study were obtained from Hofstede's Web site (Hofstede 1967–2003). The only Hofstede measures to indicate a mild degree of correlation were power distance (PDI) $r = -0.24$ and individualism IDV $r = 0.27$.

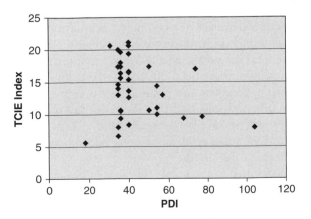

Fig. 13.6 Hofstede's (1967–2003) power distance index (PDI) and TCIE index

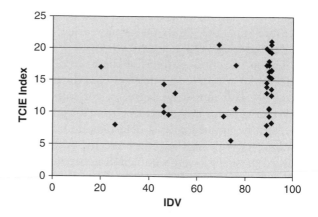

Fig. 13.7 Hofstede individualism (IDV) and TCIE index

The slight negative association apparent for power distance indicates self-service on the Internet may be more likely to flourish in those cultures which are more egalitarian. The slight positive correlation for IDV suggests that it is a cultural trait that may encourage the development of Web-based self-service. This result suggests obtaining goods and services via a computer-based mechanism appeals more in cultures oriented toward self reliance than those where more socially orientated behaviors predominate. Interacting with a Web site is individualistic in nature. On the basis of these results, we therefore conclude that countries which exhibit egalitarian tendencies and those where individualism ranks highly are more likely to encourage the development of Web-based self-service. The precautionary remarks relating to the data underpinning this analysis made in the previous sections apply here also.

13.7 Discussion

The social impact of e-commerce is an important and emerging area of study. Although exploring mechanisms to aid the pursuit of corporate efficiency remains high on the agenda of information systems academics, there is a need to examine the social effects of these initiatives as they invoke changes to existing practices and behaviors. Mechanisms for self-service are initiatives of the organizations that provide them and increase its extent. Self-service Web sites that operate from organizational Web servers and run on personal Web browsers are a relatively recent phenomenon and their social consequences relatively uncharted.

As stated at the outset this study does not seek to extend this "science" but rather to define, document, categorize, measure and theorize about the phenomenon within the e-commerce arena. Some of our initial suppositions have been confirmed as a result of the application of the instrument reported here. The initial model postulated that industry, income, technological development, and culture were likely explanatory variables for the incidence of TCIE. This analysis has provided confirmation of this initial model presented in Fig. 13.1. The Industry dimension possesses the strongest support for inclusion, followed by technology and income, and to a lesser extent Hofstede's cultural dimensions of power distance and individualism.

The main limitation relating to our application of the TCIE instrument, apart from the statistical biases which we have mentioned earlier, is that it has only examined dimensions visible from the Web sites themselves. Additional data that could expand upon this study would be measurements of the intensity of Web traffic on the sites in question as well as consumer studies of those who avail themselves of these services.

13.8 Conclusion

This research in progress outlines an approach that has been taken to researching the TCIE phenomenon as it is manifested in information systems. It outlines the development of a measurement instrument and its application to a number of industries in a number of different countries and cultures. This research provides industry, technology, economic, and culturally based insights into the Web-based self-service phenomenon. We have provided some additional measures to assess the penetration of this activity to build on those provided in earlier studies. We have developed an explanatory model and provided justifications for the explanatory variables selected. The process of applying the instrument is ongoing and further results may be forthcoming.

Appendix: TCIE Measurement Instrument

☐ Prepurchase decision making	
1. Customers can see a display of products/services with product details	Yes / No
2. Customers receive an online invoice	Yes / No
3. Customers can use diagnostic tools to help them define their needs	Yes / No
4. Customers can sample or try products for free before purchasing them (receiving sample reports, trying on a virtual dress, etc.)	Yes / No
5. Customers can compare different products by the same company	Yes / No
6. Customers can get information on products of other companies (directly or through banners)	Yes / No
7. Customers can see other customers' comments on products before they make the purchase	Yes / No

(continued)

☐ Prepurchase decision making	
8. Customers receive suggestions based on their own past purchases on what products to consider	Yes / No
☐ Purchase	
9. Customers can see a display of transaction options	Yes / No
10. Customers can order online	Yes / No
11. Customers can pay online	Yes / No
12. Customers can pay by phone	Yes / No
13. Customers can pay face-to-face	Yes / No
14. Customers are able to track the merchandise until they get it	Yes / No
15. Customers are able to measure and report usage of a service (for example, gas usage, electricity usage, etc.)	Yes / No
16. Customers receive a printable receipt and/or e-mail confirmation of purchase	Yes / No
17. Customers are able to establish an account with the company so as to simplify all future transactions with the company	Yes / No
18. Customers receive coupons for future purchases upon completion of the transaction	Yes / No
19. Customers get rewards for recommending the product to others	Yes No
20. Customers are invited to receive regular information from the company on new products and services (via a newsletter or direct e-mails)	Yes / No
☐ Post purchase service and support	
21. Customers can view their itemized bills	Yes / No
22. Customers can view their payment history	Yes No
23. Customers can view a comparison of their bill to the bills of other customers	Yes / No
24. Customers can complain or ask questions online	Yes No
25. Customers can complain or ask questions by phone	Yes / No
26. Customers can complain or ask questions face to face	Yes / No
27. Customers have access to online community of customers for questions and support	Yes / No
28. Customers have access to face-to-face community of customers for questions and support	Yes / No
29. Customers are provided with online advice on how to fix faulty merchandise	Yes No
30. Customers are provided with a physical address for returning faulty merchandise and receiving a refund.	Yes / No

References

Bitner MJ, Ostrom AL, Meuter ML (2002) Implementing successful self-service strategies. Academy of Management Executive 16(4):96–108

Conneighton C (2004) Self-Service Comes of Age - Part III. http://www.crm2day.com. Accessed 4 March 2006

Glaser B, Strauss A (1967) The Discovery of Grounded Theory: Strategies for Qualitative Research. Aldine, Chicago

Halbesleben JRB, Buckley RM (2004) Managing customers as employees of the firm - new challenges for human resources management. Personnel Review 33(3):351–372

Harris K, Baron S, Davies B (1999) What sort of soil do rhododendrons like? Comparing customers and employees responses to request for product-related information. Journal of Services Marketing 13:21–37

Hofstede G (1967–2003) Geert Hofstede™ Cultural Dimensions. http://www.geert-hofstede.com/. Accessed 31 May 2006

Hofstede G (1980a) Culture Consequences: International difference in work related values. Sage Publications, Beverly Hills, CA

Hofstede G (1980b) Motivation leadership and organization: do American theories apply abroad? Organizational Dynamics 9(1):42–63

Hofstede G (1984a) The cultural relativity of organizational practices and theories. Journal of International Business Studies 14:75–89

Hofstede G (1984b) The cultural relativity of the quality of life concept. Academy of Management Review 9:389–398

Hofstede G (1994a) The business of international business is culture. International Business Review 3(1):1–14

Hofstede G (1994b) Management scientists are human. Management Science 40(1):4–13

Keh HT, Teo CW (2001) Retail customers as partial employees in service provision: a conceptual framework. International Journal of Retail and Distribution Management 29:370–378

Krawczyk A (2007) Determining Improvement Directions for Transactional and Relational Components of Websites. Paper presented at the 20th Bled eConference on eMergence: Merging and Emerging Technologies, Processes, and Institutions, Bled, Slovenia

Landis JR, Koch GG (1977) The measurement of observer agreement for categorical data. Biometrics 33:159–174

Lengnick-Hall CA (1996) Customer contributions to quality: a different view of the customer oriented firm. Academy of Management Review 21:791–825

Meuter ML, Ostrom AL, Roundtree RI, Bitner MJ (2000) Self-service technologies: understanding customer satisfaction with Technology-based service encounters. Journal of Marketing 64(3):50–64

Mills PK, Chase RB, Margulies N (1983) Motivating the client/employee system as a service production strategy. Academy of Management Review 8:301–310

Mills PK, Morris JH (1986) Clients as partial employees of service organizations: role development in client participation. Academy of Management Review 11:726–735

Oliver D, Romm Livermore C, Farag NA (2005) Are You Being Served? – Exploring the Role of Customers as Employees in the Digital World. Paper presented at the CollECTeR Europe conference, Furtwangen, Germany

Oliver D, Romm Livermore C, Farag NA (2007) Self-service on the Internet: An Explanatory Model. Paper presented at the 20th Bled eConference, on eMergence: Merging and Emerging Technologies, Processes, and Institutions, Bled, Slovenia

Romm Livermore C, Farag NA, Oliver D (2005) Turning Customers Into Employees - Research In Progress. Paper presented at the 6th Annual Global Information Technology Management (GITM) conference, Alaska, USA

Sayers J (2003) The JIT Service Labour Process And The Customer: New Possibilities For Resistance/Misbehaviour And Consumption In: The Labour Process? Paper presented at the Critical Management Studies: 3rd International (CMS3) Conference, Lancaster University

Schneider B, Bowen DE (1995) Winning the Service Game. Harvard Business School Press, Boston, MA

Strauss A, Corbin J (1990) Basics of Qualitative Research: Grounded Theory Procedures and Techniques. Sage, Thousand Oaks, Sage, Thousand Oaks

Strauss A, Corbin J (1997) Grounded Theory in Practice. Sage, Thousand Oaks, CA

VirginBlue (2006) Flight Bookings. http://bookings.virginblue.com.au/skylights/cgi-bin/skylights.cgi. Accessed 11 May 2006

World Bank (n.d.) Data & Statistics. http://web.worldbank.org/WBSITE/EXTERNAL/DATASTATISTICS. Accessed 10 January 2007

Young D, Benamati J (2000) Differences in Public Web Sites: The Current State of Large US Firms. Journal of Electronic Commerce Research 1(3):94–105

Index

Printed in the United States of America